THE
DAYS OF
THE FRENCH
REVOLUTION

BY THE SAME AUTHOR

MILITARY HISTORY

WOLFE AT QUEBEC
THE DESTRUCTION OF LORD RAGLAN
CORUNNA
THE BATTLE OF ARNHEM
AGINCOURT
THE BATTLE OF ANZIO

HISTORY

KING MOB
THE ROOTS OF EVIL
THE COURT AT WINDSOR
THE GRAND TOUR
LONDON: THE BIOGRAPHY OF A CITY
THE DRAGON WAKES: CHINA AND THE WEST, 1793–1911
VERSAILLES
THE PEN AND THE SWORD
THE HOUSE OF MEDICI
THE GREAT MUTINY: INDIA 1857
THE COURT OF ST. JAMES'S

BIOGRAPHIES

BENITO MUSSOLINI
GARIBALDI AND HIS ENEMIES
THE MAKING OF CHARLES DICKENS
CHARLES I
THE PERSONAL HISTORY OF SAMUEL JOHNSON
GEORGE IV: PRINCE OF WALES, 1762–1811
GEORGE IV: REGENT AND KING, 1811–1830
EDWARD THE UNCROWNED KING
THE ROYAL VICTORIANS: KING EDWARD VII, HIS FAMILY AND FRIENDS
GILBERT AND SULLIVAN AND THEIR VICTORIAN WORLD
DISRAELI AND HIS WORLD

THE
DAYS OF
THE FRENCH
REVOLUTION

CHRISTOPHER HIBBERT

MORROW QUILL PAPERBACKS
New York   1981

Library of Congress Cataloging in Publication Data

Hibbert, Christopher, 1924-
  The days of the French Revolution.

  "Morrow quill paperbacks."

  Bibliography: p.
  Includes index.
  1. France—History—Revolution, 1789-1795.
I. Title.
DC161.H5 1981   944.04   81-9666
ISBN 0-688-03704-6   AACR2
ISBN 0-688-00746-5 (pbk.)

Printed in the United States of America

7 8 9 10

FOR

TERRY AND MOYRA

CONTENTS

LIST OF ILLUSTRATIONS

WITH ACKNOWLEDGEMENTS

1. Louis XVI
2. Marie Antoinette as a young mother
3. Versailles in 1722
4. Louis XVI giving money to a poor family by Debucourt
5. Market people celebrating in Les Halles by Debucourt
6. A caricature satirizing the inequality of taxation
7. The duc d'Orléans and the marquis de Lafayette carry aloft Jacques Necker
8. The opening ceremony of the Estates General at Versailles on 5 May 1789
9. The Abbé Sieyès
10. Camille Desmoulins
11. J. L. David's painting of the deputies taking the oath in the tennis-court at Versailles on 20 June 1789
12. Troops encamped on the Champ de Mars on 14 July 1789
13. The storming of the Bastille on 14 July 1789
14. Mirabeau, sketch by David
15. Jean-Sylvain Bailly
16. The King arriving at the Hôtel de Ville
17. A contemporary print depicting the departure of the heroines of Paris for Versailles on 5 October 1789
18. The arrival of the women at Versailles
19. The celebrations on the first anniversary of the fall of the Bastille, 14 July 1790
20. The burning of a Tree of Feudalism, 1792

21. The mob looting a nobleman's house
22. Pierre Victurnien Vergniaud
23. The King is apprehended in Sauce's house in Varennes
24. The King announces the declaration of war to the acclaim of the deputies
25. The attack on the Tuileries on 10 August 1792
26. 'The Victory of Equality, or the Plots Baffled'
27. 'La Femme du Sans Culotte'
28. Sans Culottes
29. A revolutionary committee during the Terror
30. Georges Jacques Danton
31. The royal family walking in the grounds of the Temple
32. The trial of Louis XVI in the National Convention, 26 December 1792
33. The execution of the King on the Place de la Révolution on 21 January 1793
34. J. L. David's celebrated 'Marat'
35. Charlotte Corday after the murder of Marat
36. Robespierre, sketch by David
37. Arrest of Robespierre
38. Antoine-Quentin Fouquier-Tinville
39. The trial of Fouquier-Tinville
40. David's sketch of Marie Antoinette on her way to execution
41. The execution of Marie Antoinette on 16 October 1793
42. The interior of Frascati's during the days of the Directory
43. A Bonapartist print depicting the 'brave Grenadiers' protecting their hero in the Orangery at Saint-Cloud
44. David's painting of Napoleon's coronation in 1804

The author and publishers are grateful to the following for permission to reproduce photographs: Photographie Bulloz, Paris, for nos. 1, 2, 4, 5, 9, 11, 12, 14, 15, 17, 22, 27, 28, 30, 31, 32, 33, 34, 36, 38, 42, 43, 44; The Mansell Collection, London, for nos. 3, 8, 13, 16, 19, 20, 23, 25, 29, 35, 37, 39, 41; Snark International, Paris, for nos. 6, 7, 18; Mary Evans Picture Library, London, for nos. 10, 21; Réunion des Musées Nationaux, Paris, for no. 40; Photographie Giraudon, Paris, for nos. 24, 26.

AUTHOR'S NOTE

This is a narrative history of the French Revolution from the meeting of the Estates General at Versailles in 1789 to the *coup d'état* of 18 *Brumaire* which brought Napoleon to power ten years later. It concentrates upon events and people rather than ideas, particularly upon those *journées* which helped to decide the course of the Revolution and upon those men and women involved in them. It is written for the general reader unfamiliar with the subject rather than the student, though I hope the student to whom the field is new may find it a readable introduction to the works of those historians to whom I myself am indebted. I want particularly to mention, and to thank, Professors Georges Lefebvre, Albert Soboul, Alfred Cobban, Richard Cobb, George Rudé, A. Goodwin and Norman Hampson. I am most grateful to Richard Cobb, Professor of Modern History in the University of Oxford, for having read the typescript and for having given me much valuable advice for the book's improvement.

I want also to thank my friends, Mr R. H. Owen, who helped me with various translations when we were working on the book in Paris, and Mr John Guest who has been my most skilful and trusted editor for over twenty years. For their help in a variety of other ways I am deeply indebted to Mrs John Rae, Mrs Francis Pollen, Mrs John Street and to my wife for compiling the index.

C. H.

Appendix 1 (page 305) provides some information about the fate of characters whose end is not recorded in the text;
Appendix 2 (page 319) is a glossary of French terms used in the text;
Appendix 3 (page 329) is a table of the principal events in France from 1788 to 1799.

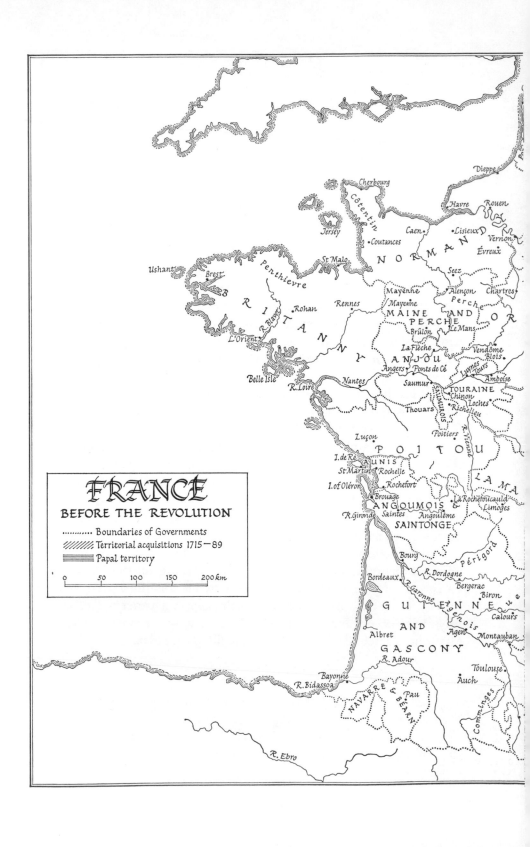

FRANCE
BEFORE THE REVOLUTION

.... Boundaries of Governments
/////// Territorial acquisitions 1715—89
≡≡≡ Papal territory

0   50   100   150   200 km

Dieppe

Cherbourg
Côtentin
Havre
Rouen
Caen
Lisieux
Vernon
Coutances
Évreux

Jersey

NORMAN
Ushant
Brest
Penthievre
St Malo
Seez
OR
Mayenne
Alençon
Chartres
Rohan
Rennes
Mayenne
Perche

BRITANNY
MAINE AND
PERCHE
Brûlon
Le Mans

L'Orient
La Flèche
Vendôme
Blois
R. Blavet
ANJOU
Belle Isle
Angers
Ponts de Cé
Luynes
Tours
Amboise
R. Loire
Nantes
Saumur
TOURAINE
Chinon
Loches
Thouars
Richelieu

Luçon
Poitiers
R. Vienne
I. de Ré
AUNIS
POITOU
St Martin
Rochelle
LA MA
I. of Oléron
Rochefort
La Rochefoucauld
Brouage
Limoges
R. Gironde
ANGOUMOIS
Saintes
Angoulême
SAINTONGE

Bourg
Périgord
Bordeaux
R. Dordogne
Bergerac
R. Garonne
Biron
GUIENNE
Cahors
AND
Agenois
Agen
Albret
Montauban
GASCONY
R. Adour
Toulouse
Bayonne
Auch
R. Bidassoa
NAVARRE & BEARN
Pau
Comminges

R. Ebro

Ostend
Nieuport
Gravelines   • Antwerp
Dunkirk
Boulogne   FLANDERS & HAINAULT   R. Lys
St Omer   • Lille
Montreuil   Douai   Valenciennes
ARTOIS   Arras   • Cambrai
Abbeville
Somme   Péronne   St Quentin
PICARDY   Amiens
Noyon
Beauvais   R. Oise   Soissons
Compiègne   Rheims
Chantilly   OF FRANCE   St Menehould   VERDUN
Pontoise   R. Marne   Châlons
St Germain   St Denis   Meaux
Versailles   Vincennes   Charenton
Sceaux   Villeneuve St Georges
Limours   PARIS   Melun
Etampes   R. Seine   Troyes
Fontainebleau   Brienne
Nemours   Sens
CHAMPAGNE
BRIE

Orléans
Gien   Blois
Auxerre
BERRY   NIVERNAIS
Bourges   Dijon
Montrond   Nevers   Bellegarde
Autun   Besançon
FRANCHE
COMTÉ
Dôle

Guéret
La Chaussade   Moulins   Gueugnon
Riom   Mâcon
MARCHE   Clermont   LYONNAIS   Bourg   Geneva
BOURBONNAIS   Beaujolais   Dombes
Trévoux   Bugey
Lyons   Valromey
Vienne   Les Sablons

LIMOUSIN
AUVERGNE   R. Po
Romans   Grenoble   Exilles
Vixille   Fenestrelles
Valence   Pinerolo
DAUPHINÉ
Embrun
Viviers   Barcelonnette
Rodez   Colmars
Uzès   ORANGE Carpentras
Albi   Avignon
LANGUEDOC   Nîmes   Venals
Castres   Montpellier   Arles   PROVENCE   Antibes
Béxiers   Aix   Is. de Lérins
Castelnaudary   Narbonne   Marseilles   Fréjus
Amiers   Carcassonne   Château d'If   Toulon
Alet   Is. d'Hyères
FOIX   Perpignan
ROUSSILLON

R. Meuse
R. Rhine
R. Main
Bouillon
Charleville
Sedan   Stenay   Longwy
Rethel   Jametz
Clermont-en-Argonne   Metz   R. Moelle
MESSIN
Bar   Bar-le-duc   Nancy   Lunéville
LORRAINE   ALSACE   Strassburg
R. Danube
Héricourt   Mulhausen
Montbéliard   Basle   R. Rhine
R. Doubs

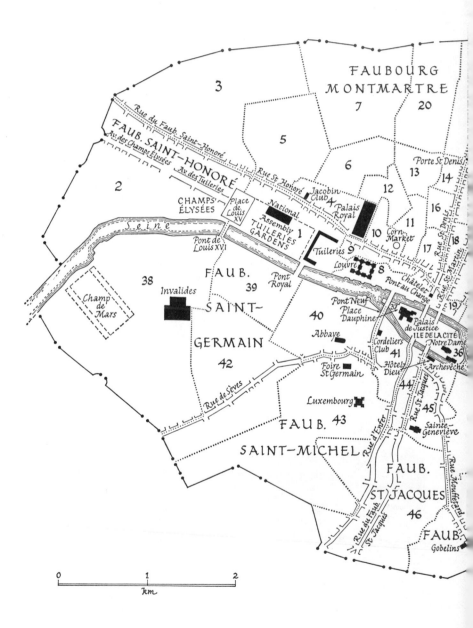

PARIS in 1790

FAUBOURG MONTMARTRE

7 20

3

5

6

13 14

Porte St Denis

2

Rue du Faub. Saint-Honoré

FAUB. SAINT-HONORÉ

Av. des Champs Élysées

Av. des Tuileries

Rue St Honoré

CHAMPS ÉLYSÉES

Place de Louis XV

National

Jacobin Club

Palais Royal

12

11 16

Rue St Denis

17 18

Assembly 1

TUILERIES GARDENS

10 Corn Market

Seine

Pont de Louis XVI

Tuileries 9

Louvre 8

Châtelet *Pont au Change*

Rue St Martin

19

FAUB. 39

Pont Royal

38

Invalides

Champ de Mars

SAINT-

40

Pont Neuf Place Dauphine

Palais de Justice

ILE DE LA CITÉ Notre Dame 36

Abbaye

GERMAIN

42

Foire St Germain

Cordeliers Club 41

Hôtel Dieu

Archevêché

Luxembourg

44

Rue St Jacques

45

FAUB. 43

Rue d'Enfer

Sainte-Geneviève

SAINT-MICHEL

FAUB.

St JACQUES

46

Rue du Faub. St Jacques

Rue Mouffetard

FAUB.

Gobelins

0   1   2

km

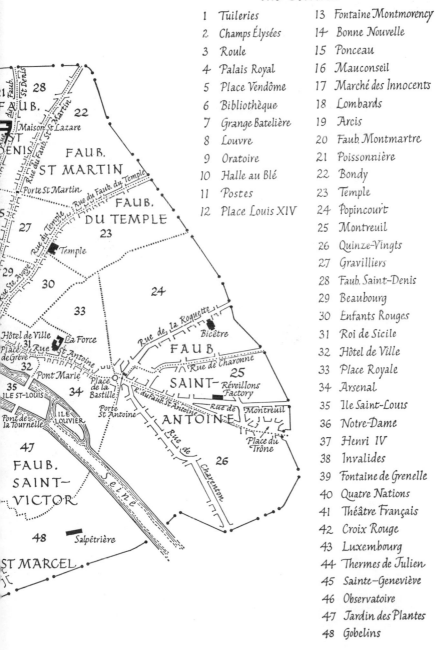

The Sections

PROLOGUE

COURT AND COUNTRY

*'Never was any such event so inevitable
yet so completely unforeseen'*

ALEXIS DE TOCQUEVILLE

In a quiet corner of the park at Versailles stands that delightful little *pavillon* of honey-coloured stone known as the Petit Trianon. Designed for Madame de Pompadour, King Louis XV's entertaining mistress, it had become His Majesty's favourite retreat. He was staying here in April 1774 when it was noticed by the light of a candle as he bent over a table that his cheeks were blotched with red marks, symptoms of smallpox. At sixty-four, with a constitution weakened by excess, he was not expected to recover. With little hope of doing so himself he said that he would like to die where he was. He was advised, however, that the setting was inappropriate. So the doctors wrapped him in a cloak, carried him down to a waiting coach and had him transported back to the palace. And here, in his bedchamber, while priests listened to his confession and his face became swollen and dark, a candle was placed in the window to be snuffed out when he died.

His grandson, who was to succeed him, repeatedly glanced at the candle through the windows of his own room. It was still burning when he went to bed on 9 May. But in the early hours of the following morning the flame was extinguished. The Lord Chamberlain came out into the antechamber known as the Oeil de Boeuf to announce to the courtiers waiting behind the railings, 'Gentlemen, the King is dead.'

The new King, Louis XVI, was nineteen years old. Although kind and generous by nature, his manner was usually brusque, cold and formal, marked by fits of ill humour and sharp retorts. His Keeper of the Seals had 'never known anyone whose character was more contradicted by outward appearances'. He was 'really good and tender-hearted'. You could 'never speak to him of disasters or accidents to people without seeing a look of compassion come over his face, yet his replies [were] often hard, his tone harsh, his manner unfeeling'. Hesitant, reserved and ungainly, his appearance, too, was unprepossessing. He had clear blue eyes and abundant fair hair, but his mouth was over-full and flabby and his chin was pale and fat.

He was so short-sighted that he could not recognize anyone at a distance of more than three paces [one of his wife's ladies-in-waiting, the Comtesse de La Tour du Pin, wrote in her memoirs]. He was stout, about five foot six or seven inches tall, square shouldered and with the worst possible bearing. He looked like some peasant shambling along behind his plough. There was nothing in the least stately in his clothes, putting on whatever was offered to him . . . His sword was a perpetual embarrassment to him.

Possessed of great physical strength, he spent days on end hunting, galloping at reckless speed through his forests after stags and deer, roebuck and boar, but he could never keep his weight down for his appetite for rich food was voracious. Religious and most exact about Mass, he ate nothing between breakfast and supper in Lent, but at other times of the year he indulged himself to the full. It was said that one morning before going down to the stables he had consumed 'four cutlets, a chicken, a plateful of ham, half a dozen eggs in sauce and a bottle and a half of champagne'. Even at his wedding banquet—though he had appeared nervous, embarrassed and gloomily apprehensive at the preceding marriage ceremony – the guests in their tiered boxes in the Salle de Spectacle had seen him put down his head with gusto at the royal family's balustraded table in the centre of the floor. 'You really should not stuff yourself so on a night like this,' his grandfather had admonished him. 'Why not?' he had asked. 'I always sleep better after a good meal.'

He had been fifteen then. His bride, Marie Antoinette, was just over a year younger, though she looked little more than twelve years old. Alert, affectionate, highly strung and wilful, she was the daughter of the formidable Empress Maria-Theresa of Austria who who had given birth to her, the fifteenth of her children, in an armchair at the Hofburg and had then almost immediately returned to the examination of her state papers which the labour pains had briefly interrupted. Marie Antoinette had been extremely badly educated but, although she had few interests and was not in the least intellectual, her mind was much sharper and she was far more vivacious. When she had said goodbye to her family – and had been carried away in a vast cavalcade to an island in the Rhine where she had been stripped of all her Austrian clothing in a tent before being handed over naked to the French – she had burst into tears. But on arrival at Versailles she had soon recovered herself. She had found the Dauphin, whom she had been sent to marry, not nearly so 'horrid' as she had feared he might be, and on the day of the wedding she was seen to be looking quite happy and calm. Occasionally she betrayed a hint of nervousness during the service; yet, beside the trembling, blushing figure of her husband, she seemed a model of composure, and, indeed – with her lovely complexion, clear blue eyes and shining fair hair – of beauty.

The Dauphin's nervousness was understandable. Not only had he never known a girl of his own age, but he had been brought up in the belief that attractive women were a danger to the soul. His gloomy, fastidious father, who had died when he was eleven, had pointed out his grandfather's many mistresses to him as representatives of the kind of excess against which he himself must always be on his guard. So had his mother, a kindly, pious woman who had not long outlived her husband. So had his maiden aunts with whom he had spent much of his time after his parents' early death. Nor was it only attractive women against whom he had been warned: he had been taught to beware of the wiles of Austria, France's traditional enemy. A pretty Austrian girl was, therefore, doubly hazardous.

After supper on his wedding night he and his bride were escorted to the Dauphine's bedroom on the ground floor. Watched by numerous courtiers, the Dauphine's ladies ritually removed her jewellery, shoes and dress as custom dictated; the Dauphin then undressed while the King stood ready to hand him his nightshirt. Bride and bridegroom then climbed into the marital bed, whose sheets had been sprinkled with holy water, and were addressed by a bishop with reverentially hopeful prayers. The curtains were then drawn back to reveal the seated couple before being closed again. Soon afterwards the Dauphin went to sleep.

For a long time after their first uneventful night together, the Dauphin did not venture again into his wife's bedroom; and when, eventually, he did so, having overcome his early suspicions and fallen in love with her, it seems from Marie Antoinette's letters to her mother that he derived as little pleasure from these visits as he was able to give her. It was the stated opinion of the Austrian Ambassador, Comte Florimond Claude de Mercy, who was naturally anxious to blame Louis rather than Marie Antoinette for their failure to have children, that the Dauphin was hampered by a physical deformity. Marie Antoinette's brother, who became Emperor Joseph II on their mother's death, believed, on the contrary, that Louis's 'laziness, clumsiness and apathy were the only obstacles'. 'As for my sister,' he added, 'she is not amorously inclined and when they are together they are a couple of awkward nincompoops.' Certainly Marie Antoinette appears to have been extremely modest: in her bath she wore a flannel shift, buttoned from neck to ankle, and when she emerged she required her maids to hold up a sheet as a screen between her body and her ladies. But there were those who hinted that this modesty was merely the affectation of a fundamentally libidinous nature. It was rumoured not only that the King was impotent but also that the Queen sought her pleasures elsewhere, both with men and with women.

Neither the King nor the Queen was an unpopular figure with the people as a whole in the early years of their marriage; on their first visit to Paris they were warmly welcomed by cheering crowds in streets decorated with flowers and triumphal arches. But pamphlets, at first attacking Marie Antoinette as a meddlesome, troublesome foreigner, then accusing her of adultery and lesbianism, had already begun to appear and were soon in wide circulation. Her passionate friendships with the excessively sensitive widow, the Princesse de Lamballe, the Superintendent of her Household – who lost consciousness so readily that she once swooned away at the sight of a lobster in a painting – and with the pretty, high-spirited Duchesse de Polignac, were described in these pamphlets in obscene terms that gave much satisfaction to her enemies. It was said that these two ladies, on whom she lavished money, offices, apartments and gifts, helped her widen '*la porte de Cythère*' so that her husband's '*jeanchouart*', '*toujours molle et toujours croche*', could more easily enter it.

Whatever the difficulties of the young couple may have been, it was not until August 1773, over three years after the marriage and

22

thanks, so some reports had it, to an operation performed on the Dauphin's foreskin, that Marie Antoinette was able to report to her mother, and then rather doubtfully, 'I think our marriage has been consummated.' And a further four years were to pass before she could write more confidently that the marriage had at last been '*parfaitement consommé*', that she was '*dans le bonheur le plus essentiel pour toute ma vie*'. In the spring of 1778 she discovered herself to be pregnant, and just before Christmas that year, following the *accoucheur*'s announcement, 'The Queen is entering labour', a crowd of Ministers, Court dignitaries and others rushed into her bedroom to witness the delivery, two men clambering on to a sofa to obtain an unobstructed view of the bed, which had been placed near the fire, behind a low screen. So intense was the crush, so hot the room that the Princesse de Lamballe lost consciousness for several hours. For fear lest his wife might suffocate, the King with unaccustomed decision tore off the tapes which hermetically sealed the windows to let in some air. A few moments later, the child, a daughter, was born.

Three other children followed her, a brother in 1781, another brother, the future Louis XVII, in 1785 and a sister in 1786. But, while his family grew, the King's self-assurance did not. He continued hesitant, undignified, clumsy, reticent and self-doubting. He appeared to have no will of his own, to act only under pressure. 'Imagine,' said one of his brothers, 'a handful of oiled ivory balls that you are trying to keep together!' Had he had any choice in the matter he would certainly not have been a king: he once remarked to one of his Ministers who relinquished office, 'How lucky you are! Why can't *I* resign, too?' Still impressionable and sensitive, his true feelings remained concealed behind a façade at once blunt and severe. As kind-hearted as ever, he could not bring himself to be gracious to his courtiers, to offer them sympathy in grief or illness, to speak to them other than off-handedly or with harsh and tactless banter. He still indulged in horseplay and tiresome practical jokes, trying to trip his pages up with his *cordon bleu*, making a face and childishly running away when his nightgown was handed to him, walking with his breeches hanging around his ankles. Laboriously painstaking, he occupied himself for hours with petty details, minor cash accounts and lists of game killed in the forests, as though to avoid consideration of the wider, complicated problems of the state. He preferred to work with his hands, beating out bronze and copper, carving wood, constructing locks, building stone walls – all of which tasks he performed with competence – rather than to discuss with his Ministers their departmental affairs. He gave the impression of studiousness: he built a fine white and gold library at Versailles, he purchased a second-hand set of the *Encyclopédie*, he read a great deal – both newspapers and books, he taught himself to read English and, after a fashion, Italian and Spanish. But he rarely seemed to profit from his study or to show that he remembered what he had read.

His day began at six o'clock when one of his four *valets de chambre*, who had passed the night on a truckle bed, threw back the curtains of the four-poster to awaken him. He rose immediately, put on his dressing-gown, shaved, dressed in the clothes that the valets ceremonially presented to him, had the Star of the Holy Spirit – France's highest order – fixed to his left breast. When his hair had been satisfactorily curled, powdered and decorated with a silk ribbon round the queue, he went for a walk, returning precisely at eight o'clock for the *petit lever* during which Ministers and officials of the Household were admitted to discuss business with him. He then went up to his private apartments to read or tinker in his work-shop. Mass was said at noon.

Dinner, which was usually over at half-past one, was eaten in public. The King and Queen sat next to each other in armchairs, their backs to the fireplace, a row of stools arranged in a semi-circle in front of their small table. On these stools sat various female members of the royal family and the senior ladies of the enormous Household, and behind them stood other ladies of the Household and as many spectators as could be admitted into the room. One day in November 1775 these spectators included Samuel Johnson and his friend, Hester Thrale. 'They had a damask tablecloth neither coarse nor fine,' Mrs Thrale noticed. 'Their dishes were silver . . . and their dinner consisted of five dishes at a course. The Queen ate heartily of a pye which the King helped her to. They did not speak at all to each other, as I remember, but sometimes talked to the Lord-in-Waiting.'

In the afternoon the King and Queen sometimes went to a play performed for their benefit in the Salle de Spectacle; and in the evening the Court settled down to play card games, billiards, backgammon or cavagnole, the King disapproving of – but refraining from objecting to – the high stakes gambled by his wife and his two brothers.

These two extravagant brothers, whose debts the King always paid, were the Comte de Provence, later Louis XVIII, and the Comte d'Artois, later Charles X. Provence, known as Monsieur, was a year younger than the King, an intelligent, sometimes witty, well-read, rather sickly young man with highly expensive tastes and a rigid belief in absolute monarchy. The Comte d'Artois was not so intelligent but much more athletic and dashing, taking a lively interest in women, clothes and race horses. He shared Monsieur's political views and was to be much given to declaiming his wish to fight for the monarchy, to draw 'the sword of his fathers'. The King was ill advised by both of them and trusted neither.

Marie Antoinette was as extravagant and as indulged by her husband as were her brothers-in-law. In the early days of their marriage, according to the Austrian Ambassador, there had been frequent squabbles between husband and wife. She had objected in particular to his passion for hunting and to his eating so much at hunt suppers at which he was led astray by his grandfather and his grandfather's sensual, grasping mistress – Madame de Pompadour's successor – the former prostitute, Madame Du Barry. After her husband had suffered from a particularly bad attack of indigestion, Marie Antoinette evidently 'had all the dishes containing pastry removed from his table and peremptorily forbade any more pastry to be served until further notice'.

Other observers besides de Mercy had attributed Marie Antoinette's pert and saucy behaviour to her husband's failings as a lover. Insecure and dissatisfied, she seemed to go out of her way to shock and surprise. She did not attempt to conceal her impatience with the ridiculousness of Court protocol which required, for instance, that when she was being dressed in the morning her chemise had to be handed to her by her *dame d'honneur* or, if a royal Princess were in the room, the chemise must first be passed to the Princess before being passed to the Queen. Once, when the dressing ceremony was about to begin, there was a scratch at the door and the Duchesse d'Orléans was admitted. The chemise was, therefore, passed to her for presentation to the Queen; but before the Queen could take it another scratch announced the entry of the Comtesse d'Artois who had precedence over the Duchesse. The Duchesse could not, however, hand it directly to the Comtesse but had to pass it first through the hands of the *dame d'honneur*. While these movements were being performed, with appropriately stylized emphases, the Queen stood shivering in the cold and draughty room, murmuring to herself in the German accent which she never entirely lost, '*C'est odieux!*'

It was further held against the Queen that she made no attempt to disguise the feelings which were always reflected in the expressions that fleeted across her pretty face. If she felt like laughing she laughed. If she felt like teasing the King she did tease the 'poor man' as she called him. If the mood took her to throw her hat into a lake she did so. She thought it absurd that it was considered impolite to clap musicians and dancers at royal performances, so she applauded them. She considered it preposterous that she should always be expected to be driven about by a coachman, so she bought a cabriolet and drove it herself, extremely fast. She called one of the senior and most staid of the Court ladies, the Comtesse de Noailles, to whom a pin misplaced on a gown was a tragedy, 'Madame l'Étiquette'. And on one celebrated occasion when she fell off a donkey she laughingly refused to be helped to her feet. 'Leave me on the ground,' she said. 'We must wait for "Madame l'Étiquette"! She will show us the right way to get up having fallen off a donkey.'

She was often bored and even more often frightened of being bored. 'To escape the terrible obsession,' she said, 'I must have bustle; I must have endless change.' She could not bear to be still. She played with children and dogs; she dressed up in a plain muslin dress, net fichu and straw hat and pretended to be a dairymaid in the miniature village she had built at enormous cost in the grounds of the Trianon; she took part in amateur theatricals; she arranged and rearranged the flowers in her room; she went to horse-races and to balls; she did embroidery and frustratedly put the silks and canvas down to play the clavichord, then left that to gamble. Looking for a part to play in life, she became a patron of the opera and of the ballet; she became a leader of fashion, rejecting the elaborate dresses of her day and choosing to wear those simple and natural clothes which so well suited her, buying three or four new dresses every week, and spending far more than her allowance permitted, turning to the King to supplement it and never turning in vain.

Indulgent as the King was towards her, however, and influenced as he was by her opinions, the King did not allow the Queen to interfere as meddlesomely in affairs of state as public opinion was led to suppose and her own naturally proud and authoritative nature seemed to suggest. Once, when she came into his room while he was working on some official papers, he said to her quietly but firmly, 'Madame, I have business to attend to.'

At the beginning of his reign he had called upon the services of the clever, witty Comte Jean-Frédéric de Maurepas, a former Minister who had been appointed Secretary for the Navy at the age of fourteen but who, having offended Madame de Pompadour, had been dismissed from office and had spent the past twenty-five years on his country estate. With the guidance of Maurepas, and of Maurepas's intimate friend and confessor, the Abbé Joseph Alphonse de Véri, Louis had gradually and nervously replaced his grandfather's Ministers with others more efficient and honest, including Anne-Robert Turgot, Baron de Laune, whom in 1774 he appointed Controller General of Finances. He had also decided to recall the *parlements* including the ancient Paris *parlement*.

This *parlement*, quite unlike the Parliament which had developed across the Channel, was one of thirteen appeal courts which had assumed the right of registering laws, principally royal edicts connected with taxation, but which aspired to the right of veto as well as of registration. Its jurisdiction covered about ten million people in northern France and since its influence was so much greater than the other provincial *parlements*, which were inclined to follow its lead in remonstrating against edicts its members disliked, it was usually referred to simply as *parlement*. Its members were far from being representative of the people as a whole. Their predecessors had been granted hereditary nobility in the reign of Louis XIV in 1644, and the principal offices had come to be held by some of the most renowned and wealthy dynasties in France. Proposals for the admission of commoners were always strongly resisted.

In the past, when *parlement* had proved recalcitrant, the Crown had enforced its will by a special session known as a *lit de justice*,* or had exiled the members from Paris in the hope, usually justified, that the damage to their legal business in Paris would induce them to give way to the royal will. In 1771 *parlement* had been exiled to Troyes; and two other provincial *parlements*, those of Rouen and Douai, had been suppressed.

There had been a public outcry against Louis XV's action as, although *parlement* was far more concerned with its own interests than with those of the nation at large, it had come to be regarded in the people's mind, largely as a result of its own propaganda, as their champion; and it did, indeed, do quite as much to promote and publicize liberal political theories as the *philosophes*. Louis XVI was aware of this and would have been well advised in the interests of the monarchy to curb its powers as his predecessors, with varying success, had repeatedly attempted to do. But he chose instead to follow the advice of Maurepas who argued that he must listen to public opinion and follow it; that a monarch who recalled *parlement* would be 'considered a friend of the people'. 'I should like to be loved,' he had once declared and had since reiterated this ambition. And so, although he had known he would be making difficulties for himself by doing so, he had recalled the exiled *parlement* from Troyes. On 12 November 1774 he had driven to the Palais de Justice in Paris where the reconvened members had knelt before him in their red robes; then, rising to their feet, they had listened quietly to the King as he had assured them that they could rely upon his protection so long as they did not challenge his authority.

With the recall of the *parlements* and the appointment of fresh Ministers, the people began to hope that a new age might be

* An explanation of French terms such as this will be found in Appendix 2.

dawning. In Paris a placard bearing the legend '*Resurrexit*' was hung around the statue of that revered monarch, Henri IV, and portraits of the new King who, it was believed, was prepared to follow the example of his popular predecessor, were displayed in shop windows. 'All the nation shouts in chorus,' Jean Le Rond d'Alembert, the mathematician and philosopher, reported to Frederick the Great, ' "A better day dawns upon us" ... The priests alone make sound apart, murmuring softly.' But this approval did not last long. The King's intermittently painstaking industry, his desire to be respected and loved by his people, and the cautious, tentative reforms of Turgot, Maurepas and the Minister of War, the Comte de Saint-Germain, did little to alleviate the plight of a nation whose fundamental grievances remained without remedy.

The population of France in the late eighteenth century was about 26,000,000. Of these about 21,000,000 lived by farming, many of them owning the land on which they lived. But although over a quarter of the land in the country was owned by peasants, few possessed more than the twenty acres or so which were necessary to support a family, and these few acres were generally farmed in an antiquated manner indicative of their owners' distrust of scientific agriculture. So, while some country people were able to maintain their independence in comfort and security, most were forced to work for at least part of the year as poorly paid labourers on bigger farms, or to borrow livestock, wagons and implements from richer farmers who in return claimed a share, usually a large share, of the crop. Conditions varied widely from one region to another, and French peasants were generally less ill-fed than those of Russia and Poland, but in times of scant harvests or epidemics of murrain many went hungry. Arthur Young, the observant and well-informed English landowner who travelled extensively in France at this time, frequently recorded examples of the most abject poverty, of countrywomen and ploughmen without shoes or stockings, of hungry-looking children 'terribly ragged, if possible worse clad than if with no cloaths at all'. One little girl of six or seven years, playing with a stick, made his 'heart ache to see her'. 'They did not

beg,' he wrote, 'and when I gave them anything seemed more surprised than obliged. One-third of what I have seen in this province
[he was then at Montauban in Brittany] seems uncultivated, and
nearly all of it in misery.' A few years before, another English
traveller, the splenetic novelist Tobias Smollett, was even more
appalled by the sight of the peasants he encountered travelling
across France; they had the appearance more of 'ravenous scare-
crows' than of human beings.

The poverty of many and the grievances of nearly all French
peasants were much aggravated by their liability for taxes from
which noble landowners might well be immune, and for increasingly
burdensome feudal dues which were required of them by the local
seigneur. It was also exasperating for the poor peasant that the tithe
which he might perhaps have paid without undue complaint to the
village *curé*, or as a contribution to the village church, was liable to
go instead to some rich abbot of aristocratic birth whose monastery,
though it might well be decaying, had as little need of the money as
the abbot himself.

The clergy in France then numbered rather less than 100,000, yet
they owned over one-tenth of the land, that is to say about 20,000
square miles. Despite these rich and rolling acres, most of the
clergy were poor, for there existed in the Church a hierarchy quite
as distinctly stratified as in the other orders of society. The bishops
were all nobles, and canonrics were often considered the perquisites
of well-to-do bourgeois families. Moreover, in many towns there
were far more canons than there were hard-worked parish priests.
In Angers, for example, where Church buildings and gardens took
up half the area of the town, there were seventy canons but less than
twenty priests.

Yet, although many priests were extremely poor, the Church as
an institution was not only very rich but also powerful. It paid no
taxes, voluntarily contributing instead a grant to the state every five
years, and, as the amount of this grant was decided in the quin-
quennial Church Assemblies, the clergy were able to exercise a
considerable influence over the policies of the Government. Nearly
all schools were in the hands of the Church which had, in addition,
its own courts of law. It also controlled most sources of information,

since it had taken upon itself the responsibilities of censorship. For those who could not read, the clergy were the means by which Government decrees and intentions became known.

The charges made against the Church by the *philosophes* of the Enlightenment were often unjust: most clergy, particularly those of the humbler orders, were neither corrupt nor unfeeling, nor even harshly intolerant of religious dissent. But the Church's great privileges, the scrupulously, not to say severely, businesslike manner in which many of its large estates were run, the number of absentee abbots and of well-endowed religious houses whose members were exclusively aristocratic, the gradual decline in belief of the virtues of a life of religious contemplation and the spread of scepticism among the influential middle class of the larger towns, all contributed to the growing spirit of anti-clericalism.

High as feelings ran against the Church in certain quarters, the general dislike of the aristocracy, from which its leaders came, was much more intense. King Louis XIV, while recognizing the social privileges of the nobility had done his best to exclude them from the exercise of power which he endeavoured to keep in his own hands and in those of his chosen Ministers. But, despite the resistance of Louis XVI's Ministers, the aristocracy were, in the later years of the eighteenth century, beginning once again to tighten their hold on the machinery of government; and, bent upon the eventual destruction of royal absolutism, which was declining but by no means extinct, were determined, in the meantime, to resist any encroachments upon their privileges. These privileges were extensive: only they could become ambassadors; only they could reach the highest offices in the Church; only they could command regiments in the army. Indeed, since 1781 it had become virtually impossible to obtain a commission in the army at all unless four generations of aristocratic birth could be proved. The nobility were further privileged by being exempt from the direct tax known as the *taille* which fell largely upon the peasants – *taillable* being a social indignity as well as a burdensome expense – and from the *corvées royales* which obliged those liable, again mostly peasants, to pay for the construction and maintenance of roads and for the supply of wagons for the transport of troops. And although legally liable to

31

pay those other more recent taxes levied in relation to income, the *capitation* and the *vingtièmes*, nobles enjoyed certain exemptions from these as well and were generally able to make a bargain with the *intendant* so as to escape paying the full amount.

Then there were seigneurial privileges by which noble landlords exercised control over manorial courts and over hunting rights and by which they enjoyed such *droits* as *droits de colombier*, which ensured that their pigeons were fed at their tenants' expense, and *banalités* which ensured them a monopoly of the local corn mill, wine press and oven. These feudal rights, demanded with ever-increasing severity, were often farmed out to lawyers and other experts who squeezed as much profit as they could out of them, who were constantly discovering forgotten *droits*, reimposing obligations, appropriating common lands, planting trees along the edges of peasants' fields and expelling them from forests. The 'feudal reaction', as it came to be called, naturally increased the peasants' resentment against the social order which made such impositions possible, and which imposed upon them, and upon them alone, the obligation to draw lots for service in the militia.

The nobility were not, however, a unified force, except in their not unjustified belief that their order, by encouragement and patronage as well as by the exertions of some of their members, had made France the most civilized country on the continent of Europe. There was once a time – some considered that the time had not passed – when the nobleman chose to suppose himself the heir of the Frankish invaders, and that the commoner, so far beneath him, was the descendant of those Romano-Celtic peoples, timid and unwarlike, whom his ancestors had conquered. The nobleman had, in fact, been a member of the *noblesse d'épée* who followed the King to war and, as a feudal landowning class, helped him to rule the country in peace. But in more recent times this could no longer be maintained. The Kings of France had not only created a new aristocracy, the *noblesse de robe*, by granting hereditary titles to their Ministers and other useful servants, but had sold these titles, together with public offices, to rich and socially ambitious members of the bourgeoisie. Daughters of these newly ennobled bourgeois families, bringing with them large dowries from their fathers, had married into less well-off families of the *noblesse d'épée*, while matches were also made between the *noblesse d'épée* and the *noblesse de robe*. Some of the more ancient families, particularly those of the *noblesse de court*, continued to look down upon this new aristocracy from whom they were still distinguished by being allowed certain privileges denied to the *noblesse de robe* such as full membership of the Order of the Holy Spirit, whose blue ribbon the King habitually wore.

Sharp as distinctions were between certain jealous families of the *noblesse d'épée*, the *noblesse de robe* and the *noblesse de court*, the distinctions between the rich and poor nobility were, of course, far sharper still. The nobility as a whole, numbering some 400,000 people in all – about half of whom had acquired their noble status within the previous two centuries – owned about a fifth of the land in France, twice as much as the Church. But, whereas some nobles owned thousands of acres which brought in immense incomes, and some increased their fortunes by speculating on the Stock Exchange, by investing in industry or by developing their estates, others lived and worked on small farms which provided them with the barest of meagre livings. And from these small and often ramshackle farms there was little chance of escape into more profitable enterprises, all but a few of which, such as the glass industry and maritime commerce, were traditionally closed to noblemen. Nor could they escape into the army where – despite the Comte de Saint-Germain's decree that the price of commissions should be reduced every time they changed hands so as to attract officers of birth rather than fortune – commissions were usually reserved for gentlemen who could afford to maintain themselves in style.

Many noblemen, in fact, were far less well off than the increasingly prosperous urban middle class whom they considered quite as great a threat to their privileged existence as royal absolutism. Yet most of the bourgeoisie – whether in business or in the professions, manufacturers or merchants, doctors or lawyers – were for the most part anxious to break down the barriers that excluded them from aristocratic preserves rather than to destroy the aristocracy that had brought those preserves into existence. For centuries, as Professor Lefebvre has said, 'the bourgeois, envious of the aristocracy, had aimed only at thrusting himself into its ranks ... This ambition was not extinct ... Bourgeois of old stock were frankly proud of their lineage, careful not to form an improper marriage ... Nothing was more pronounced than the ordering of ranks in this bourgeois society. The wife of a solicitor was called "Mademoiselle", the wife of a councillor was "Madame" without dispute, and the wife of a barrister was usually saluted with the same title. Distinctions no less fine were placed between the doctors and the surgeons; the former had entered the bourgeoisie; the latter were knocking at the gates. In short, the bourgeoisie, looked down upon by the high born, copied them as best they could. It has therefore often been thought surprising that this class whose spirit was far from democracy, should have been so imprudent, in attacking the aristocracy, as to strike at the very principle of social hierarchy itself. But the bourgeoisie had its reasons. The abolition of the legal hierarchy and the privilege of birth seemed to it by no means incompatible with the maintenance of a hierarchy based on wealth, function or calling.' The limitations imposed upon the talents of the bourgeoisie, particularly upon those of ambitious lawyers, were to make them the aristocracy's most formidable opponents.

If the grievances of the middle classes were social rather than economic, the poorer people in the towns were more concerned about money. It is impossible to generalize about France as a whole: in the late 1780s Bordeaux was a thriving port which to Arthur Young seemed far more prosperous than Liverpool, whereas the silk industry in Lyons was passing through a period of severe depression with over half its looms at a standstill. Yet it does seem evident that French trade and industrial production were generally expanding, even though manufacturing processes were for the most part antiquated with very few factories using steam, and with mines so dependent upon manual labour that coal production was only one-twentieth that of England. But while wages were slowly rising they failed to keep pace with the more rapidly growing rate of the cost of living, and industrial unrest was becoming common. Most master craftsmen and their journeymen still remained on friendly terms: after all, they usually lived under the same roof, sharing the same interests, and, as Professor Hampson has put it, 'when food prices rose the journeyman was more disposed to blame the baker, the farmer and the speculator in foodstocks than to demand higher wages'. All the same, master craftsmen were trying to perpetuate 'their own privileged position at the expense of their journeymen and to confine recruitment to their own families. The journeymen's attempts to organize themselves and to resort to strike action found the Government on the side of the masters and the municipal authorities – royal edicts prohibited the association of workmen for collective bargaining ... The urban population was therefore a prey to deep internal divisions, with some of the wealthier merchants aspiring to become large-scale industrialists, the master craftsmen and journeymen united in resisting the pressure to reduce them to a mere proletariat' but at the same time sometimes at loggerheads with each other.

The attempts of the King's Finance Minister, Turgot, to tackle some of the country's problems were neither reassuring to the people nor welcome at Court where his manner, too, caused offence. He was tactless, high-minded, impatient and touchy; he interfered officiously, so it was said, in departments other than his own. A thoughtless remark of his to the effect that if a woman were to have influence on the King's decisions it was better that this woman should be Marie Antoinette rather than de Pompadour or Du Barry annoyed both the King, who had attempted to keep his wife out of politics, and the Queen who resented being compared with royal mistresses. Accordingly, in May 1776, having lost the confidence not only of the King and Queen and the Court but of the financiers, the Church and *parlement*, and being considered too much of a *physiocrate* by the interventionists, Turgot was dismissed.

The following year, the Swiss financier, Jacques Necker, the Director of the Royal Treasury, was appointed Director-General of Finance, a post which had to be specially created for him since, being a foreigner, he could not serve on the King's Council of Ministers, all of whom, unlike himself, were French noblemen; and, being a Protestant, he could not be naturalized. It was the common opinion in Paris – an opinion fostered by his formidably clever and inextinguishably romantic wife who held sway over a literary salon in their smart house in the Rue de Cléry – that Necker was a financial genius. It was an opinion with which he himself would not have quarrelled. Silent, ponderous and ruminative, with half-closed eyes in a pallid, yellowish face, he seemed to be constantly lost in thought. If any man could bring order to France's economy, it was maintained, surely it was he. After all, he had made a fortune for himself as a banker in Paris; and a self-made millionaire could scarcely be other than an improvement on the noble Finance Ministers of the past.

At first all appeared to go satisfactorily. The King and his new Minister got on well together, even though Necker's silences when broken tended to be succeeded by economic speculations, prognostications and lectures of inordinate length. His cuts in Household expenditure at Versailles naturally aroused resentment at Court, where his vanity soon aroused as much antagonism as Turgot's high-handedness and where he made a particular enemy of the Comte de Provence whose request for over a million *livres*, which he claimed was due from his father's estate, was rejected. Yet it was generally agreed that these reductions of expenditure at Court were not only necessary but inevitable.

When he came to study the country's inequitable tax system, though, Necker was faced with complicated and intractable problems which he was quite incapable of resolving. The various taxes and duties levied in France – the *gabelle*, the *traites*, the *aides* as well as the *capitation* and the *vingtièmes* – were all, as he discovered, subject to variations, exemptions, inequalities in distribution and abuses in collection that made the evils of the system one of the principal causes of social unrest. Yet the increasing expenses of government and public works and the costs of the country's wars – in particular France's participation in the War of American Independence which involved expenditure of about 2,000 million *livres* – rendered the collection of further and more burdensome taxes inevitable unless the state were to slide ever deeper into bankruptcy. Necker thought that he had the answer to this problem: arguing that the limits of taxable capacity had already been passed, he proposed to raise the money required by borrowing, on the dubious assumption that a swollen public debt would not place an insupportable burden on the country's finances. He offered generous rates of interest and in order to attract investors published his *Compte Rendu au Roi sur les finances de la Nation*, a grossly optimistic and complacent document which transformed an actual deficit of 46,000,000 *livres* into a fictitious surplus of 10,000,000. Although the public at large, having no means of checking Necker's figures, accepted his pamphlet with satisfaction and bought thirty thousand copies of it within a week, its fraudulence was immediately noticed by most of the King's other Ministers. 'It's about as true as it is modest,' Maurepas commented when asked what he thought of it. A few weeks later, after a confidential memorandum written by him for the King's consideration and proposing a limitation of the *parlement's* fiscal powers had been copied and distributed by his enemy, the Comte de Provence, Necker felt his position so undermined that he demanded admittance to the Council of Ministers. The King refused, and Necker resigned.

Necker was succeeded as Director-General of Finance by Charles-Alexandre de Calonne, a cheerful, amiable, red-haired man of forty-seven who had been an *intendant* of Flanders. A collector of pictures and the proud possessor of no less than ten Titians, Calonne had a far more pleasant and easy manner than either Turgot or Necker and was well liked at Court. He became an even more welcome figure there when, soon after entering office, he raised further loans which allowed him to be far less severe with taxes than it was feared he might have been. It was not long, however, before Calonne realized in what a perilous state the country's finances were and that fundamental and wide-ranging reforms were essential to save them from utter collapse and to obviate the risk of the monarchy collapsing with them. He therefore drew up a detailed programme which included, together with many other less contentious measures of both economic and administrative reform, a new tax on land which was to be imposed without regard to the status of its owners and which would accordingly fall most heavily upon the privileged orders. This tax was to be a permanent one, not requiring registration for renewal by the *parlements*, and would enable the King's Ministers to disregard the *parlementaires'* remonstrances which had been the bane of their previous existence. The apprehensions of the nobility and the clergy that this new tax would prove not only financially burdensome but also the first step towards the extinction of their privileged positions were exacerbated by Calonne's further proposal that its assessment should be supervised by newly created provincial assemblies where local landowners would have votes in proportion to the amount of land they owned rather than in accordance with their social rank.

Well aware of the opposition that his proposals aroused among both the privileged orders and the members of the *parlements*, who were now confirmed in their belief that a strong and favoured aristocracy was a necessary bulwark against royal absolutism, Calonne suggested that they should be submitted for approval to a special Assembly of Notables, a convention nominated by the King, of which Henri IV had been able to make successful use in the past.

This Assembly of 144 members, including mayors and magistrates as well as nobles and prelates, met in February 1787, and Calonne, revealing the existence of an immense annual deficit, opened the proceedings with challenging words: 'Only in the abolition of abuses lies the means to answer our need. The abuses which we must wipe out for the public good are of the widest extent, enjoy the greatest protection, have the deepest roots and the most spreading branches.' But already the opponents of Calonne's policies were combining to render them unworkable. Both the Comte de Provence and the King's cousin, the Duc d'Orléans, voiced their disapproval of him. So did Loménie de Brienne, the sickly, ingratiating and scarcely less than agnostic Archbishop of Toulouse, who hoped to succeed him. So did Étienne d'Aligre, one of the leading magistrates in the Paris *parlement*. So did the adherents of Necker who chose to believe their hero's assertion that France had been solvent at the time of his enforced resignation. So did the influential Archbishop of Narbonne who declared, 'M. de Calonne wishes to bleed France to death. He is merely asking us whether to make the incision on the feet, the arms or the jugular vein.' So did Marie Antoinette, who strongly condemned Calonne's publication of an *avertissement* which, distributed free all over France as an appeal to public opinion, was condemned by a member of her

Household as 'a terrible diatribe against the clergy and the nobility'. Obliged to listen to these voices raised in condemnation of his Minister, the King at first supported him, then wavered, and constantly asked for advice. 'He asked advice of everybody,' wrote Pierre Malouet, a well-informed government official, 'and seemed to be saying to every person he approached, "What can I do? What should be done?"' In the end Calonne was dismissed and exiled to his estates in Lorraine, whence, threatened with proceedings against him by the Paris *parlement*, he fled to England, the first of the *émigrés*.

Brienne replaced him; but when he presented to the Notables a shadowy version of the proposals he had formerly rejected out of hand, the Notables were in no mood to accept from the Archbishop even so mild a concoction of the medicines that they had refused to take from Calonne. Their Assembly was dissolved and they went home, having demonstrated the firm determination of most of their number to prevent the King's Ministers tampering with their privileges.

The land tax and other measures which the Notables had rejected now had to be presented to the Paris *parlement*. And *parlement*, among whose members were several who had sat with the Notables, was equally determined not to let them pass, protesting that any new taxation required the assent of the Estates General, a consultative body of clergy, nobles and representatives of the Commons or Third Estate, which had not met since 1614 in the reign of Louis XIII. Confronted by the intransigence of *parlement* and worried by a crisis in foreign affairs, the King and Brienne, backed by Chrétien de Lamoignon, Keeper of the Seals, the one strong man in the Government, decided to use force. They dispatched troops to the Palais de Justice and had two of the leading and most intractable *parlementaires*, Jean Jacques Duval d'Eprémesnil and Goislard de Montsabert, arrested. Three days later, on 8 May 1788, after the King had invoked his right to enforce various edicts to which they had objected, the Paris *parlement* and all the provincial *parlements* were deprived of their power of opposing the monarch's will.

That summer violence erupted all over France. 'In Dauphiny and other Provinces,' reported the *chargé d'affaires* at the British

Embassy in Paris, 'no Taxes whatever can be collected, and accounts
of some fresh act of Revolt and disobedience arrive every day from
different parts of the Kingdom.' Protesting that they were acting in
defence of the *parlements*, nobles and magistrates came together to
block the Government's attempt to impose equality of taxation.
There were riots in Brittany, Burgundy, Béarn and Provence. In
Pau and Rennes violent demonstrations were provoked among the
population by local *parlementaires*. In Dauphiné there were clashes
between troops and the townspeople of Grenoble in which twenty
soldiers were wounded and two demonstrators killed. In Paris
there was fighting in the streets and an effigy of Brienne was burned
before cheering crowds.

As the prospect of national bankruptcy grew more daunting,
Brienne turned in desperation to the clergy, but they, in an extraordinary meeting of their Assembly, condemned the Government's
reforms and granted only a small proportion of the money for
which they had been asked. Forced to accept defeat, Brienne
announced on 5 July that the Estates General would be summoned
to Versailles in May the following year; and a few weeks later he
handed in his resignation. The King had now no alternative but to
reappoint Necker, to recall the *parlements* and to agree to the replacement of de Lamoignon by the supposedly more moderate
Charles de Barentin.

The general satisfaction aroused by the announcement that the
Estates General were to be reconvened was, however, soon overcast
by the further declaration by the Paris *parlement* that they should be
composed as they had been in 1614, which was to say that the three
orders whose representatives were to meet at Versailles, the clergy,
the nobility and the Third Estate, or Commons, were to have an
equal number of delegates. This meant that, if each order were to
vote separately, the clergy and nobility could always combine in
defence of their privileges to thwart the aspirations of the Third
Estate. The popularity of *parlement*, which the middle class had
formerly been inclined to view as a bulwark against despotic
government, collapsed, as Professor Goodwin has observed, overnight. 'Thus it was that, in the autumn and winter of 1788, the
struggle between the monarchy and the aristocracy was trans-

formed into a social and political conflict between the privileged and unprivileged classes. As the issues broadened, the solidarity of the privileged orders weakened. A split appeared even in the ranks of the *parlement* of Paris between the conservative magistrates and those with liberal inclinations ... The Third Estate also found champions of its claims among the lay and clerical aristocracy ... Lastly, there was formed in these months, in opposition to the coalition of the conservative aristocracy, a combination of liberal theorists and politicians who assumed the style of the "patriotic" or "national" party.' 'The controversy has completely changed,' wrote a contemporary witness, Jacques Mallet du Pan, the journalist. 'King, despotism and constitution are now relatively minor questions. The war is between the Third Estate and the other two orders.'

Politics now became of all-consuming interest. Noisy discussions took place every night in the coffee-houses of the Palais Royal where there passed from hand to hand a stream of freshly printed pamphlets, propounding the ideas of a new declaration of rights, new conceptions of national sovereignty, and France's need of a constitution.

The business going forward in the pamphlets shops is incredible [Arthur Young was soon to write]. I went to the Palais Royal to see what new things were published, and to procure a catalogue of all. Every hour produces something new. Thirteen came out today, sixteen yesterday and ninety-two last week ... This spirit of reading political tracts, they say, spreads into the provinces, so that all the presses of France are equally employed ... Is it not wonderful that, while the press teems with the most levelling and even seditious principles that if put in execution would overturn the monarchy, nothing in reply appears, and not the least step is taken by the Court to restrain this extreme licentiousness of publication? It is easy to conceive the spirit that must be raised among the people. But the coffee-houses in the Palais Royal present yet more singular and astonishing spectacles; they are not only crowded within, but other expectant crowds are at the doors and windows, listening *à gorge deployée* to certain orators, who from the chairs or table harangue each his little audience. The eagerness with which they are heard, and the thunder of applause they receive for every sentiment of more than common hardiness or violence against the present government, cannot easily be imagined.

These orators and journalists harangued the customers in the Café de Foy, the Régence, the Caveau and the Procope. Meetings were held in the fashionable salons of Madame de Tessé and Madame de Genlis. In masonic lodges the theories and writings of the *philosophes* were disseminated. Political clubs, which had been suppressed by the Government, reopened and found scores of new members; and new clubs were founded and soon fully subscribed. In cities all over France, the common practice of the upper floors of buildings being occupied by bourgeois families and the lower by the common people made the dissemination of revolutionary ideas between classes all the more rapid and effective.

'Scarcely six months had passed since I left France,' wrote Jacques Pierre, the pamphleteer, after a visit to America. 'I scarcely knew my fellow countrymen on my return. They had advanced an enormous distance.' Some of the liberal sentiments expressed by the 'patriots' were highly suspect in their sincerity: there were professedly progressive bishops who had their idea on ministerial appointments, there were *soi-disant* 'nationalist' lawyers anxious to dissociate themselves publicly from their conservative colleagues who had now become so unpopular. But most of the leading and more influential members of the 'patriotic' party were genuinely attached to the cause of liberalism and reform.

Nearly all these leaders were members of a secretive body known as the Committee of Thirty of which very little is known. The Committee, founded in November 1788, usually met at the house of a rich magistrate and *parlementaire*, Adrien Duport. Many of its other members were equally rich, able to finance the authorship and distribution of pamphlets, the circulation of lists of grievances which were intended to serve as models for others, and the dispatch of agents to the provinces. They included the Duc de La Rochefoucauld-Liancourt and the Duc d'Aiguillon, the Marquis de Condorcet and the Vicomte de Noailles. Among their number were also three men whose influence on the course of events during the next few months was to be far more profound. One of these was the Abbé de Talleyrand-Périgord who became Bishop of Autun in January 1789 and lived to become known to the world as Prince Talleyrand. Another was the Marquis de Lafayette, a tall, thin, solemn, conceited young man with a long nose, reddish hair and a receding forehead who had fought with distinction in America and dreamed, it was said, of becoming a kind of 'George Washington under Louis XVI'. The Third was the Abbé Sieyès.

Emmanuel-Joseph Sieyès was forty years old. Although of a naturally reflective, analytical turn of mind, he had wanted as a boy to go into the army rather than the Church. But his pious and ambitious middle-class parents had overborne his own wishes and he had spent ten years in a seminary. There, however, he spent more time in the study of political philosophy, of Locke, Condillac and Bonnet, than of those religious writers pressed upon him by his tutors who concluded that they might turn him into a 'gentlemanly, cultured canon, yet he was by no means fitted for the Ministry of the Church'.

He nevertheless entered the Church on the completion of his studies, and began slowly to rise in its hierarchy, though without any hope of becoming a bishop since he was not a member of the aristocracy, a class whom he consequently viewed with peculiar animosity. Ordained priest in 1773, he became secretary to the Bishop of Tréguier two years later, then Chancellor of the Diocese of Chartres and a member of the Provincial Assembly of Orléans. A small, thin man, austere, rather cynical, unfailingly if distantly polite, he made few friends, appeared indifferent to the society of women and was ill at ease with his social inferiors. As one of the twelve clerical representatives at the Provincial Assembly of Orléans, however, he did display a deep concern for the plight of the poor and argued for a programme of radical reform. But he was no orator: his voice was weak, his manner formal, his delivery, as one who listened to him commented, 'ungraceful and ineloquent'. He made little impression and was soon discouraged. So, seeing scant hope for any improvement in the social order, disliking the Church, distrusting the *parlements*, and despairing of the monarchy's ability to escape from the thrall of a reactionary nobility, Sieyès made up his mind to emigrate to America. And, having saved about 50,000 *livres*, he was just about to sail when the outburst of political discussion which erupted in France in 1788 persuaded him to change his mind. He took to writing. Never having published anything before, he made no mark with his first two pamphlets; but his third, 'What is the Third Estate?', powerfully persuasive though rather boringly written, was as influential as any other pamphlet produced at this time. Formulating the grievances of the unprivileged classes and identifying the Third Estate with the nation as a whole, Sieyès answered the question of his pamphlet's title, 'What is the Third Estate?' – 'Everything. What has it been up till now in the political order? Nothing. What does it desire to be? Something.' That 'something' included the rights to have as many representatives as the other two orders combined as well as to have its votes counted by head rather than by order. It also included the right to share in the framing of a constitution free from interference by any outside influence.

While the great political debate, fired by such pamphlets as Sieyès's, raged in the cafés, clubs and salons of Paris, Necker gave much thought to the problems posed by the forthcoming convocation of the Estates General. In the hope that they might be persuaded to give way to popular demand by allowing the Third Estate as many representatives as the other two orders combined, as 'What is the Third Estate?' demanded, he summoned another Assembly of Notables. But the Notables were not to be persuaded. They held by a large majority to the view that the presumptions of the Third Estate were to be firmly resisted. Disregarding the Notables' verdict – and concerned by warnings from the *intendants* in the provinces that civil war would break out if the privileged orders were allowed to have their way – Necker set about persuading his fellow Ministers and the royal family to issue an edict granting what had become known as 'double representation' to the Third Estate.

There were heated discussions at Court where both the King and Queen, as well as the Comte de Provence, were eventually persuaded to support Necker's views, and on 27 December it was announced that the Third Estate would, indeed, have 'double representation'. It was not, however, made clear whether voting would be by head, in which case the Third Estate – relying on the liberals among the nobility and the clergy – would be able to count on a majority, or by order, which would mean that their apparent advantage of numbers would be nullified.

Early in the New Year the elections began. Almost everyone aged twenty-five and over whose name appeared on the taxation rolls – or, in Paris, who did not pay less than six *livres* in *taille* – was entitled to vote; and voting in most areas was heavy. In all, 1,201 representatives were elected, 291 nobles, 300 clergy and 610 members of the Third Estate. Apart from the Duc d'Orléans there were few members of the *noblesse de cour* amongst the noble representatives, most of them being landowners of a conservative cast of mind from the provinces, though there were about ninety nobles who regarded themselves as liberals, including such celebrated figures as the Marquis de Lafayette, who was elected, with difficulty, at Riom. Less than a sixth of the representatives of the clergy were prelates; most were parish priests, many of whom had studied the *Encyclopédie*. Among the Third Estate middle-aged professional men were dominant, especially lawyers, though there were a few who were elected from outside their order, for example the Abbé Sieyès, who was chosen as one of the twenty deputies for Paris after being rejected by the clergy of Montfort-l'Amaury.

Before selecting their delegates, the electors of each of the three orders had drawn up a list of their grievances and of suggestions for reform known as a *cahier de doléances*. These *cahiers* were virtually unanimous in their condemnation of royal absolutism but none wished to do away with the monarchy altogether or questioned the King's right to choose his Ministers and initiate legislation. They were also almost unanimous in their desire for a constitution with the voting of taxes and approval of new legislation taking place in regular meetings of the Estates General, in their demands for elected Provincial Estates, for individual liberty and freedom of the press. Many asked for unification of laws and standardization of weights and measures, an end to government wastefulness, to abuses in public finance and internal customs barriers, and for reforms in the Church, though not for its separation from the state. But it was clear that the Clergy were bent upon retaining their independence; the Nobility their social rank and feudal dues.

45

At the end of April the various deputies, travelling from all over France, made their way by private carriage and public coach towards the palace of Versailles. It had been arranged that they should meet here close to 'the King's own dwelling', 'not in any way to fetter their deliberations, but so that he could preserve in regard to them the character that lies nearest his heart – that of adviser and friend'.

THE DAY OF THE
TENNIS-COURT OATH

20 June 1789

'No National Assembly ever threatened to be so stormy
as that which will decide the fate
of the monarchy, and which is gathering in such haste
and with so much mutual distrust'

MIRABEAU

On Saturday, 2 May 1789, the King waited in the Hall of Mirrors at Versailles to receive the deputies of the clergy and the nobility. The clergy, as the pre-eminent order, came in first, the double doors being opened wide and then firmly closed behind them. The nobility were also received in private although, in accordance with the usual ceremonial practice, the doors were not fully closed after their entry but left slightly ajar. As though to emphasize their inferior status, the Third Estate were not received in the Hall of Mirrors but, after being kept waiting for over three hours, were presented to the King in another apartment where they were ushered past him in file. The King, standing between his two brothers, could not bring himself to address a single word to any of them other than one old man of exceptionally benign appearance to whom he said, 'Good morning, good man.' The others, having made their bows, turned away, feeling much disheartened by the King's inability to display the least indication of friendliness and by the courtiers' haughty reserve.

The next day was Sunday, a day of preparation, argument and discussion, during which it became clearer than ever that none of the three orders was completely united in its aims. Among the clergy there were passionate radicals such as the Abbé Henri Grégoire from Nancy; there were defenders of the *ancien régime* like the clever and articulate Abbé Maury, the son of an artisan, who set his face firmly against change from the beginning; and there were those who followed the Archbishop of Vienne in preaching moderation. Among the Nobility there were many who supported the fat and fiery Duval d'Eprémesnil and the brilliant orator Jacques de Cazalès, a dragoon officer from a minor noble family in the south, in advocating an uncompromising stand in defence of their privileges. But there were also those, like the Duc de La Rochefoucauld-Liancourt and the Duc de Clermont-Tonnerre, who, more accommodating and, incidentally, of more imposing pedigree, were prepared to compromise. There were equally pronounced differences among the members of the Third Estate, some of whom believed that their ends should be obtained by agreement with the King and with the the other two orders, and others of whom insisted that there must be no compromise even at the risk of violence. The delegates from

Brittany, for example, and many of those from Provence and Franche Comté, soon came to be recognized as the most uncompromising, while those from Dauphiné were generally far more moderate.

On Monday, 4 May, the deputies of all three orders came together for a procession through the streets of Versailles to a Mass of the Holy Spirit at the Church of Saint Louis. As on Saturday, the members of each order were separated and distinguished by their dress: the Third Estate, all wearing tricornes and clothed in plain, official suits of black cloth with cambric ruffs, led the way immediately behind the guard; the nobles followed them, splendidly attired in plumed hats, satin suits with lace ruffs, silver waistcoats and silk cloaks, swords hanging from their belts. Lagging behind the rest, as though unwilling to be associated with them, was the Duc d'Orléans, the debauched, hard-drinking and witty demagogic Prince of the blood, who was believed to have designs on the throne and certainly spent a great deal of money in making himself popular with the people, and in the furtherance of mysterious plots. Behind him marched the parish priests in black habits, followed by the bishops in their episcopal robes and the King's musicians. 'Neither the King nor the Queen appear too well pleased,' wrote Gouverneur Morris, soon to become American Minister in Paris and that day a guest at Versailles of the *Intendant* of the Royal Gardens. 'The King is repeatedly saluted as he passes along with the *Vive le Roi* but the Queen receives not a single acclamation. She looks, however, with contempt on the scene in which she acts a part and seems to say, "For the moment I submit but I shall have my turn."'

When she appeared in the church, sparkling with jewels, some deputies cheered but others murmured 'Shame!' for she had kept them waiting for no less than three hours. The King, however, was well received, pleasing the Third Estate by smiling approvingly at the end of the sermon, which had been given by the Bishop of Nancy who had taken the opportunity to deliver a lecture to the Court, the burden of which His Majesty had missed since he had fallen asleep.

The next day the meetings began. Various buildings had been set aside for the deputies, including the Hôtel des Menus Plaisirs on the Avenue de Paris, which was normally used for storing theatrical scenery and costumes and was now specially decorated with tasselled hangings and gold and white painted columns, and a hall behind it in the Rue des Chantiers, which had recently been built for the Assembly of Notables and had just been enlarged and re-decorated.

It was in this hall that the deputies of all three orders came together for the official opening of the convention. Gouverneur Morris was there, sitting on a cramped bench, to watch them arrive: 'When M. Necker comes in he is loudly and repeatedly clapped and so is the Duke of Orleans, also a bishop who has long lived in his diocese and practised there what his profession enjoins ... An old man who refused to dress in the costume prescribed [for the Third Estate] and who appears in his farmer's habit, receives a long and loud plaudit ... The King at length arrives ...' 'He waddled in clumsily,' the Comtesse de La Tour du Pin observed. 'His movements were graceless and abrupt; and, as his sight was so poor and it was not customary to wear spectacles, he screwed up his face' as he peered at the deputies.

He was wearing a suit of cloth-of-gold, a huge diamond in his hat which he carried in his hand. The Queen, accompanied by Charles de Barentin, Keeper of the Seals, followed him in a white silver-spangled dress, a heron plume in her now thinning hair. The King, welcomed by shouts of '*Vive le Roi!*' sat down on his velvet-covered throne and put on his plumed hat, a sign that the privileged orders might put on theirs. And, as they did so, the Third Estate, either unaware of the custom or in defiance of it, put theirs on, too. The King immediately, therefore, took his off again, all the deputies following suit. He then replaced his hat as the Queen sat down in an armchair next to him.

He thereupon rose to make a short address. 'Gentlemen,' he said. 'The day I have been eagerly waiting for has at last arrived, and I find myself surrounded by the representatives of the nation which it is my glory to command ... A general restlessness and an exaggerated desire for change have captured men's minds and would end by leading public opinion completely astray were they not to be given proper direction by your wisdom and moderation.' He made a brief allusion to the inequality of taxation, added that he hoped all three orders would cooperate with him for the good of the state, and sat down to respectful applause. Barentin then spoke, but he spoke so softly that few of his sentences could be heard, and those that were were most unimpressively delivered. The deputies, some of whom were plainly annoyed by his condemnation of the 'false and exaggerated maxims' of the recent spate of pamphlets, were thankful when he sat down, leaving it to Necker to explain in more detail the condition of the country's finances. This Necker did at inordinate length, boring Madame de La Tour du Pin so much that the speech seemed 'never ending'. Occasionally passing sheets of facts and figures to an assistant who read them out for him in a tedious monotone when his own voice failed, he spoke for over three hours. He detailed the present situation of the Treasury, propounded its past achievements, elaborated on its future prospects, but made only passing references to proposed measures of constitutional reform, largely limiting himself to giving vague advice and inviting the delegates to reflect upon the Government's difficulties. No firm instructions were given either as to procedure or to the vital matter of voting. The speech was heard with a certain restlessness but politely and without interruption, and after it was over and the King arose to depart, there were loud cries of '*Vive le Roi!*' To Gouverneur Morris's surprise and satisfaction there were also cries of '*Vive la Reine!*', the first he had heard in several months. The Queen had sat throughout the proceedings with 'great dignity', wrote Madame de La Tour du Pin, though 'it was plain from the almost convulsive way in which she used her fan that she was very agitated'. She now acknowledged the cheers with a low curtsey; this produced a louder acclamation and another, lower curtsey.

Despite the polite cheers for the King and Queen, in which far from all the deputies joined, the Third Estate left the hall in a mood of obvious disappointment. 'Necker,' complained one of them, 'said nothing at all about a constitution and seems to accept the division of the three orders.'

In 1614 each of the three orders had retired to examine the credentials of its deputies on its own. Now, in 1789, they were again expected to conform to this rule, and the next day both nobles and clergy, meeting in the halls allocated to them, began to do so; but the Third Estate contended that the credentials of every deputy should be examined at an assembly of the entire convention. They remained in the large hall in the Rue des Chantiers. No rostrum had yet been built there; and the public, who were freely admitted, crowded round the deputies, offering them advice, shaking them by the hand, clapping them on the back, cheering popular speakers, booing others. The confusion of the early debates was aggravated by the deputies not yet knowing one another, by conflicts between those who favoured conciliation and those who did not, by their disinclination to adopt any rules of procedure which might indicate that they were organized as a separate order and thus at the mercy of the combined voting power of the privileged orders. A dean was appointed to supervise the debates, Jean-Sylvain Bailly, a respected astronomer and member of the French Academy whose father had been a court painter and custodian of the royal art collection at Versailles. But he found it impossible to exercise much control over them.

By the end of the month it had at least been decided that a concerted effort must be made by the Commons to persuade the parish priests among the clergy to come to join them. There were good grounds for hope that many of these priests would respond with enthusiasm. It was certainly well known that they were quite out of sympathy with the more conservative of the prelates and that there had been bitter exchanges during debates in the clergy's hall. An abbé who had spoken slightingly of the Third Estate had been roughly told by a priest to hold his tongue; another priest had forcefully reminded the bishops, 'In this place, my lords, we are all equal'; a third told the reactionary Abbé Maury, 'The village priests may not have the talents of Academicians but they have at least the sound common sense of villagers!'

Encouraged by these disputes among the clergy, a large delegation from the Third Estate, led by the enormously fat Gui Jean Baptiste Target, a deputy from Dauphiné, proceeded to the hall where the clergy were assembled. 'The gentlemen of the Commons,' announced Target, 'invite the gentlemen of the clergy, in the name of the God of Peace and for the national interest, to meet them in their hall to consult upon the means of bringing about the concord which is so vital at this moment for the public welfare.' A number of the clergy greeted these words with cheers and would have accepted the invitation immediately had not the more conservative amongst them insisted on discussing it first. The deputation thereupon returned to the Commons who decided to remain in session until the clergy's answer arrived. Hours passed and the answer did not come. The invitation was repeated; the clergy replied that they needed further time to consider it; the Commons said they were prepared to wait all day and all night if necessary.

Alarmed by the overtures being made to the priests and by the growing unrest in Paris and Versailles which was exacerbated by food shortages, the bishops turned to the King and asked him to intervene. Consequently, on 4 June, Necker proposed that each order should examine the credentials of its own members but allow the others to raise objections when the results were announced. If no decision could be reached, the King was to act as arbitrator.

On the day that this proposal was announced, however, the Dauphin died at the age of eight. Overwhelmed with grief the King shut himself up in his rooms at Versailles then withdrew for a week to Marly. While he was away, the Parisian deputies, whose elections had been delayed, began to settle themselves into the rooms reserved for them at Versailles and to harden the Commons' determination 'to appear formidable in the eyes of their enemies'. Among the Parisian deputies was the Abbé Sieyès who proposed that the clergy and nobility should now be asked to join the Commons, that those who did not should be considered to have forfeited their rights as representatives – in other words, that the Third Estate should constitute itself the representative body of the nation as a whole without the King's consent.

A roll on which the names of clergy and nobles willing to join the Commons was accordingly opened on 12 June. Over the next few days not a single noble put down his name; as an order they merely promised to consider the Third Estate's request 'with their most studied attention'. But on 13 June three *curés* from Poitou appeared at the entrance to the Commons' hall. They agreed, they said, to having their names put down on the roll. Their words were greeted

with an outburst of clapping and cheering as deputies rushed towards them, embracing them with tears in their eyes. The next day
another six priests, and two days later a further ten, followed their
example.

Encouraged by this break in the privileged orders' ranks, Sieyès
now proposed that, as the Third Estate represented ninety-six per
cent of the nation, they should immediately start the work the
country was waiting to see performed. As a first step the name of
Estates General should be officially abandoned and the Third should
confer upon itself a title that implied its unique authority.

The debate that ensued was stormy, and at the centre of the
storm was a vehemently gesticulating figure with bloodshot eyes
and a massive neck, the Comte de Mirabeau.

Honoré Gabriel Riqueti de Mirabeau was then forty years old.
His great-grandfather, whose ancestors had been rich merchants of
Marseilles, had been created a marquis after acting as a suitably
indulgent host to King Louis XIV; his outspoken grandfather had
been so badly wounded at Cassano in 1705 that, obliged thereafter
to wear an arm in a sling and his head supported by a silver stock, he
was wont to say that it was a battle in which he had lost his life; his
father had also served as a soldier for a time, but had resigned his
commission early to become a farmer and the author of various
radical books, which brought upon him the disfavour of the
Government who required him to remain upon his farm to the
south of Fontainebleau.

Honoré, his eldest surviving son, was born here in 1749 with two
teeth in his mouth and an inexhaustible energy which was to be
the despair of his family and household. At the age of three he contracted smallpox which left his face deeply pitted for life and thus
increased his ugliness and contributed to the dislike his difficult
father felt for him. After attending a military school in Paris he
received a commission in the cavalry regiment which his grandfather had once commanded, but, like his father, he did not remain
in the army long. Unattractive as his appearance was, his vivacity,
charm, adventurous high spirits and entertaining conversation made
him attractive to women for whom he himself had a voracious
sexual appetite, making love to anyone who would have him and

committing incest, so it was said, with his sister. A young lady to whom his colonel was attached fell in love with him and this led to a scandal which ended with his being imprisoned on the Île of Ré. In the hope that he might settle down and restore the family fortunes, he was, upon his release, married to the plain and extremely rich daughter of the Marquis de Marignane from whom he soon parted and, deep in debt, was incarcerated in prison once again. Removed from the Château d'If to a less rigorous confinement near Pontarlier, he made use of his relative freedom to visit the town where he was introduced into the house of a local nobleman whose pretty if rather vapid and ill-educated wife, Marie-Thérèse de Monnier, or Sophie, as he called her, fell helplessly in love with him. He fled to Switzerland where Sophie joined him; from Switzerland they travelled together to Holland where he made a precarious living by journalism and where he heard that he had been sentenced to death for *rapt et vol* at Pontarlier and beheaded in effigy; and from Holland he was brought back to France by the police and imprisoned yet again at Vincennes.

At Vincennes he occupied his time in writing passionate letters to Sophie and the obscene *Erotica biblion* as well as political works of a less self-indulgent nature, including his celebrated attack on prison abuses, *Lettres de cachet*, which was published after his release from Vincennes in 1782 and translated into English in 1787. This treatise, which led to the closure of the prison of Vincennes, added some lustre to his literary reputation, but he was otherwise regarded with as widespread misgiving as ever. He grew tired of Sophie, who consoled herself with a young army officer and then committed suicide, while he began an affair with Madame de Nehra, the daughter of a Dutch statesman, whom he was to desert in turn for Madame Lejay. At the same time he became involved in no less than three scandalous law suits, after which he had to leave France again, first for Holland, then for England.

'He had a tall, square, heavy figure,' wrote someone who met him at a dinner party at about this time. 'The abnormally large size of his head [in which the eyes were unnaturally protuberant] was exaggerated by a mass of curled and powdered hair. He wore evening dress with enormous buttons of coloured stone, and the

buttons of his shoes were equally large. His whole costume was remarkable for an extravagant fashionableness which went well beyond the bounds of good taste . . . He had a reserved expression, but
his eyes were full of fire. Trying to be polite, he bowed too low, and
his first words were pretentious and rather vulgar compliments.'

'His vanity was certainly excessive,' added another observer, the
fastidious and percipient law reformer, Sir Samuel Romilly, who
translated one of Mirabeau's political theses into English, 'and, like
many of his countrymen who were active in the calamitous Revolution which afterwards took place, not sufficiently scrupulous about
the means by which [the reform of society] was to be accomplished.'
Yet, for all his manifest faults, Mirabeau, 'in his public conduct as
well as in his writings, was desirous of doing good . . . His ambition
was of the noblest kind and he proposed to himself the noblest ends.'

Certainly, if he was rude and provocative, argumentative, over-
bearing and vain, immoral and unscrupulous both with regard to
women and to money, Mirabeau was *une force de la nature* who could
not be disregarded. 'I am a mad dog,' he said himself, 'from whose
bites despotism and privilege will die.' Charming when he chose to
be, a gifted conversationalist, possessed of a rare gift for mastering
complex issues, and combining a powerful intelligence with a deep
knowledge of the ways of the world, Mirabeau was bound to be one
of the most dominant figures in the Third Estate to which, having
been rejected by his own order, he was elected as deputy for Aix.
He was also one of the most distrusted. The Comtesse de La Tour
du Pin described in her memoirs the effect he had upon the other
deputies when he first appeared amongst them:

He entered the Chamber alone and took his place near the middle of the
rows of backless benches which stretched one behind the other. There
arose a very low but widespread murmur – a *susurro* – and the deputies
already seated in front of him moved one bench forward, while those
behind him moved back a little. He thus remained isolated in the middle of
a very obvious space. Smiling contemptuously, he sat down.

During the debate on the Third Estate's new title he aroused
further distrust by his apparent desire to stem the tide of feeling that

was pushing the Commons towards appropriation of complete sovereignty to itself. He proposed that the Third Estate should re-name themselves 'Representatives of the French People', and was immediately asked whether he would have translated 'people' as *populus*, meaning the whole nation including the privileged orders, or – what was, in fact, his intention – as *plebs*, meaning the Commons alone. Made aware of the ambiguity in Mirabeau's title, the Third Estate then turned to the consideration of other names, and tempers rose as some deputies made suggestions that others considered inappropriate or misleading. Voices grew higher and more angry, while outside the hall a summer storm raged, the wind howling at the windows. Bailly was urged to bring the session to a close, but he remained in his place, cool and imperturbable, until the tempest subsided and the most violent of the protesters left the hall. He then proposed that the rest of the deputies should also withdraw to meet again in calmer mood the following morning.

It was in such an atmosphere of confusion and uproar that so many of the debates were conducted. Often a hundred or so deputies were on their feet at the same time; and usually there was an impatient throng of them pushing against each other by the iron steps that led up to the rostrum. According to Arthur Young, who occasionally joined the noisy spectators in the public galleries, 'Monsieur Bailly was absolutely without power to keep order'. There were still no rules of procedure and when it was suggested that lessons might be learned from the House of Commons in London, the proposal was rejected contemptuously as yet another example of that intolerable anglomania which the Comtesse de La Tour du Pin said had become so extreme at Court that people took to affecting English accents. So the debates remained uncontrolled: tedious speeches, prepared beforehand, were read out at length irrespective of whether or not they were relevant to the issues in dispute, petitioners arrived at the doors insisting that their griev-ances be immediately considered and from the galleries there came an almost continuous roar of approval or disapprobation and the occasional piece of rotten fruit.

When the debate on the Commons' new title was resumed on 17 June, however, the atmosphere in the hall was less uproarious than usual. And when a deputy from Berry, prompted it seems by Sieyès, proposed the simple and explicit name 'National Assembly', it was approved by 491 votes to 89. On learning that this title had been assumed by the Third Estate, those of the clergy who wished to join them pressed harder than ever for union. A vote was taken on the issue, and as the result was announced, a priest threw open one of the windows of the hall and shouted to the crowds waiting expectantly outside, '*Won! Won!*' Soon the bishops and the priests who had voted in favour of the motion came out of the hall to be surrounded by a wildly cheering throng who bore them away triumphantly, many of them in tears, shouting, 'Long live the good bishops! Long live the priests!'

The next day, when the members of the self-styled National Assembly met to continue their deliberations, they found the door of their hall locked against them. Pressed by the Queen and by his family to make a stand against the revolutionary behaviour of the Third Estate, the King had decided to hold a meeting of all three orders, a *séance royale*, presided over by himself, and to announce that the actions of the Commons were illegal. In the meantime they and the clergy must be prevented from meeting.

But, undeterred by the locked doors of their hall, and at the suggestion of Dr Joseph Ignace Guillotin, one of the Paris deputies, most of the members of the National Assembly hurried off to an indoor tennis-court nearby. It was a large building with bare walls and a blue ceiling picked out with golden fleurs-de-lis. There were no seats other than a bench which was used as a desk, and an arm-chair which was offered to Bailly who refused it. Outside a huge crowd of people, who had followed the deputies from their locked hall, shouted '*Vive l'Assemblée!*' by way of encouragement. Some of them demanded admittance, but two deputies were posted at the door to prevent them. The Commons' deliberations, they were told, must be continued without interruption or distraction. Soon the tennis-court keeper arrived to take over the duties of door-keeper, and the two deputies returned inside the building. Here Jean-Joseph Mounier, a handsome young barrister from Grenoble whose weak voice had obliged him to give up his practice, silenced talk of withdrawing to Paris to seek the protection of the people by declaring that they must all take an oath 'never to separate' until an acceptable constitution was established 'on solid foundations'. With only a single exception the delegates came forward, their arms raised in dramatic salute, to take the oath before the tall figure of Jean-Sylvain Bailly who stood on a table made from a door wrenched off its hinges. They then took it in turns to sign a document on which the words of the oath had been inscribed. The one dissentient deputy, Martin d'Auch, insisted on signing his name with the word '*opposant*' next to it. Cries of protest were raised against him, and Bailly tried to persuade him that, while he was perfectly entitled to refuse to sign the declaration, he could not register his opposition to it. But d'Auch refused to give way and was eventually allowed to register his dissent 'out of respect for the liberty which all members of the Assembly enjoyed'.

The Court was now thoroughly alarmed, and the King, for the moment rejecting the idea of forceful coercion though still convinced that the acts of the Third Estate must be declared null and void, was ready to make some concessions at the *séance royale*. But this meeting, announced for 22 June, had to be postponed to allow time for the removal of the public galleries in which demonstrations by unruly spectators might have taken place. The Third Estate were able to take advantage of the delay by welcoming the majority of the clergy into their new meeting-place, the Church of Saint Louis, whose doors had been opened for them by the parish priest when the Comte d'Artois thought he would deny them a place of meeting by booking the tennis-court for a game. Two nobles from Dauphiné also joined them and were greeted with enthusiastic applause. These were soon followed by a group of nobles from Guyenne.

Three days after the oaths had been taken in the tennis-court, on 23 June, the Commons walked down the Rue des Chantiers for the *séance royale*. They found the door of the hall locked against them. Bailly knocked for a long time in vain. At length it was opened. He was told that they had arrived too early, and the door was shut again in his face. It was now pouring with rain and the deputies were about to go away when Bailly knocked yet again. At last they were admitted and hurried into the hall. One of them, who had noticed the ranks of soldiers on guard duty outside, recalled how oppressive was the atmosphere, how bedraggled and dispirited his colleagues looked.

The King arrived to a fanfare of trumpets and the rolling of drums, escorted by cavalry and a company of Household Guards. He 'affected to smile,' wrote one observer, 'but it was with an ill grace. The ironical gaiety of the Comte d'Artois seemed much more natural. He had the air of one riding in triumph and leading the King bound as his captive.' The King was welcomed with cheers by the people outside the hall and by most of the nobility and clergy as he entered it. The Commons, though, were silent.

Barentin stood up, after a short introductory speech by the King, to define the rules by which the three orders' future sessions should be governed. Then the concessions which the monarchy was prepared to make were enumerated: there were to be various fiscal reforms; consideration was to be given to the abolition of the hated *lettres de cachet* – letters signed by the King, countersigned by a minister and stamped with the royal seal, by which men could be subjected to imprisonment without trial or the opportunity of defence; steps were to be taken towards the establishment of a free press; there were to be no taxes 'without the consent of the nation's representatives'. Yet, despite this apparent abandonment of Bourbon absolutism, there were so many reservations in the royal declaration that it was clear that the *ancien régime* was not to be dismantled. And, as though to emphasize this, the wording of the King's speech had been more threatening than conciliatory. Still grieving for the loss of his son, he 'had appeared sad and gloomy', and had sounded flat and unconvincing, yet he made it clear all the same that the separateness of the orders and the existing social hierarchy were to be maintained, that any reforms which were to come would be granted by himself and not won by demand. 'If you abandon me in this great enterprise,' he concluded, 'then I will work alone for the welfare of my peoples ... I will consider myself alone their true representative ... None of your plans or proceedings can become law without my express approval ... I command you to disperse at once and to proceed tomorrow morning to the separate rooms set aside for your orders so that you may resume your deliberations.'

With these words he walked out of the hall, followed by the Comte d'Artois, looking 'full of pride', by the contented nobles, who had been assured of their continuing privileges, and by some of the clergy, leaving it free for further debate by the Commons unrestrained by his presence. Mirabeau seized his opportunity. 'Gentlemen,' he called, rising to his feet, his powerful voice echoing round the walls while trumpets sounded outside as the royal coach rattled away. 'We are being dictated to in an insulting manner . . . I demand that you assume your legislative powers and adhere to the faith of your oath. It allows us to disband only after we have made the Constitution.'

The twenty-seven-year-old Grand Master of the Ceremonies, Henri-Éverard de Dreux Brézé, interrupted him to remind him of the King's order to disperse. But Mirabeau stood his ground. 'Yes, Sir,' he replied. 'We have heard the orders that the King has been advised to give. But you have no right to speak here. Go tell your master that we are here by the will of the people and that we shall not stir from our seats unless forced to do by bayonets.' Sieyès and Bailly both supported him. 'The assembled nation,' Bailly asserted, 'cannot be given orders.' The question of their inviolability was then put to the vote and carried by 493 votes to 34.

According to the Duc d'Orléans, Brézé then rushed off to report to the King what had happened; and 'the King went pale with anger and uttered strong oaths. "Well then, clear them out by force," he ordered . . . Brézé returned to carry out this order but found that the Deputies had by then dispersed.' Other witnesses, however, reported that the King responded to the Third Estate's revolt with weary resignation, saying '*Eh bien, foutre! Qu'ils restent.* Well, damn it, let them stay.' Certainly, on 27 June, when most of the clergy and forty-seven of the nobility led by the Duc d'Orléans had joined the National Assembly, he decided that he would have to give his approval to a measure which he felt no longer able to prevent. After news had been received from Paris that unless he authorized joint meetings of all three orders, a mob thirty thousand strong would besiege the palace, he asked the remaining clergy and the rest of the nobility to follow the example of their colleagues.

The first stage of the Revolution was over and had been achieved without bloodshed. 'History,' Mirabeau proudly declared, 'has too often recounted the actions of nothing more than wild animals, among which at long intervals we can pick out some heroes. Now we are given hope that we are beginning the history of man.'

But while the National Assembly, under the Presidency of the Archbishop of Vienne, turned to the business of framing a constitution, the King turned to the army to save him from forces over which he was losing all control. He ordered six regiments up from the eastern frontier, then, following riots in Paris, another ten. As these troops converged upon Paris and Versailles the atmosphere in the capital and in the country at large grew ever more tense. There were increasingly frequent outbreaks of violence, a military prison was invaded by the mob, passers-by who declined to declare their support of the Third Estate were attacked in the streets. As the price of bread rose, there were riots in protest against the landowners, tithe-owners and merchants who were held responsible. In many towns the liberal-minded upper bourgeoisie encouraged the *petite bourgeoisie* to voice their protests against the reactionary attitudes of the aristocracy. They urged them to provide a lead for the journeymen and workers, to ensure that the hopes of a fairer society aroused by the calling of the Estates General would not be shattered so soon.

'Oh my fellow-citizens,' ran one of the numerous pamphlets published at this time and written by a member of the upper bourgeoisie, a doctor, 'keep close watch on the conduct of the King's Ministers ... Their aim is to dissolve our National Assembly, and the only means whereby they can do so is civil war. In private, Ministers are talking of ... sending against you a formidable force of soldiers and bayonets!'

'A large number of troops already surround us,' Mirabeau declared in a violent speech on 8 July. 'More are arriving each day.

Artillery are being brought up ... These preparations for war are obvious to anyone and fill every heart with indignation.'

Already the troops, mostly foreign mercenaries, had reached the high ground around Paris and were dispatched to protect strategic points such as the bridges of Sèvres and St Cloud and the Royal Treasury. The National Assembly protested at these movements, asking why a King, who was loved by twenty-five million Frenchmen, should surround the throne 'at such great expense with several thousand foreigners'. The King replied that the troops were in Paris to protect it from disorder, not to overawe it, but his words were rendered suspect by his dismissal of Necker whose place was filled by the sternly conservative Baron de Breteuil. To supervise the military actions, the experienced Maréchal de Broglie, a confirmed royalist, had already been summoned from Alsace to take over the Ministry of War.

The news of the dismissal of Necker caused the utmost consternation amongst the 600,000 people of Paris: treasury notes slumped in value, stockbrokers held an emergency meeting and closed the Stock Exchange, financiers and investors spoke gloomily of bankruptcy, artisans, journeymen and workers feared that the price of bread which had already almost doubled within the past two months would become more expensive still. They had long suspected that the aristocrats and land-owners had advocated the hoarding of grain so as to destroy the Third Estate. Now their suspicions seemed fully justified.

Concerned to defend property against the mobs that were rampaging about the town, breaking into gunsmiths' and sword-cutlers' shops and threatening the houses of the richer citizens, the Electors who had made the final selection of the Parisian deputies in the Estates General met at the Hôtel de Ville. Here they established themselves as an unofficial municipal authority and decided to organize a militia. Mostly well-to-do themselves – of the 379 men who attended the meeting the majority were lawyers, doctors and merchants – they agreed that the militia, soon to be called the National Guard, should be a bourgeois body composed only of respectable citizens prepared to serve one day in four, more than most wage-earners could afford to do.

As one Elector observed 'the situation in Paris [was] becoming highly ominous'. In the Place Vendôme a band of demonstrators hurled stones at the troops of the Royal Allemand Regiment; near the Tuileries a regiment of dragoons, commanded by the Prince de Lambesc, were also stoned and bombarded with garden chairs. Two companies of *Gardes-françaises*, confined to barracks for insubordination, broke out and rushed off shouting, 'We are the soldiers of the nation! Long live the Third Estate!' They were arrested and incarcerated in the Abbaye prison but were released by the mob. Other mobs marched through the streets pillaging bakers' shops and threatening to burn down the theatres if they did not close immediately, since people had no right to enjoy themselves in the midst of public misfortunes. Wax busts of Necker and the Duc d'Orléans, borrowed from Curtius's waxworks, were paraded about accompanied by black and white standards, symbols of 'mourning for the disgrace of an idolized Minister'. And in the gardens of the Palais Royal huge crowds collected. These gardens, which were surrounded by some of the most expensive shops and brothels in Europe and which had been thrown open to the public by the Duc d'Orléans, had long been the haunt not only of men-about-town and ladies of fashion but also of political agitators and public orators, and so it was here that people anxious for news, eager to spread rumours, or hungry for excitement naturally gathered. Most of them were delighted now to learn that the detested customs barriers which encircled Paris in order to exact heavy tolls upon all meat, wines, vegetables and other commodities entering the city, had been destroyed.

Among the crowd, standing on a table outside one of the cafés, was a tall young lawyer with a yellowish complexion and long, curly hair, Camille Desmoulins. The son of an official from Guise, Desmoulins had been admitted to the bar four years before, but a painful stammer as well as an unattractive manner and appearance had prevented his obtaining many briefs. He was then living in Paris in a poverty which his copying of legal documents and his authorship of several radical pamphlets had not done much to alleviate. There was, however, little trace of any impediment in his speech now as he excitedly harangued the people around him, referring to the dismissal of Necker as 'the tocsin for the St Bartholomew of the patriots', and calling them to arms and to the barricades. He had recently had a good deal of practice at this kind of demagogy.

It's simpler to go to the Palais Royal [he told his father, having failed to get elected to the Assembly], because you don't have to ask the President's permission to speak or to wait your turn for a couple of hours. One proposes one's own motion. It is supported and the audience gets the speaker to stand on a chair. If he is applauded he calls the crowd to order; if he is booed or whistled at, he steps down. The Romans ran their forum this way ... At the Palais Royal the patriots form a great chain with cavalry men, dragoons, chasseurs, Swiss guards, artillerymen, putting their arms round them, pouring out money in making them drunk or toasting the health of the Nation.

On this occasion Desmoulins, reckless, immature and uncontrollably passionate, drew two pistols from beneath his coat, declaring that he would never fall alive into the hands of the police who were closely watching his movements. He climbed down from the table into the arms of the crowd who loudly repeated his call 'To arms!' on every side. He had fastened a green ribbon to his hat as an emblem of spring and hope and liberty. And he urged everyone else to wear some sort of green cockade in token of their support for the 'common cause'. Hundreds did so, some of them pulling off the leaves of the horse chestnut trees for the purpose, until, as Gouverneur Morris discovered, it became dangerous to be seen out of doors without a hat garnished with foliage. Then they all marched off into the city to search for arms. The crowd was becoming an irresistible force.

THE DAY OF THE
VAINQUEURS DE LA BASTILLE
14 July 1789

'Yes, truly we shall be free!
Our hands will never wear shackles again'

DUQUESNOY

The morning of Tuesday, 14 July 1789, was overcast; heavy clouds threatened rain. Throughout the night the atmosphere in Paris had been growing more and more tense as rumours flew from street to street of thousands of troops on the march. In the Hôtel de Ville a Permanent Committee established by the Electors issued urgent orders for the erection of barricades, for the organization of those *Gardes-françaises* who had declared themselves on the citizens' side, for the protection of the banks, and for the arrest of all carts and carriages found entering or leaving Paris. Scores of these vehicles were assembled beneath the windows of the Hôtel de Ville in the Place de Grève which was soon littered with piles of stores and provisions of vegetables, with furniture, baskets, boxes and empty powder-barrels whose contents had been distributed the night before to those who had guns.

As yet, few citizens did have guns, and soon after dawn a crowd of about 60,000 people gathered on the parade ground in front of the Invalides demanding to be supplied with them. They had already made similar demands at the Hôtel de Ville where one of the leaders of the Permanent Committee, an elderly merchant Jacques de Flesselles, had aroused their distrust by his unhelpful, prevaricating manner. The Governor of the Invalides refused to deliver the arms up without authority. On Monday he had referred an earlier request for arms from a delegation of Electors to the Swiss General Baron de Besenval, Marshal Broglie's second-in-command, who had told him he must do nothing without authority from Versailles and had taken the precaution of ordering the pensioners on duty at the Invalides to render the muskets useless by unscrewing the hammers. The pensioners, unwilling to help their masters, set about this task with such extreme laboriousness that in six hours they had unscrewed scarcely more than twenty hammers of the 32,000 muskets awaiting their attention. The Governor told Besenval 'that a spirit of sedition was rife in the hospital,' so the General recorded, 'and that for the past ten days the soldiers had had their pockets full of money. A legless cripple, whom no one suspected, had introduced into the establishment hundreds of licentious and subversive songs. In a word, the Governor concluded, it was hopeless to count on the pensioners, who, if they received orders to load their cannon, would turn them on the Governor's apartment.'

While they were still at their leisurely work, a representative of the Electors left the Hôtel de Ville with instruction to persuade the Governor to give way to the peoples' demand. He found the crowd, larger than ever now, pressing round the gate of the Invalides, waving hats adorned with cockades and shouting for muskets. He forced his way up to the gate which was opened just wide enough to let him through. Inside, the Governor told him that no instructions had yet been received from Versailles and that he was, therefore, powerless to help him. The Governor then went out to try to explain this to the mob. But he could not make himself heard above their shouts and, as he withdrew, crowds of men rushed after him, forced the gate wide open and streamed into the building, while others clambered across the moat and up the parapet walls.

The guards of the Invalides stood by their cannon, disinclined to open fire, while 5,000 troops, encamped less than a quarter of a mile away on the Champ de Mars, also remained inactive. Indeed, Baron de Besenval could find no soldiers at all prepared to interfere. One after another their commanding officers told him that their men refused to march, and that, unless they were withdrawn from Paris, they were more likely to join the rioters than act against them.

So the crowd surged down the steps into the cellars of the Invalides undisturbed, seizing armfuls of muskets and dragging out whatever other weapons they could lay their hands on, pressing weapons on anyone who looked in need of them, including two servants of the British Ambassador who had wandered over to see what was going on. But although the rioters got away with over ten cannon as well as 28,000 muskets, they discovered very little powder and very few cartridges. And for these they turned to the Bastille in the Faubourg Saint-Antoine.

Among them was Jean Baptiste Humbert, a watchmaker born in Langres who had come to Paris in 1787 having learned his craft in Switzerland. He had made first for a shop in the Place de Grève where he had bought some nails which he hoped might serve instead of shot. On leaving the shop, so he later recorded:

> I was accosted by a citizen who told me they were now issuing shot at the Hôtel de Ville. So I hurried there and was given a few pellets of buckshot. I then immediately set out for the Bastille, loading my gun as I went. I was joined by a group of people who were also on their way to the Bastille. We found four foot-soldiers of the Watch, armed with guns and I urged them to come along with us. They replied they had neither powder nor shot. So we clubbed together to give each of them enough for two shots. Thus armed they were pleased to join us. As we were passing in front of the Hôtel de la Régie we saw that two cases of bullets had just been broken up and their contents were being freely handed out. I filled one of my coat pockets with them to give to anyone who was short . . . [Then], passing through the courtyard of the Arsenal, we arrived at the Bastille.

The Bastille, a huge building of eight round towers linked by walls eighty feet high, had originally been built as a fortress in the fourteenth century. Since then it had been used as a state prison for men who had been arrested in accordance with *lettres de cachet* but who were not guilty of an offence punishable under common law. It was surrounded by an air of mystery. Prisoners, so it was said, their names not divulged to the gaolers with whom they were forbidden to talk, arrived in coaches with drawn blinds, and when they were escorted inside, the soldiers on duty had to turn to face the wall. Its sinister reputation – sustained by legends that owed much to the gruesome and imaginative *Mémoires sur la Bastille* by the lawyer and journalist, Simon Linguet, who published them soon after his release in 1782 – was much increased by stories of 'the man in the iron mask', of the imprisonment of writers like Voltaire and the Abbé Morellet, and of Latude whose thirty years of intermittent incarceration began when he was accused of attempting to poison Mme de Pompadour. Yet the Bastille was, in fact, one of the least unpleasant of Paris's prisons. The food was adequate, prisoners were allowed to bring in their own possessions, and the dreaded dungeons, where it was believed scores of wretches lay in chains, had not been used for years. Indeed, the Bastille was never crowded, there being rarely more than ten prisoners inside its massive walls. Discussions had recently been held as to the advisability of maintaining so expensive an establishment for the incarceration of so few offenders, and a suggestion had been put forward that the unsightly structure should be demolished and a square laid out on its site. The architects and contractors who supported this plan were encouraged when informed in the late spring of 1789 that the Bastille contained no more than seven prisoners, none of whom was of much importance. Four were forgers who had been transferred there from some other, overcrowded prison; one was a mentally unbalanced Irishman who, believing himself to be alternately Julius Caesar and God, was supposed to be a spy; the sixth, also deranged, was suspected of being involved in an attempt to assassinate the King; the last was the Comte de Solages whose family had arranged for him to be committed by a *lettre de cachet* for incest.

To the people of Paris, however, unaware either of its proposed demolition or of the number of prisoners held there, the Bastille was the symbol of an intolerable régime; and it was not merely to obtain powder for their muskets and to release the men held there that they marched so determinedly upon it this Tuesday morning.

For several days now the Governor of the Bastille, the Marquis de Launay, had been anticipating their arrival with the utmost apprehension. Neither a decisive nor an assertive man, de Launay was quite incapable of instilling his officers with any confidence. One of them, Lieutenant Louis Deflue, who had been sent with a detachment of thirty-two Swiss soldiers to reinforce the garrison of eighty-two superannuated soldiers or *invalides*, described him as being 'without much knowledge of military affairs, without experience and without much courage'.

'I could clearly see from his constant uneasiness and irresolution' [Deflue afterwards wrote in a letter to his brothers],

that if we were attacked we should be very badly led. He was so terrified that at night he mistook the shadows of trees for enemies so that we had to be on the alert throughout the hours of darkness. The staff officers . . . and I myself often tried to assure him that our position was not as weak as he complained and to persuade him to attend to important matters rather than to expend his energy on trifles. He would listen to us, appearing to agree with our advice. But then he would do just the opposite before changing his mind yet again.

Nervous and indecisive as he evidently was, de Launay had nevertheless done much to prepare the Bastille for an attack. Expecting that he would not have to hold out for long before troops came to disperse a hostile mob, he had not troubled to lay in more than two days' supply of bread; but in the cellars he had a large stock of powder contained in 250 barrels which had been transferred there from the Arsenal. He also had numerous cannon. There were fifteen eight-pounders standing between the battlements on the towers, a further three eight-pounders below them with their muzzles levelled at the approaches to the entrance gate, as well as twelve smaller rampart guns. In order to give these guns a wider field of fire the embrasures had been widened. Other apertures and windows had been blocked up, the drawbridge across the deep dry moat had been strengthened and the defences generally repaired and improved. Loads of paving-stones had been dragged up to the top of the towers from which they could be hurled down through the machicolations on to the heads of any rioters who managed to approach the foot of the towers.

But if these measures gave some confidence to de Launay's officers, his increasingly prevaricating manner certainly did not. Nor did the attitude of their men. Most of the *invalides* of the regular garrison were known to be in sympathy with the people of the surrounding *faubourgs* in whose shops they bought their tobacco and in whose cafés they sat drinking wine. It was hardly to be expected that they would eagerly obey orders to open fire on them, and not at all unlikely that they would flatly refuse to do so. Lieutenant Deflue's Swiss soldiers did not share the same close ties with the people of Paris, but they were by no means hostile to their aspirations. They were rumoured already to have sworn to spike their own guns if they were ordered to fire on the crowd, and the next day seventy-five men of the same regiment, the Salis-Samade, billetted in Issy, Vaugirard and Sèvres, were to desert. Besides, the thirty-two men from the Salis-Samade in the Bastille had been

73

occupied throughout the night in carrying the heavy and cumbersome barrels of powder from the Arsenal down into the cellar, and by the morning of the 14th they were tired out.

To the people of the *faubourgs*, though, the Bastille, the muzzles of its guns depressed towards the Rue Saint-Antoine, the Rue des Tournelles and the Rue de Jean Beaussire, appeared not so much in a ready state of defence as in preparation for attack. And in response to their protests, a delegation of Electors went to the Bastille to ask the Governor to withdraw the guns which were both provocative and alarming. When they arrived shortly after ten o'clock, the Governor was about to sit down to his morning meal which was then usually eaten in France about this time. He invited the delegates to join him. He was a perfectly agreeable host, and entirely amenable to their demands. He readily consented to having the guns pulled back out of sight and to having the embrasures blocked up with planks.

By the time the meal was over, however, the relaxed atmosphere in the Governor's dining-room had been suddenly shattered by noise from the streets outside. The crowds that had raided the Invalides had now arrived beneath the walls of the Bastille and had been joined by hundreds of demonstrators from the Faubourg Saint-Antoine and the surrounding districts who pushed their way into the outer court, the Cour du Passage, which was flanked on either side by shops and the barracks of the *invalides*. When they saw the cannon in the towers above them being withdrawn they presumed that the gunners were about to load them. It was also supposed that the delegates from the Electors, who had not yet risen from the Governor's dining-room table, had been arrested and were being held as hostages.

Responding to the frantic appeals of a group of demonstrators, a second delegation of Electors, led by a lawyer, Thuriot de la Rozère, went up to the Governor's lodging where they met the other delegates on their way out. Thuriot de la Rozère told the Governor that the people outside, believing that the guns had been withdrawn from view only to be loaded, were now demanding that a citizen's militia should be allowed into the stronghold to hold it in the name of the city. The Governor protested that the guns were certainly not being loaded, and he invited Thuriot – who knew the Bastille well having often visited one of his clients there – to satisfy himself that no attack on the people was intended. He took Thuriot up to the top of the towers to show him the unloaded guns and the blocked-up apertures; he urged him to believe that he would never open fire unless he were attacked; he gave his word of honour that he intended no harm to anyone and, in Thuriot's presence, he asked the garrison to swear that they would not use their arms except in self-defence, an undertaking which they were only too willing to give. So eager, in fact, was the Governor to display his good intentions that Thuriot believed he would have agreed to accept a citizens' militia had not his officers declared that they would all be dishonoured if they gave in so meekly.

When Thuriot came out again into the Cour du Passage, the crowds thronging the courtyard had become threatening and angry. A few, impatient with the unsatisfactory negotiations, shouted abuse at him. Others cried out, 'We want the Bastille! Out with the troops!' The mob was denser than ever now, the new arrivals pushing forward so that those in front were forced towards the edge of the moat that separated the Cour du Passage from a second courtyard, the Cour du Gouvernement. The two drawbridges which spanned the moat, the pedestrian and the wider one for carriages, had both been pulled up.

In the towers high above these bridges the *invalides* looked down at the swirling mass of cockaded hats and heaving shoulders of the crowds that now stretched as far as the Rue des Tournelles. They shouted at them to retreat, as the cannon were loaded now and the Swiss troops might be persuaded to open fire. They waved their caps in the air and made warning gestures. The sound of their words was lost above the roar of voices in the Cour du Passage, but the gesticulations were observed and apparently misinterpreted as signs of encouragement. For at that moment two men, followed by several others, clambered on to the roof of one of the shops that lined the northern side of the Cour du Passage, dashed along the walk at the top of the rampart wall and jumped down into the Cour du Gouvernement on the other side of the moat. Here they broke into the guardhouse, emerged with axes and sledge-hammers, and began to slash at the pulleys of the drawbridges. There was a sudden rattle of chains; the drawbridges began to move. The men on the far side of the moat pushed furiously against the bodies behind them in an effort to get back from the edge as the immense bound planks, now fully released, fell towards them. But one man was killed and another badly hurt by an impact they could not avoid. The crowd behind them rushed over their bodies into the Cour du Gouvernement.

To their right were the Governor's lodgings; to their left the main gate of the Bastille itself, its huge entrance blocked by a further raised drawbridge across another deep moat. For a moment the leaders seemed to hesitate, wondering what to do. Then the crackling sound of musketry fire rang out, followed by the boom of a cannon.

Afterwards there was bitter controversy as to who first started firing. According to the assailants it was the defenders who opened fire on them as soon as they debouched from the narrow passage between the Governor's lodgings and the guardhouse, shouting 'Down with the drawbridge!' But Lieutenant Deflue insisted that it was the besiegers who 'fired the first shots at those on top of the towers ... The assailants were asked what they wanted, and the general demand was for the bridge to be lowered. They were told that this could not be done and that they must withdraw, or else they would be shot. They renewed their cries, "Down with the bridge!" It was then that the order to fire was given.'

Finding themselves under a heavier fire than they were able to return, the assailants took shelter in a range of buildings to the right of the gate which contained the Bastille's kitchens. From here several ran out to attack the drawbridge but were driven back by the fire of the garrison. So two carts filled with straw were brought up from Santerre's brewery, set alight and dragged in front of the drawbridge to afford the protection of a smoke screen.

It was now about two o'clock in the afternoon. And it was at this time that yet another delegation from the Permanent Committee at the Hôtel de Ville, led by Delavigne, the Chairman of the Assembly of Electors, and the Abbé Fauchet, arrived at the Bastille hoping to prevent further bloodshed by persuading the Governor to hand over the fortress to a citizens' militia who would 'guard it in conjunction with the troops of the existing garrison' and who would be 'under orders from the city'. But so great was the noise of firing and shouting that they could not make themselves heard above the din; nor was the slightest notice taken by the garrison of the white handkerchiefs which the Electors' delegates waved above their heads. 'We do not know whether our signals were noticed and understood,' they subsequently reported. 'But the firing never stopped.' Eventually they managed to affect a partial ceasefire in the Rue Saint-Antoine. 'Although we renewed our signals, however, the garrison went on firing at us,' the report continued. 'And we experienced the pain and mortification of seeing several citizens, whose brave fight we had interrupted, fall at our sides. The assailants therefore resumed their fire with as much indignation now as courage. And we could do nothing to prevent them. They were no longer interested in our deputation. What they wanted now, and loudly clamoured for, was the destruction of that fearful prison and the death of its Governor.'

At the Hôtel de Ville the Permanent Committee, concerned by the failure of Delavigne's delegation to restore order at the Bastille, decided to make one final effort to persuade the Governor to agree to their terms. Wounded men were being carried into the building on makeshift stretchers and in the arms of their friends. Others arrived to demand more ammunition and then shouted abuse at Flesselles who was disbelieved when he declared that he had none left to give them. It was even feared that if the slaughter continued unavailingly at the Bastille, the people might turn upon the Hôtel de Ville in their fury. So Ethis de Corny set out with five other delegates, carrying a large flag and accompanied by a drummer of the *Gardes-françaises*.

As the delegation approached the Bastille by the Cour de l'Orme, the flag was vigorously waved and the *Garde-française* loudly beat his drum. Two of their number, Boucheron and Piquod de Saint-Honorine, forced their way through the crowds across the Cour du Passage and over the drawbridges into the Cour du Gouvernement where, persuading the assailants to stop firing for a moment, Boucheron shouted to the garrison at the top of his voice that the city had sent a delegation to discuss terms but that they must all hold their fire and lay down their arms.

'A person in a coloured coat, in the middle of a group of *invalides* who were all holding their hats in their hands, answered me from the summit of the citadel,' Boucheron recorded. 'He said he was willing to receive the delegation but the crowd must withdraw.'

Behind Boucheron and Piquod de Saint-Honorine, the other members of the delegation could see that the *invalides* were quite ready to accept their terms. They were waving their hats in the air and turning their muskets upside down; one went so far as to wave a white flag. But these friendly gestures suddenly ceased, being brought to a halt, so the *invalides* later maintained, by the Governor who insisted that the delegates did not really represent the city but were leaders of the mob, intent on trickery.

The delegates now saw a cannon levelled in their direction. At the same time a volley of musketry fire killed three people who had come up to talk to them, tore a hole in the hat of another, and struck an epaulette from a delegate's coat. Cursed by the crowd, who blamed them for the deaths of the three men who had just fallen at their feet, the delegates now hastily returned to the Hôtel de Ville where, in their absence, a dramatic scene had taken place.

At about three o'clock a thirty-one-year-old former non-commissioned officer in the *Gardes-françaises*, Pierre Hulin, had arrived in the square. A large, excitable man, he had recently returned to Paris from Geneva where, as an official in government service, he had taken part in the rebellion of 1782. He had made inflammatory speeches to the crowds in the Palais Royal two days before, and now, finding himself confronted by two companies of *Gardes-françaises* outside the Hôtel de Ville, he began to harangue them with the same stridency and passion, tears pouring down his cheeks.

'Brave *Gardes-françaises*,' he cried. 'Can't you hear the cannon? ... That villain de Launay is murdering our brothers, our parents, our wives and children who are gathered unarmed around the Bastille. Will you allow them to be massacred? ... Parisians are being slaughtered like sheep. Will you not march on the Bastille?'

They replied that they would if he would lead them. So, with

Hulin at their head, some sixty *Gardes-françaises* followed by about 300 armed civilians with four cannon, marched off towards the Bastille where they were joined by another band of armed citizens under the command of Lieutenant Jacob Élie, who after twenty years in the ranks had recently been granted a commission in the Queen's Regiment of Infantry.

While Hulin's cannon opened fire ineffectively on the fifteen-foot-thick walls of the Bastille, Élie made up his mind that the only way of taking the fortress would be to attack the drawbridge and effect an entry through the main gate. So, accompanied by a few civilian volunteers, he ran forward to drag away the carts whose loads of burning straw had earlier provided the assailants with a smoke screen. While he was performing this dangerous operation, during which two of his companions were killed, the crowds of armed men and *Gardes-françaises* behind him maintained a continuous fire on the towers.

They did not shelter behind retrenchments while they did so [in the words of a contemporary account]. They stood in the very courts of the Bastille and so close to the towers that M. de Launay himself repeatedly made use of the paving-stones and other debris that had been taken up on to the platforms. It cannot be denied that there was much confusion and disorder ... Yet the *invalides*, who had been through many sieges and battles, have assured us that they never experienced such musketry fire as that of these besiegers. They dared not raise their heads above the parapets of the towers.

Having dragged the carts out of the way, Lieutenant Élie gave orders for two cannon to be brought forward into the Cour du Gouvernement and levelled at the underside of the raised drawbridge.

Opposite them, on the other side of the drawbridge, were three eight-pounders, mounted on naval gun carriages. But these remained silent, for the Governor, seeing the besiegers' cannon in the courtyard facing the gate, now decided to surrender. He ordered a drummer to march round the platform behind the battlements of the towers beating a retreat and two men to accompany him waving large white handkerchieves. But the crowds below took not the least notice of these signals, continuing to fire their muskets as energetically as ever, shouting 'Down with the bridges! Down with the bridges!'

Hearing these cries, de Launay went into the Council Chamber beside the Tour de la Chapelle on the far side of the Bastille where he wrote a note which read: 'We have twenty thousand pounds of powder. We shall blow up the garrison and the whole neighbourhood unless you accept our capitulation. From the Bastille at five in the evening. July 14th, 1789, Launay.' He handed this note to Lieutenant Deflue who went down into the Grande Cour and pushed it through a slit which he had himself cut earlier in the gate by the drawbridge to enable his men to fire on the people outside.

Seeing the note being waved through the slit on the other side of the moat, a group of men, led by a clerk, ran off to fetch some planks from a carpenter's workshop in the Rue des Tournelles. The longest of these was pushed forward over the edge of the moat. While three or four men leant on one end of it to hold it down, a cobbler walked gingerly towards the other end, but lost his balance and fell over into the moat, breaking his elbow. Another man then tried and, managing to retain his balance as the plank bent under his weight he seized the note and ran back with it to Hulin.

When its contents became known there were renewed shouts of 'Down with the bridges!' 'No capitulation!' Hulin marched purposefully towards the guns as though about to give the order to open fire, while, inside the fortress, Lieutenant Deflue 'was expecting the Governor to keep his word and blow up the fort'. But, to Deflue's 'great surprise', de Launay suddenly decided to open the gate. He took out a key from his pocket, handed it to a corporal who unlocked the gate and lowered the drawbridge. The siege was over and the crowd rushed in.

I was about the eighth or tenth man to enter the courtyard [the watchmaker, Jean-Baptiste Humbert, wrote]. The *invalides* shouted, 'Lay down your arms!' Apart from one Swiss officer they all did so. I went up to this officer and threatened him with a bayonet, repeating, 'Lay down your arms!' He appealed to the others, saying, 'Gentlemen, please believe me, I never fired.'

'How dare you say you never fired,' I immediately replied, 'when your lips are still black from biting your cartridges?' As I said this I made a grab for his sword.

'They disarmed us immediately,' confirmed Deflue. 'They took us prisoner, each of us having a guard. They flung our papers and records out of the windows and plundered everything.' Deflue, and those of his men who were captured with him, were marched away to the Hôtel de Ville, and all the way were 'met with threats and insults, and a clamour from the whole mob that [they] ought to be hanged'. 'The streets through which we passed and the houses flanking them (even the roof-tops) were filled with masses of people shouting at me and cursing me,' Deflue wrote. 'Swords, bayonets and pistols were being continually pressed against me. I did not know how I should die but felt that my last moment had come. Stones were thrown at me and women gnashed their teeth and brandished their fists at me.' He firmly 'believed that but for the efforts of an officer of the *Arquebusiers* to protect the Swiss prisoners' none of them would have escaped with their lives.

Other defenders of the Bastille were not so fortunate; three of the *invalides* were killed, so were three of the Governor's staff. The Governor himself was seized by one of the *Gardes-françaises* and Marie Julien Stanislas Maillard, a tall, dark man, suffering from consumption, who claimed to have walked the plank to snatch the ultimatum. As a hostile crowd gathered round de Launay, shouting for his death, his sword was snatched from his side. Hulin and Élie tried to get him away to the Hôtel de Ville, Élie, leading the party and carrying the text of the capitulation on the point of his sword; but on the way he was attacked by an out-of-work cook named Desnot. Kicking out wildly de Launay caught Desnot an agonizing blow in the testicles. Desnot cried out, 'He's done me in', whereupon someone else stabbed de Launay in the stomach with a bayonet. The mob gathered round him as he lay in the gutter, firing pistols at him and thrusting the blades of swords and bayonets into his now lifeless body. A man bent down and tore the queue from his scalp as a souvenir, another ripped the Cross of Saint Louis from his coat and fixed it to his own. There was a call for his head to be cut off so that it could be displayed to the people as that of a traitor. 'Here,' said a man to Desnot, handing him a sword. 'You do it. It was you he hurt.' Desnot knelt down to do so, but could not manage the operation with the sword; then, having swallowed some brandy mixed with gunpowder, he finished the job with his pocket-knife.

Jacques de Flesselles, accused of hindering the people's search for arms, was also killed and decapitated. And the two dripping heads were then carried through the streets on pikes to what a witness described as loud applause from the spectators.

No one knew for sure how many men had been killed in the fighting. Deflue reported that only one *invalide* was killed on top of the towers and three or four wounded. None of his own soldiers was hurt, but he afterwards 'learned that two were massacred by the populace on their way to the Hôtel de Ville'. He could 'never discover the exact number of casualties among the besiegers'; he had heard them put as high as 160 but he thought this figure must be exaggerated. Subsequent estimates suggested that eighty-three of the assailants were killed, fifteen died from wounds, and seventy-three were wounded.

Most of them were artisans from the Faubourg Saint-Antoine who had been born outside Paris whence they had come to find work. Of those who survived the assault 954 were awarded the title of *Vainqueur de la Bastille* the following June. As the occupation of more than two-thirds of these are known, it is possible to form some idea of the kind of people who were involved in the assault, allowing for the probability that a good number were not anxious to claim the title of *Vainqueur* as they were already in trouble with the police. There were several men from bourgeois homes, including the oldest 'conqueror' of all, a man of seventy-two. The youngest was a boy of eight. Thirty-five described themselves as merchants, fourteen, more specifically as wine merchants, four were *rentiers*, three were industrialists, and one, Antoine Santerre of whom much more was to be heard, owned the nearby brewery. Eighty were soldiers. Of the artisans, most worked in the furniture industry which was largely centred in the Faubourg Saint-Antoine. Ninety-seven were cabinet-makers of whom four were unemployed. There were twenty-eight cobblers, twenty-three workers of gauze, nine jewellers, nine dyers and nine masons, nine nailsmiths, nine hatters and nine tailors. There was one woman, a laundress.

All were eventually granted a certificate describing their services, and those able to bear arms were rewarded at public expense with a uniform coat as well as a sword and musket, their names engraved on blade and barrel. It was also decreed that an honourable certificate would 'similarly be sent ... to the widows and children of those who died, as a public record of the gratitude and honour due to men who brought about the triumph of liberty over despotism'.

During the evening of 14 July most of these *Vainqueurs de la Bastille* were to be seen in the streets of the city celebrating the great victory which they had helped to bring about and which the officers of the King's army, aware of the feelings of their men, had been unable to prevent. They marched up and down joyfully shouting the news of the Bastille's fall, while guns fired in salute of their triumph.

At the same time crowds of sightseers surged into the Bastille to see the inside of the fearful place of which they had heard so many grisly tales. They were shown parts of a suit of fifteenth-century armour which was described as a kind of strait-jacket used to keep prisoners in tight constraint, and a confiscated printing-press which they were told was an instrument of torture. Later they were regaled with bones, probably of soldiers killed in a long-forgotten siege, but ascribed to poor unfortunate prisoners of much later date.

The next morning, a contractor specializing in the demolition of old buildings submitted an application he had put forward before to pull the building down, supporting his claim for consideration by making the unfounded assertion that he had played a leading role in its capture. He was given the contract and, having taken on a thousand workmen to fulfil the Permanent Committee's instructions that the Bastille 'should be demolished without delay', he made a great deal of money in providing the people of France with relief plans of the fortress carved on stones and with souvenir paper-weights, boxes, inkpots, doorstops and key-plates made from the irons in which the prisoners had allegedly been locked.

*

While Paris celebrated the fall of the Bastille, voices were heard in the crowds urging the people to follow up their triumph by marching on Versailles and demanding the recall of Necker. But more cautious men suggested that, so long as there were so many troops in and around Paris, it would be better to wait and see what the King would now do. In the meantime the tocsin rang repeatedly to warn them that the danger was not past, and the more determined and wary citizens continued to tear up paving-stones and to build barricades. Before nightfall a heavy rain began to pour down, driving the revellers home and bringing their celebrations to an end.

THE DAY OF THE MARKET-WOMEN

5-6 October 1789

'We must have a second fit of Revolution'

LOUSTALOT

The King had been out all day hunting. Returning tired, he went to bed early and was awakened by the news of the fall of the Bastille. 'Is this a rebellion?' he is said sleepily to have asked the Duc de La Rochefoucauld-Liancourt, the Grand Master of the Wardrobe. 'No, Sire,' the Duke replied emphatically, 'it is a revolution.'

Within an hour the Duke was hurrying over to the National Assembly to tell the deputies that the King was coming to address them. The deputies greeted this announcement warmly, but their applause was cut short by Mirabeau who stood up to advise them, 'Wait until the King has let us know what friendly overtures we may expect from him. Let our first greeting to him at this distressing moment be marked by a cold respect . . . The silence of the people is a lesson for kings.'

Mirabeau's warning was justified. The King's submission was, as Thomas Jefferson, the American Minister, described it, only a 'surrender at discretion'. He did say that he had ordered the withdrawal of troops from Paris and Versailles, but, while denying that he planned any action against the National Assembly – to which he referred by that name – he undertook neither to dismiss Breteuil nor to recall Necker. All the same, grateful for his concession regarding the troops, the delegates respectfully escorted the King back to the palace and were followed by a cheering crowd. Even the Queen was applauded for a short time when she appeared on a balcony of the Cour de Marbre.

Soon afterwards a delegation of eighty-eight deputies left Versailles to convey the King's reassurances about the troops to the people of Paris. They drove 'in splendid weather in an atmosphere like that of a public festival'. 'Our journey,' wrote Bailly, 'was one long triumph. At several places we came upon troops marching away from the capital, and crowds of people shouting, "*Vive la Nation!*" as our carriages drove past.' In Paris, where most workshops were closed and groups of tense people had been gathered in the streets since dawn, the deputies were greeted with delight, their carriages were surrounded, they were handed flowers and cockades, hugged and kissed. 'Every window was crammed,' Bailly continued. 'The crowds were immense; but everything was very orderly. On all sides the enthusiasm was open and sincere.'

At the Hôtel de Ville there were speeches full of compliments and mutual congratulations. Lafayette, who read out to the Assembly of Electors the speech which the King had just made in Versailles, said that His Majesty had been misled by his advisers, but now understood the true position. In replying for the Electors, Moreau de Saint-Méry, their second President, asked the Marquis to tell the King how much they appreciated his gesture and to assure him of their loyalty. As a demonstration of regard for their personal qualities and for the National Assembly which they represented, the Electors appointed Bailly Mayor of Paris and Lafayette commander of the citizens' militia which was shortly to become the National Guard. The militiamen were authorized to wear cockades of red and blue, the colours of Paris, to which was added a band of white, the colour of the King, thus joining in the tricolour the old France with the new.

The pleasant atmosphere in the Hôtel de Ville was not matched for long, however, by the mood of the people outside. For, when it became known that although the King had agreed to withdraw the troops, he had made no promises about Breteuil or Necker, crowds gathered, loudly demanding a change of Ministers. Barricades were erected in the streets, new trenches were dug across them, the Electors were besieged in the Hôtel de Ville, passers-by were stopped by armed citizens who demanded proof of their identity. And when the deputies and Electors proceeded together for a service of thanksgiving in Notre Dame, conducted by the Archbishop of Paris, they were surrounded by people clamouring for further concessions by the King.

At Versailles, too, deputies dissatisfied with the King's promises were now demanding more. Antoine Barnave, representing Dauphiné, supported by Mirabeau, pressed for the recall of Necker. So did the Marquis de Lally-Tollendal, one of the deputies for the Parisian nobility, who passionately declared, '*Messieurs*, as we have seen and heard, in the streets and squares, on the *quais* and in the markets, the cry is "Bring back Necker!" ... The people's request is an order. We must therefore *demand* the recall of M. Necker.'

By now the King had himself reluctantly concluded that this was, indeed, what he must do. On the morning of 16 July, at a council meeting attended by his Ministers, the Queen and the Comtes de Provence and Artois, he asked them all to consider whether or not it was still possible to resist. The Comte d'Artois strongly urged him to do so, but Marshal de Broglie, the War Minister, advised him that resistance would be impossible with the troops in their present mood. Well, then, the King asked, what were the possibilities of withdrawal to a less disaffected part of the country where the Estates General could be reconvened and protected by loyal troops? This idea, which had already been discussed, met with the approval of the Queen who urged them to withdraw the Court to Metz on the north-east frontier. But once again de Broglie objected: he could not trust the army to escort the royal family through a countryside on the verge of revolt.

The King, therefore, decided he had no alternative but to give way. He had a message sent to the National Assembly to inform them of his decision, and unwillingly prepared himself for the twelve mile journey to Paris where the people were demanding his presence. He said his prayers, he made his will and, while the Comte d'Artois made haste to flee abroad with his wife and mistress, his sons and the Polignacs, he created the Comte de Provence Lieutenant-General of the Kingdom with full powers to act in his name while he was absent from Versailles.

Bailly, who had now returned to Versailles, rose very early the next morning to give himself time to prepare a speech of welcome before leaving at seven o'clock for Paris where, as Mayor of the city, he was to receive the King.

When I went out [Bailly recorded in his memoirs] I was met by all the coachmen who gave me a tree bedecked with flowers and ribbons ... I had to allow them to fasten this tree to the front of my coach. All the coachmen accompanied me, letting off fireworks, although it was broad daylight, right to the end of the avenue ... In the Place Louis XV, I left Mme Bailly and went on to the Hôtel de Ville in a hired coach. I arrived at ten o'clock and joined everyone there busily preparing to receive the King.

The King, accompanied by bodyguards, about thirty deputies and a vast crowd of workers and their wives, proceeded slowly up the Rue Saint-Honoré which was lined on either side with men and women, and even monks and friars, carrying guns, swords, lances, pikes, scythes and cudgels. They cried out, '*Vive la Nation!*' '*Vive Monsieur Lafayette! Et les deputés! Et les electeurs!*'

Bailly said that there were shouts, too, of '*Vive le Roi!*' But another witness, Bertrand Barère de Vieuzac, a deputy from Gascony, recorded that there was 'great difficulty in certain districts in restraining the indignation of citizens outraged by the measures that had provoked the insurrection'. And the Austrian Ambassador reported, 'It is certain that during his journey there were very few cries of "*Vive le Roi!*" ... whereas on all sides there were shouts of "*Vive la Nation!*" ' The British Ambassador, the Duke of Dorset, said that His Majesty was treated more like a captive than a King. He was led along like 'a tame bear'.

On entering the Hôtel de Ville the King was offered the tricolour cockade which had already become the emblem of the revolution, the original green cockade having been discarded when it was realized that green was the colour of the Comte d'Artois. Bailly, who had been asked to make the presentation, 'did not know quite how the King would take it, and whether there was not something improper about the suggestion'. The King, however, accepted the cockade without protest and fastened it to his hat. He then went up the staircase of the Hôtel de Ville. He had no guard with him now, but instead was surrounded by a number of citizens. They were 'all holding swords and forming an arcade of blades over his head'.

In response to the speeches made to him in the great hall, the King endeavoured to frame suitable replies. But he had prepared nothing and could think of little to say appropriate to the occasion. After uttering a few disjointed sentences, he walked out on to the balcony where he was joyfully greeted by the crowds who, seeing the cockade in his hat, were now prepared to give him the wholehearted ovation they had previously reserved for the Electors and deputies. 'Well done!' they cried. 'Well done! He now belongs to the Third Estate!' And the Comte d'Estaing said to him excitedly,

'Sire, with that cockade and the Third Estate you will conquer Europe!'

'Applause and shouts of "*Vive le Roi!*" welcomed him on every side,' said Bailly. 'All eyes, filled with tears, were turned towards him. The people held out their hands to him. And when he was placed on the throne which had been prepared for him, a voice from the back of the assembly uttered the heartfelt cry: "*Our King! Our father!*" At this applause, the excitement, the shouts of "*Vive le Roi!*" redoubled.'

This happy mood continued in Paris for some days after the King had returned to Versailles. A new municipality or Commune was formed, while the National Assembly were granted fresh powers to accelerate reform and frame a constitution. Shops and theatres opened their doors again; men returned to work, encouraged by the Commune's offer of six *livres* to all who produced a certificate of attendance from their employers. Yet it seemed to many of the poorer people all over the provinces that the Assembly had utterly failed to tackle or even to appreciate their problems. And, with bread still expensive and in short supply, with unemployment increasing in the wake of the bad harvest of 1788, riots erupted in numerous towns and villages. Millers and farmers suspected of hoarding grain were assaulted, walls and fences were pulled down, forests were devastated, stags and rabbits were slaughtered whole-sale while gamekeepers hid in their cottages, fishponds were dredged, pigeons were shot in the courtyards of manor houses. In several places the deserted manor houses themselves were looted or burned down, and in others the owners were made to sign away their *droits*. At Agde the bishop was dragged from his house and forced to relinquish all rights to his mill; at Troyes the mayor was killed; and at Caen an army officer who had become involved in arguments about the wearing of medals bearing the head of Necker, was also murdered. At Rennes the royal garrison was prevailed upon to desert and at Marseilles it was disbanded by armed citizens. Forts and prisons were stormed, arsenals were seized, hôtels de ville were invaded under the eyes of complaisant guards, customs duties were withheld, unpopular mayors were ousted from office and more amenable ones elected in their place, *intendants* fled. Gangs of beggars roamed intimidatingly through the streets and down the country lanes. A combination of brigands, hungry peasants and a middle-class intent upon the replacement of their authority for that of the royal government was producing an irresistible revolutionary power.

As the King's *intendants* abandoned their offices and central authority collapsed, provincial towns established their own committees which agreed to respect the decrees of the National Assembly only when they coincided with the wishes of the local population. Attempts were made to put down the disturbances by raising companies of militia, but as most of those enrolled were in sympathy with the demonstrators, the disorders continued with angry crowds marching upon town halls crying for bread at prices they could afford, surrounding the homes of rich merchants and *rentiers* and, in some cases, pillaging them.

In the capital a deputy lamented that there was 'no more army and no more police', and Bailly admitted that 'everybody knew how to command but nobody knew how to obey'. The *lieutenant de maire* of Saint Denis on the northern outskirts of Paris was chased through the streets by an angry crowd for contemptuously refusing to reduce the price of bread. Chased to the top of the church steeple, he was stabbed to death and decapitated. One of the Ministers in Breteuil's reactionary government, Foullon de Doué, who was believed to have been speculating in the grain trade and plotting a counter-revolution, met an even more horrible fate. Accused of having said that the people should be made to eat hay if they were hungry, a collar of nettles was placed around his neck, a bunch of thistles was thrust into his hand and a fistful of hay was stuffed between his lips. He was then hanged on a nearby lampost. His son-in-law, Bertier de Sauvigny, the *Intendant* of Paris and the Île de France, was accused of similar abuses and murdered as well. His heart was torn out of his body and brandished at the windows of the Hôtel de Ville. Then his head was cut off and paraded with that of his father-in-law on a pikestaff through the streets and down the arcades of the Palais Royal, the one head being pushed against the other to cries of 'Kiss papa! Kiss papa!' Here Gouverneur Morris saw the 'populace carrying about the mangled fragments with a savage joy'. 'Gracious God,' Morris thought. 'What a people!'

There were strong protests against these murders, but they had their apologists, too. 'Is this blood then so pure,' asked Barnave defiantly in the National Assembly, 'that one should so regret to spill it.' Others cried that more heads would have to roll before justice for the people could be secured.

While the debates in the Assembly continued urgently but inconclusively, the wildest rumours, intensified by newspaper reports, were passed from mouth to mouth: the aristocrats were conspiring to suppress the National Assembly; the Queen had inspired a plot to blow it up; huge armies of hired brigands were on the march; foreign powers were preparing to invade the country to restore the King's lost power; nobles were emigrating to enlist the help of mercenaries; the British fleet had been sighted off Brest; Polish troops had landed at Dunkirk; Spaniards were about to disembark at Bordeaux; Austrian soldiers had been seen on the march at Lyons.

Stories such as these, spreading through the country districts, led to waves of panic which were to become known as the Great Fear. As castles, manor houses, abbeys and tax and salt monopoly offices were invaded and sometimes set on fire, villagers fled in terror from their houses at reports of assassins paid to wreak revenge, and sought refuge in forests and church belfries. Fear led to further violence. Protesting that they were acting in the name of the King against aristocrats who were conspiring to thwart his wishes, the peasants grew ever more violent in their demonstrations against manorial dues, disregarding all authority. 'There no longer exists either executive power, laws, magistrates or police,' the Venetian Ambassador reported. 'A horrible anarchy prevails.'

To the National Assembly the problem of restoring order seemed insuperable until the delegates from Brittany hit upon a clever tactical move by which certain of the liberal nobles were to offer to renounce some of those feudal privileges against which the peasants were so violently protesting. It was hoped that other nobles would then be persuaded to follow their example in a rising flood of emotional renunciations. These renunciations were to be provoked by the Duc d'Aiguillon, the greatest landowner in France, who was believed to have an annual income of 100,000 *livres* from his feudal rights alone. The debate was planned for the evening of Tuesday, 4 August.

It almost failed in its purpose: the Vicomte de Noailles, a young man who had fought in America with his brother-in-law, Lafayette, and who evidently had a mind to steal the thunder of those who were in the Breton plot, leapt to his feet before the Duc d'Aiguillon. His proposals for a programme of aristocratic self-denial were naturally not too well received, coming as they did from one who did not personally have much to lose. After the Duc d'Aiguillon's speech, however, the mood the Bretons had been hoping for was created. One after the other, noblemen and prelates alike, stood up voluntarily to renounce rights and privileges in an atmosphere that became almost hysterical. Spurred on by the excited self-immolation of the earlier renunciants, spokesmen for *parlements* and privileged towns jumped up to offer further sacrifices in a stream of oblation so rapid that the Assembly's clerks could not keep up with it and the Marquis de Lally-Tollendal, by now an exasperated conservative, passed a message to the President: 'Suspend the session. They have all gone quite mad.'

But the session, which Mirabeau and Sieyès had both declined to attend, continued enthusiastically apace in what one witness described as 'a contagion of sentimental feeling' until two o'clock in the morning, deputies weeping and embracing one another, cheering each other's selflessness or giving away, so one observer caustically commented, that which they did not own. 'What a nation! What glory!' declared Duquesnoy, a deputy from Bar-le-Duc, 'What an honour to be French!'

With daylight however, came doubt and apprehension. There was talk of having to consult constituents for the endorsement of what one noble deputy termed the 'annihilation of a whole property system'. There was a feeling that perhaps Mirabeau was right when he complained that it was just like Frenchmen to spend weeks squabbling over syllables and then within a single night to 'overthrow the entire traditional order of the monarchy'. So, although the Assembly's decree proudly announced that it had destroyed 'in its entirety the feudal system', the debates of the next few days severely modified the sacrifices which had been promised and ensured that, while ecclesiastical tithes were abolished, the most burdensome of the feudal dues were made subject to redemption, and, until they were redeemed, the peasants were bound by them, as they had been before.

Nor were the peasants much comforted by the Declaration of the Rights of Man and Citizen which, affirming that 'men are born and remain free and equal in rights', was adopted by the National Assembly later on that month. For, encouraged by disagreements within the Assembly, the King withheld his consent both to the Declaration and to the ratification of the decrees in which the sacrifices of the privileged orders had been formulated and published. 'I will never consent to the spoliation of my clergy or my nobility,' he assured the Archbishop of Arles. 'And I will not sanction decrees which seek to despoil them.' So, faced by the passive resistance of the King, the 'patriots' decided that force would have to be used again. The Revolution required another dramatic *journée*.

The form that the *journée* was to take was indicated in a conversation between Dussaulx, a member of the Paris Commune, and Augeard, an official of the Queen's Household, as they walked past the Tuileries one day.

'When the King is living there,' Dussaulx said pointing at the old, neglected palace, 'this business can be settled. It was a great mistake not to keep him in Paris when he came here on 17 July. The King's place of residence should be in the capital.'

Augeard objected that the King could not be told where he must live. But Dussaulx maintained, 'He can be forced when the good of the country is at stake. We will *have* to come to that.'

On 29 September the Flanders Regiment arrived at Versailles. It was customary, when a new regiment came into garrison there, for a banquet to be given in its honour by the *Gardes du Corps*. The King saw no reason to interfere with this tradition. So the usual banquet was held on 1 October in the Opera House where the boxes were filled with spectators from the Court. It turned out to be just the provocation for which the 'patriots' and the newspapers that supported them were waiting: several of the guests got drunk; there were rowdy demonstrations of loyalty to the throne; insults were showered upon the National Assembly; soldiers tore off their red and blue cockades. At the appearance of the King and Queen, who walked around the table, the band struck up one of Grétry's popular royalist airs, while the ladies of the Court, who had for several weeks been provocatively wearing lilies pinned to their dresses, distributed cockades of pure white in honour of the Bourbon dynasty.

In Paris, where the bread queues had been growing ever longer, accounts of this 'orgy', suitably embellished with reports that the national cockade had been trampled disdainfully underfoot, were soon spread far and wide. Camille Desmoulins renewed the call for the King to be brought to Paris away from the corrupting influence of the Court. Other popular orators leaped upon the tables shouting for a march upon Versailles, many of them combining that call with demands for a reduction in the price of bread.

Bread was the people's staple diet. Most workers, who consumed about three pounds a day, spent half their wages on it, as opposed to about fifteen per cent on vegetables, oil and wine, five per cent on fuel and one per cent on lighting. Skilled workers such as locksmiths and carpenters earned about fifty *sous* a day in 1789, masons about forty, labourers no more than twenty to thirty, so when the price of bread, normally about eight *sous* for a four-pound loaf rose above ten or twelve *sous* they had to face the prospect of hunger, and disturbances became commonplace. In August that year the price of bread was not unduly high at twelve *sous* for a large loaf, but a prolonged drought had resulted in millers being unable to grind corn, so there was an acute shortage and a consequent increase in outbreaks of violence: fighting erupted in bread queues where women were pushed aside by men, bakers were threatened with hanging and guards had to be posted in their shops. At Versailles a furious crowd attempted to murder a baker who started to sell bread at eighteen *sous* to those who could afford it, and stale loaves at a rather less exorbitant price to those who could not. In several other places women seized cartloads of grain, and on the morning of 5 October huge crowds of women gathered in the central markets and in the Faubourg Saint-Antoine shouting for bread, forcing the bell-ringer of the Sainte-Marguerite church to ring the tocsin and calling upon the citizens to take up arms to force the Government to help them. They were mostly *poissardes*, fishwives, working women, prostitutes and market stall-holders, but among them were several quite smartly dressed *bourgeoises* who appeared as angry as the rest. Together they marched towards the Place de Grève.

They arrived there at about half-past nine and stormed up the steps of the Hôtel de Ville. The guards were disarmed and their weapons handed to men who had now joined the demonstration and were encouraging the women in their demands. As some of them burst through the door leading to the bell tower to sound the tocsin, others invaded the main building, searching for arms and powder, tearing up documents and ledgers for good measure. Persuaded that their best hope was to petition the King, they then set off for Versailles under the not entirely willing leadership of that self-proclaimed hero of the taking of the Bastille, Stanislas Maillard, who evidently considered it undignified to command such motley female troops.

Further recruits were collected on the way, not all of them willing ones. A nurse, Jeanne Martin, the wife of a porter, claimed afterwards that she was forced to march by a group of about forty women who thrust a stick in her hand, threatening to beat her with it unless she accompanied them. She protested that she had not yet had any breakfast and had not a *sou* with her; but they shouted, 'Come on, march, march! You won't need anything.' Another woman, Marie-Catherine-Victoire Sacleux, proprietor of a cleaning and dyeing shop which she had closed for the day 'because of the public clamour', made the excuse that she was urgently wanted at home and that, in any case, she was wearing the wrong kind of shoes, but she, too, was forced to go with the others and made to help drag along a cannon which had been brought from the Place de Grève.

Compelling or inviting numerous others to accompany them, the women who had invaded the Hôtel de Ville had soon mustered a force over 6,000 strong. Among them were several men – some of hem dressed as women – *agents provocateurs* in the pay of the Duc d'Orléans as well as other agitators intent upon ensuring that their female companions did not just demand bread but the acceptance of the Assembly's decrees, the King's return to Paris and the punishment of all who had insulted the national cockade. Tramping through the rain, some with muskets, others with pikes and swords, bludgeons, crowbars, pitchforks and scythes, they passed through Sèvres where they pillaged the shops, and at five o'clock in the afternoon were in sight of Versailles.

The King had been out hunting again. On his return he went immediately to a council of Ministers most of whom, with the notable exception of Necker, advised flight, though they did not know yet just what the women wanted. Louis was, as usual, hesitant. 'A fugitive King,' he murmured doubtfully, repeating the words several times. Eventually he adjourned the Council and went to consult the Queen who had spent the early afternoon in the gardens of the Trianon, which she was never to see again. She too urged him to escape while there was still time, but he could not bring himself to do so. And when, at half past five, the women stormed through the doors of the National Assembly, the King was still at Versailles. Two hours later the hall of the Assembly 'remained full of women and men armed with scythes, sticks and pikes', so Étienne Dumont, a friend of Mirabeau, reported. 'The President was wasting his strength trying to keep order ... Mirabeau raised his powerful voice and called for the withdrawal from the Chamber of all strangers. It needed all his popularity to achieve this. Gradually the crowd withdrew'. About 'a hundred women and a number of young people' remained in the gallery, however, and these shouted or kept silence at the orders of a 'harridan who addressed the deputies with coarse familiarity: "Who's that talking down there? Make the chatterbox shut up. That's not the point. The point is, we want bread. Tell them to put our little mother Mirabeau up to speak. We want to hear *him*." Then everyone shouted for "our little mother Mirabeau" (a form of affectionate expression employed by people of this class). But Mirabeau was not the man to waste his energy on occasions such as this. His popularity as he said himself, was not that of a demagogue.'

The president, Jean Joseph Mounier, had gone to consult the King

98

leaving his chair to the Bishop of Langres who was quite incapable of controlling the rabble. 'Order! Order!' the bishop called as the women clambered on to the platform. 'We don't give a fuck for order,' they shouted back at him. 'We want bread.' Several of them pushed their faces at him, demanding to be kissed. He obliged them with a sigh. Others threatened to play *boule* with the head of 'that damned Abbé Maury'. A few, who had gone into assommoirs were now quite drunk, some of them vomiting over the benches. One of the prettiest sat down on the knee of her 'little mother Mirabeau' who seemed very happy to hold her.

Eventually the King agreed to see a deputation of women in the Salle de Conseil if Mounier would take them there.

M. Mounier appeared with twenty of these women at the palace gates all of which were closed and guarded [recorded the Marquis de Paroy in a letter to his wife]. I found myself by chance inside one of the gates and, recognizing the President of the Assembly, who was being crushed by the crowd, I told the officer of the guard who he was. M. Mounier told the officer the object of his mission. They let him in with six women, and I accompanied them to the King's apartment where they were introduced. I noticed that two of them were quite well dressed and not at all of the class of person to which the others belonged, though they affected their language. They had come, they said, to ask for bread from the King.

The King walked into the room, looking rather nervous, to ask the women what they wanted. 'Sire,' replied one, a pretty girl who sold flowers at the Palais Royal, 'we want bread.'

'You know my heart,' the King told her. 'I will order all the bread in Versailles to be collected and given to you.' At these words the girl fainted. Revived by smelling salts, she asked to be allowed to kiss the King's hands. 'She deserves better than that,' His Majesty said and took her into his arms. Thrilled by their generous reception, the women whom Mounier had chosen as representatives came out again into the courtyard to find that the others who had marched with them were far from disposed to share their pleasure at the King's generosity. The deputation had been duped, they were told; even if the King meant what he said, the Queen and the aristocrats at Court would soon see that he broke his promise. A few women began to chant again, as they had done on the march, 'Bread! Bread! Meat at six *sous* the pound! No more talking ... We'll cut the Queen's pretty throat! We'll tear her skin to bits for ribbons!' The six representatives were forced to go back and obtain a written declaration. Pacified by this, some of the women then returned to Paris with Stanislas Maillard.

The King now comforted himself with the thought that the trouble was over. He sent the *Gardes du Corps* and the Flanders Regiment, which had been ordered to march to the palace, back to their barracks. But soon after nine o'clock he learned that he must shortly expect other visitors at Versailles. For in Paris hundreds of men of the National Guard had converged upon the Hôtel de Ville demanding to be led to Versailles. Their commander, Lafayette, had been reluctant to take them there. He had sat on horseback by the steps of the Hôtel de Ville, attempting to pacify them. But they refused to listen to him, going so far, as he afterwards said, to threaten to hang him from the lampost on which Foullon de Doué had been murdered unless he agreed to their demands. So, at length, the Commune gave him instructions to march off with the Guard, ordering two delegates to accompany him and to ask the King to return to Paris.

Spattered with mud, Lafayette arrived at Versailles with these delegates, and some 20,000 National Guardsmen and other armed civilians, at about eleven o'clock. Advised once again to flee by his Ministers and the Queen, and this time also by Mounier, the King at first agreed to do so. But after some Ministers had already left the palace and were rattling along with their families in coaches on the road to Rambouillet, he changed his mind following a conversation with Necker: he would stay behind after all and see what Lafayette had to say. He greeted him courteously, accepted without demur the arrival of the National Guard, agreed to approve the Assembly's decrees and the Declaration of Rights. He listened politely while the Commune's delegates made their request for his return to Paris and, while he did not immediately commit himself to this, he seemed willing to consider it.

It was now two o'clock in the morning. The crisis appeared to be past. All was quiet. An officer, looking down into the courtyard from the Aile des Ministres, could see no movement. The women had gone away to find places of shelter from the still-pouring rain; many of them had taken off their skirts and petticoats to wring out the water, shocking an officer who complained that 'the scenes which took place amongst them were anything but decent'.

Assured by Lafayette that he and his family would come to no harm, the King went to bed. So did the Queen who was suddenly awakened at dawn by the noise of trampling feet and by loud shouts on the staircase that led up to her apartments: 'Death to the Austrian! Where is she? Where is the whore? We'll wring her neck! We'll tear her heart out! We'll fry her liver and that won't be the end of it.' 'I'll have her thighs!' cried one. 'And I'll have her entrails,' called others. 'I'll have her kidneys in a fricassee!'

A gate leading into the Cour des Princes had been left unlocked. A horde of armed women had pushed it open and had poured into the courtyard led by Nicholas Jourdan, a savage-looking, bearded model from the Academy of Painting and Sculpture, whose arms were naked to the elbow and whose hands and blue overcoat were already smeared with blood. As the crowd had approached the palace one of the *Gardes du Corps* had opened fire from a window, hitting a young journeyman cabinet-maker who had fallen dead in the courtyard. Enraged by this, the crowd had rushed forward, and Jourdan, brandishing an axe, had attacked one of the other Guards and cut his head off. A second Guard had also been decapitated as Jourdan and the women had rushed across the Cour des Princes into the Cour Royale and, shouting for the 'Austrian whore', had started to mount the staircase.

An officer attempting to bar their way, the blood pouring down his face, called out 'Save the Queen!' through the anteroom door. 'Save the Queen! They are going to kill her.' As he was knocked down with the butt of a musket wielded with such force that the trigger penetrated his skull, the Queen, who had leapt out of bed, put on a shift and petticoat, picked up a pair of stockings and was about to put those on as well when two of her ladies dashed into her room and urged her not to trouble to dress but to make for the King's apartments before the mob broke down the door. So, with her stockings in her hand and a cape round her shoulders, she and her ladies rushed through the Petits Cabinets, locking the doors behind them, towards the Salon de l'Oeil de Boeuf. As they ran, the mob behind them battered down the bedroom door, poured into the room, and finding the bed empty, slashed at the sheets with their axes and swords.

The door leading into the King's apartments was locked on the inside. The Queen and her ladies battered on it, screaming for help. At length it was opened by a frightened valet. The King was not there: at the sound of the tumult he had hurried off through a secret passage to the Queen's room, and seeing that she had escaped, he had gone to fetch the Dauphin. He suddenly appeared with the boy in his arms.

By now Lafayette, who had gone to bed at the Hôtel de Noailles, had been roused from his sleep and had galloped over to the palace where the National Guard had succeeded in stopping the fighting and had cleared the mob out of the building. But the courtyards were still full of shouting demonstrators, firing their muskets in the air, parading the severed heads of the royal guards on pikestaffs and crying out, '*Le Roi à Paris ! Le Roi à Paris !*' According to the Marquis de Ferrières-Marsay, the Duc d'Orléans 'was walking cheerfully about among them, in a grey frock-coat and a round hat with a riding whip in his hand. He smiled at some and talked in a carefree manner to others. All around him the air resounded with shouts of "Our father is with us! Long live King Orléans" . . . At the same time . . . men dressed as women were spreading word among the crowd that M. de Lafayette was a traitor and that they must get rid of him. One of the leaders . . . was advising a group of men and women who thronged round him and to whom he was handing money, "We want the heads of both the Queen and M. de La Fayette. That man is a traitor. He left Paris against his will and very late in the day." At these words a man with a hideous face disguised as a woman displayed a kind of sickle and swore that he would be the one to cut off the bitch's head . . . Troops of women and men armed with pikes and muskets were everywhere hunting the men of the Bodyguard . . . The barbarous horde manifested a savage pleasure, some of them bathing their hands in the blood [of the dead Guards] and wiping it over their faces, others dancing round the bodies . . .' Everywhere there were calls for the King to go to Paris and threats to Lafayette.

Another less partisan informant, Elizabeth Girard, a *'bourgeoise de Paris'*, who later gave evidence before an official inquiry, confirmed that 'all the people, without distinction, especially the journeymen locksmiths who were there in great numbers, were saying that they had lost a day's wages, that if the King didn't come to Paris, and if the Bodyguard were not killed, Lafayette's head should be stuck on the end of a pike.' And Claude Fournier, an officer of the National Guard and well-known agitator, claimed that he had called to the fishwives, using the kind of language that they would have used themselves, *'Sacrées* bitches, can't you see that you are being buggered about by the King and Lafayette ... The whole damned lot will have to be taken to Paris.'

Eventually Lafayette himself expressed the opinion that order could never be restored until the royal family showed themselves to the people. So the King went out on to the balcony. There were a few scattered cheers but these were almost drowned by shouts of 'The Queen! The Queen!'

Marie Antoinette had recovered her composure. Her children's governess said that she appeared, indeed, quite unmoved by her ordeal: 'Her countenance was sad but calm.' Wearing a dressing-gown of yellow and white stripes, her hair disordered, she came out on to the balcony, her four-year-old son on one side, her daughter, now eleven, on the other, holding their hands. 'No children! No children!' the crowd below shouted up at her. So she turned and bent down to help the children back through the window before facing the mob once again, her head erect, unflinching as several muskets were levelled at her. For two minutes she stood there as the mood of the women changed from hostility to grudging respect. Gradually, one after the other, the muskets were lowered. A few women even cried out *'Vive la Reine!'* but these, so Jeanne Martin said, were silenced by 'the common people ... who hit them to make them quiet'. The Queen turned away and went back into the palace.

She did not conceal the fright she had had [the Marquis de Paroy told his wife]. She sighed wearily and, taking the little Dauphin into her arms again, she covered him with kisses and began to cry. This made us all cry, too. Then the Queen went back with the King into the inner cabinet room where I followed them. We were hoping that the danger had passed ... But numerous shouts were still heard, 'The King to Paris! The King to Paris! The King on the balcony!' ... The shouts of the populace grew louder and louder. The King consulted with his Ministers for a few minutes. Then he came on to the balcony again, preceded by M. de La Fayette and followed by the Queen, who said, passing in front of me, 'We are going to Paris.' For a reply I raised my eyes to heaven.

'My friends,' the King announced from the balcony, his words greeted by repeated cheers, 'I will go to Paris with my wife and children.'

That afternoon the King and Queen, their two children and the governess, climbed into the royal carriage with Monsieur and the King's sister, Elisabeth. The carriage was surrounded by women waving banners and flags, branches bedecked with coloured ribbons and loaves of bread impaled on the points of bayonets. Several were drunk, some threatening to soak the Queen's hands in the entrails of the Household Guards, others dancing in the mud, singing songs, jumping on to the backs of soldiers, knocking off their caps and bearskins and putting them on themselves, a few sitting astride the guns and horses of the National Guard, waiting for the disorderly procession to move off.

The National Guard led the way, escorting wagon-loads of wheat and flour. Then came a regiment of Grenadiers, followed by the disarmed *Gardes du Corps* and the Flanders Regiment. The royal carriage came next, Lafayette, riding beside it; and, rolling along through the mud behind it, trailed a line of carriages bearing a hundred deputies of the National Assembly who were now to transfer their debates from Versailles to Paris, where they were to meet for a fortnight in the great hall of the archdiocese, before moving to the Manège, a riding school near the Tuileries.

At the rear of the column, and on either side of the wagons of grain, marched the market-women, their decorated branches amidst the gleaming iron of pikes and musket barrels giving the impression, so one observer thought, of 'a walking forest'. It was still raining, and the roads were ankle-deep in mud, yet they all seemed content, even cheerful. Occasionally they burst into song on the six-and-a-half-hour march, passed ribald jokes down the ragged ranks or danced along, holding out their aprons. They called out to the people who stood to watch them pass by that they were bringing back to Paris the baker, the baker's wife and '*le petit mitron*', the baker's boy.

'The Queen sat at the bottom of the coach with the Dauphin on her knees . . . while some of the blackguards in the rabble were firing their guns over her head,' recorded the Comte d'Artois's Scottish gardener, Thomas Blaikie. 'As I stood by the coach one man fired over the Queen's head. I told him to desist but he said he would continue.'

The King and Queen were driven to the Hôtel de Ville, where they were obliged to listen to several speeches, and then to the Tuileries. The comfortless, sparsely furnished rooms echoed to the sound of their footsteps. Half asleep the Dauphin murmured, 'It's very ugly here, mother.'

THE DAYS OF THE *FÉDÉRÉS*
AND THE
FLIGHT TO VARENNES

14–17 July 1790 and 19–26 June 1791

'I would rather be King of Metz
than continue to be King of France
at such a time as this'

LOUIS XVI

Once established in the Manège where the debates were less disorderly and rowdy than they had been at Versailles, the Assembly settled down to face the problems of reform. The radicals sat on the President's left, the less numerous conservatives on his right, this disposition providing thereafter, in other countries as well as France, a useful addition to the terminology of politics. Between the Left and the Right there were not many less partisan voices to be heard, for many moderates, protesting against their colleagues' attitude towards the violent intervention of the mob, decided to withdraw. Mounier, their leader, went home to Dauphiné and, having failed to rouse the people there to support the policies of the *monarchiens*, took refuge in Switzerland. Lally-Tollendal, unsuccessful on a similar mission, emigrated to England. Those *monarchiens* who remained in the Assembly, such as the Duc de Clermont-Tonnerre, no longer exercised much influence there, and many conservatives attended the debates irregularly, leaving their benches almost empty after five o'clock when they went away for their evening meal. So, unhampered by powerful conservative protest and encouraged by the excellent harvest of 1789 which, safely gathered in, silenced the disturbing shouts for bread, the reformists in the Assembly were able to push through a variety of measures which would formerly have met with the most steadfast opposition. The title of the King, who was now to rule under the law and not by divine right, was changed from King of France to King of the French; the *parlements* were declared to be henceforth in abeyance. In sweeping reforms of the judicial system, judges were to be elected by the people and paid by the state, local government was transformed following upon the creation of new provincial assemblies and the abolition of *intendants*, the landed estates of the Church were nationalized and were offered for sale in exchange for *assignats* – the celebrated bonds which were to become the currency of the Revolution. This last measure did provoke strong objections both within the Assembly and outside it. It was pointed out that the properties which were to be appropriated had not been given to the Church as a whole but to particular abbeys, colleges, parishes and hospitals for specific purposes; that the country would have to assume the extremely expensive responsibility for both charitable work and education; that it was economically inadvisable to break up large holdings into so great a number of smaller plots; that there would be a huge depreciation in their value, since the market was to be flooded with them at a time of such uncertainty. But the advocates of the measure were undeterred. 'The *assignats* will soon be dispersed all over the country,' argued one of the most persuasive of the radical clergy, Thomas Lindet, a *curé* soon to be rewarded with a bishopric, 'and, in spite of himself, every man who holds them will become a defender of the Revolution.' So, by a very small majority, the annexation of the estates of the Church was approved by the Assembly.

Although he approved of this particular enactment, Mirabeau rose again and again to condemn the flood of revolutionary measures which, before being debated in the Assembly, were often discussed at meetings of the Society of the Friends of the Constitution. This Society, which met at the convent of the Jacobins in the Rue Saint-Honoré and was to become famous as the Jacobin Club, was already profoundly influential. The more advanced Breton deputies had been among the first to join, and soon nearly all the deputies of the Left attended their meetings. In the formulation of radical opinion its influence spread all over France where the number of similar clubs in the provinces grew month by month until there were over four hundred of them.

Mirabeau came to some of the meetings in the Rue Saint-Honoré but he was concerned now to contain the Revolution rather than to promote it. 'When you undertake to run a revolution,' he said, 'the difficulty is not to make it go; it is to hold it in check.' Appalled by the rapidity of its progress, he used all his powers of persuasion and oratory to stem the tide – to release the King from virtual captivity, to reduce the increasing powers of the Assembly and above all to reverse the decree which forbade any deputy from becoming a Minister of the Crown. But, since it was well known that he longed to be a Minister himself, his condemnation of this last decree was naturally supposed to be dictated by self-interest. His great powers were recognized in the Assembly but his motives were suspect there; and, while his usefulness was acknowledged at the Tuileries, he was never fully trusted there either. It was accepted that he was a royalist at heart, but it was a matter of concern that he believed so strongly that the authority of the Crown should rest on the sovereignty of the people. The King, who abhorred Mirabeau's reputation as an adulterer, nevertheless undertook to settle his enormous debts and to pay him a generous salary in addition to a very large capital sum if his efforts on the monarchy's behalf proved successful. These sums were not entirely wasted: by persuasive advocacy in the Assembly, Mirabeau was able to prevent the erosion of certain of the King's prerogatives and to ensure that he continued to enjoy his limited freedom of movement in spite of calls for his closer confinement. Yet Mirabeau's championship of the monarchy was more frequently derided than respected, while his advice to the King and Queen, conveyed to the Tuileries in numerous secret messages, was rarely adopted. In the end, the King, disregarding Mirabeau's urgent warnings, took a step which was to place him beyond the help of his most formidable adviser or, indeed, of anyone else.

The King was persuaded to take this step largely by the Assembly's policies towards the Church. The most contentious of these policies had been drafted by one of the specialist committees to which the Assembly delegated certain of its proposed legislation. They were contained in a document misleadingly called the Civil Constitution of the Clergy and involved not only a considerable reduction in the number of bishoprics but also the popular election of both bishops and priests and the severance of those ties which had traditionally bound them to Rome.

In the hope of averting this schism, the clergy appealed to the Pope to authorize them to accept the Civil Constitution which was passed by the Assembly on 12 July 1790. The Pope hesitated before replying to their request. So the Assembly required them all to take an oath of loyalty to the new Constitution, its own clerical members being ordered to show their brethren a good example. Some of them, led by the radical Abbé Grégoire, did so; but most, including all the bishops who were present, declined to follow their example. Outside the Assembly about half of the lower clergy also refused to take the oath; and only seven bishops accepted it. The Church was thus split into two opposing camps, one aghast at the schism, the other inclined to support the Jansenist lawyer, Armand Gaston Camus, in his answer to the question, 'What is the Pope?' 'The Pope is a bishop, the minister of Jesus Christ, just like any other, whose functions are circumscribed within the limits of the diocese of Rome. It is high time that the Church of France, which has always been jealous of her liberties, should be freed from this servitude.'

As the divisions deepened, the laity, too, took sides, friends and families quarrelling bitterly, peasants in many areas enthusiastically supporting the priests who refused the oath, condemning those who had taken it, and thereby giving popular support to the forces of counter-revolution. The Assembly endeavoured to pacify the un-rest by giving pensions to priests opposed to the Civil Constitution and by allowing them to continue in their parishes until they were replaced. But the breach was not healed and remained a source of angry dispute until Napoleon's Concordat with the Papacy in 1801.

Before the Civil Constitution of the Clergy caused such upheaval in France, attempts to raise the provinces against the Assembly in Paris had met with little success as Mounier and Lally-Tollendal had discovered. In some areas enthusiasm for the Revolution was not marked and there were occasional outbreaks of violence against it; but most people welcomed it, and in many districts towns and villages had come together in fraternal friendship, forming them-selves into *fédérations* in commemoration and celebration of the country's rebirth. In February 1790, in one typical, moving cere-mony at Pontivy, delegates from Anjou and Brittany joined hands to swear that they were 'neither Angevins nor Bretons, but citizens of one and the same community'. On the anniversary of the storm-ing of the Bastille thousands of National Guardsmen and soldiers from all over France converged upon Paris for a splendid *Fête de la Fédération*. The celebrations centred upon the Champ de Mars, a large open space between the École Militaire and the Seine. It had been planned to dig out the earth from the centre and to pile it up around the sides to create a vast amphitheatre capable of containing tens of thousands of spectators. But, although twelve thousand workmen were employed on this ambitious undertaking, it was realized as the day of the festival approached that it would never be ready in time. So, 'in an instant the whole population was transformed into labourers'. Priests and prostitutes, watchmakers and watermen, sempstresses, shopkeepers and soldiers, men and women of every age and class, marched to the site to the sound of drums and under banners of different colours emblazoned with patriotic emblems. Lafayette came to lend a hand. So did several ladies who, fainting after their unaccustomed exertions, were cheerfully pushed away in wheelbarrows by sturdy fishwives.

Rich people, poor people, well-dressed people, people in rags, old men, boys, comedians, clerks, actors, scholars, nuns, Carthusians grown old in solitude ... exhibited to the astonished eye a scene full of life and bustle [recorded the Marquis de Ferrières]. There were songs and shouts of joy, the sound of drums and military instruments, the voices of labourers calling to each other ... As the clock struck nine the groups separated, each citizen returned to his family and friends. They all marched off to the sound of drums, preceded by torches, singing from time to time the famous *Ça ira* [which had become a kind of theme song of the Revolution] ... Meanwhile the *fédérés* were arriving from every part of the country. They were lodged in private houses where they were happily supplied with beds and sheets, wood and food, everything, in fact, that would help to make their stay in Paris agreeable.

At length the great day came ... The *fédérés* set out from the site of the Bastille under the eighty-three banners of the departments of France ... They were greeted on their way with the acclamations of an immense concourse of people who filled the streets, the quays and the windows of the houses on either side. A heavy rain was falling but it neither upset nor slackened the march. Dripping with sweat and rain, the *fédérés* danced *farandoles*, shouting 'Long live our brothers, the Parisians!' Wine, ham, fruit, sausages were let down from the windows for them, and they were loaded with blessings. The National Assembly joined the procession at the Place Louis XV ... The rain continued to fall. No one seemed to notice it ... M. de Lafayette, mounted on a superb horse, and surrounded by his aides-de-camp, gave orders and received the homage of the people and the *fédérés* ... A man whom nobody knew, pushed through the crowd and advanced, holding a bottle in one hand and a glass in the other. 'General,' he said. 'You are hot. Have a glass.' Raising his bottle he filled a large glass and handed it to M. de Lafayette. The General took the glass, eyed the stranger for a moment and drank off the wine at a draught. The people applauded while M. de Lafayette, with a complacent smile, cast a benevolent and confiding look upon them . . .

Meanwhile more than three hundred thousand people, assembled since six in the morning, were sitting on turf seats in the Champ de Mars, drenched, bedraggled, sheltering under umbrellas; then, when the rain stopped, they adjusted their dresses as they waited, laughing and chatting, for the *fédérés* and the National Assembly to arrive.

At last the procession entered the Champ de Mars. The deputies took up their positions and the *fédérés* assembled under their respective banners while Charles-Maurice de Talleyrand Périgord, the Bishop of Autun, attended by 300 priests in white surplices with tricolour scarves, prepared to say Mass at an altar in the middle of the amphitheatre. After Mass, the Bishop blessed the *oriflamme* and the eighty-three banners of the *fédérés*; then he led the singing of the *Te Deum* to the accompaniment of an orchestra of 1,200 musicians.

The staff of the Parisian National Guard, with Lafayette at their head, followed by representatives of the army, the navy and the *fédérés*, marched up to the altar to swear to be faithful to the nation, the law and the King. Cannon thundered, banners were waved, sabres glistened and the hundreds of musicians played their instruments more loudly than ever as the President of the National Assembly repeated the same oath and the deputies and spectators, answered with shouts of '*I swear it!*'

The King then stood up and declared in the sudden silence, 'I, King of the French, swear to employ the power delegated to me in maintaining the constitution decreed by the National Assembly and accepted by me.' The Queen then, too, stood up; and, lifting the Dauphin in her arms, said, 'Here is my son! He and I both join in those sentiments.'

Vociferous cheers greeted these remarks. Thousands of voices shouted, '*Vive le Roi! Vive la Reine! Vive M. le Dauphin!*' The rain had stopped; the sun had come out.

The festivities continued the next day and the day after that. There were celebrations and parades in the Champ de Mars; there were reviews of the army and the National Guard; there were firework displays and banquets. A ball was held in the Halle au Blé, another on the site of the Bastille. Crowds of *fédérés* converged upon the Palais Royal, many of them equipped with a useful pamphlet entitled *Lists of Emoluments for the ladies of the Palais Royal, and for the other regions of Paris, comprising names and addresses,* which an enterprising publisher had brought out to help simple young men from the provinces in their dealings with such women as Madame Duperon and her four lady friends at 33, Palais Royal, who charged twenty-five *livres,* or with the less exotic Victorine who charged only six. In the Champs Elysées, beneath trees festooned with coloured lights, crowds of young people danced and sang, while sailors clambered up the masts greased with soap in attempts to win the prizes offered to those who could bring down the tricolour flags flying from their summits. 'You should have heard the bursts of laughter which greeted those who were forced to relinquish the attempt, and the encouragement given to those who, more lucky or more adroit, appeared likely to reach the top,' wrote one observer of this 'charming and brilliant festival'. 'A sentimental joy was diffused over every face and beamed in every eye. It reminded me of the happy pleasures of the Elysian fields of the ancients. The white dresses of the crowds of women strolling under the trees in those beautiful alleys served to heighten the illusion.'

The preparations for the festival and the festival itself had, indeed, provided a convincing display of national unity and given grounds for hope that the bitterness of the past would soon be forgotten.

In the spring and summer of 1791, however, this national unity was undermined by the Civil Constitution of the Clergy. People came out into the streets in support of recalcitrant priests wearing royalist cockades, there were riots in several towns and violent disturbances in many villages from which *curés* who refused to take the oath were evicted.

The King had signed the Civil Constitution, on the advice of a majority of his Ministers, with evident reluctance. Soon afterwards he received a long-delayed letter from the Pope expressly declaring that if he lent his approval to it he would be leading his nation into schism. This was followed by another letter suspending all priests who accepted the Civil Constitution and firmly condemning the election of clergy by the people. The King thereupon replaced his confessor who had taken the oath by one who had not, and consulted a distinguished theologian, the Bishop of Clermont, as to whether he could now take communion from his parish priest who had also taken the forbidden oath.

Up till now the Paris which the King overlooked from his first-floor windows above the Seine had remained quite calm. The upheavals of the summer of 1789 had not been repeated. While outbreaks of violence and sporadic riots were troubling several provinces – particularly in the south where many regiments were so close to mutiny that Mirabeau thought it would be a good idea to disband the whole army and 'enlist another on revolutionary principles' – the life of the capital had continued largely undisturbed. The cafés were crowded, the theatres played to full houses, the salons were as well attended as ever and rich aristocrats continued to walk the streets and patronize the fashionable shops. 'We have had several delightful tea parties the last few days,' one of these aristocrats wrote. 'We are all amusing ourselves.' To some the Revolution had become a kind of joke. Women wore Constitution jewellery and Liberty caps decorated with ribbons the colour of that vivid red known as Foullon's blood; men took pinches of snuff from boxes elegantly enamelled with the tricolour. 'Feudal' became a popular word of playful denigration to be used of coffee-grinders that failed to work or watches that refused to keep time. There was a strange light-heartedness in the air. When Madame de Simiane was hit by an apple thrown from the upper gallery of the Théâtre Français, she sent it to her brother-in-law, Lafayette, with the comment, 'Here, my dear General, is the first fruit of the Revolution that has so far come into my hands.'

In this atmosphere the King had begun to suppose that he might yet recover his lost authority. At the beginning of 1790 he had made a speech to the Assembly in which he had promised to educate his son in the new principles of constitutional monarchy, of freedom with justice, and had associated himself with those plans which the Assembly were carrying out 'for the benefit of France'. He had been loudly cheered and escorted back to the Tuileries as a hero. More recently, and more than once, he had been vociferously cheered again as he had been during the celebrations of the *Fête de la Fédération*. 'I am still King of the French,' he said with some satisfaction.

When he had first arrived at the Tuileries he had seemed listless and despairing. Although it was not suggested to him that he must forego the pleasure of hunting, he had sulkily indicated that he had lost his zest for it. Followed everywhere by six National Guardsmen who were ordered by the Assembly never to lose track of him, he had grown fat and discontented. But as the months passed his spirits revived. The Queen, too, became less unpopular. She was still the victim of libels, accused of plotting to starve the poor, of sending money to Austria, of continuing to indulge a voracious sexual appetite with both men and women. Yet deputations of citizens came to wish her well, while she herself attempted to prove herself worthy of their regard by visiting hospitals and workshops.

Encouraged by the respect which the monarchy still commanded and by a growing feeling in the Assembly, except on the Left, that the Revolution had gone far enough and it was time to conciliate the King, the counter-revolutionaries now urged him to strike back, to turn to the army and to prepare for civil war. This was the advice of the Comte d'Artois given from the safety of exile in Savoy; this was the advice, too, of their sister Elisabeth. The King, however, could not face the prospect of civil war, clinging to his hope that there were now sufficient deputies in favour of compromise with the Court to ensure a return to the quiet pleasures of Versailles. This hope was shattered by the Pope's firm stand against the Civil Constitution of the Clergy and by the King's decision that, in loyalty to his faith and conscience, he must accept the view of Bishop Bonal that he could not receive Holy Communion from a '*Constitutionnel*' priest.

The Pope's unequivocal pronouncement against the Civil Constitution, made public in a brief, led to serious disturbances in Paris where the people's anti-clericalism was fostered both by political clubs and by the theatres which, when not presenting plays celebrating civic virtue, put on others that displayed the horrors of the Inquisition, the tribulations and hypocrisy of monastic and convent life, and the greed and dissipation of real and fictional leaders of the Roman Catholic Church. Outside the theatres and in the gardens of the Palais Royal effigies of the Pope were set alight on bonfires, a severed head was tossed through the windows of the Papal Nuncio's carriage, convents were broken into and nuns assaulted and revolutionary slogans were scrawled on church doors. A mob broke into the Church of St Sulpice, calling out for the head of the *curé* who had protested against the Civil Constitution and forcing the organist to play the tune of '*Ça ira*', the words of which they sang with frightening intensity. The King was called upon to dismiss his new confessor and condemned in pamphlets as a traitor for having flouted the laws of the nation by receiving Communion from a priest whose allegiance was to the Pope rather than to the state.

In fact, the King had not yet committed this breach of the Civil Constitution, but he had made up his mind to do so, and at Easter he and his family prepared to leave the Tuileries for Holy Communion at Saint-Cloud. The gates of the palace, however, were shut against them by a shouting crowd that had intimidated the National Guardsmen on duty in the courtyard. Lafayette arrived on the scene. So did Bailly. But neither of them could persuade the mob to let the carriage pass. Nor could the King who put his head out of the window to ask for that freedom for himself which, he told them, he had given to the nation. His words were met by insults and by a rattling of fists on the carriage doors. For nearly two hours the uproar continued while the Queen, pale yet composed, comforted the weeping Dauphin and the King waited vainly for the crowds to disperse. Then he told the coachman to return to the palace.

In the Tuileries he was advised once again, as he had so often been in the past, to escape from Paris: once he had got away to the army on the frontier he would be able to persuade his brother-in-law, the Austrian Emperor, to take part in an armed congress if not actually to order an invasion of France; he would then be in a position to act as negotiator and the Assembly would be obliged to have him back on his own terms. He would also be free to worship as his conscience urged him to do. Slowly convinced by suggestions and propositions such as these, and by the Queen's strong endorsement of them, the King came to the conclusion that he must make a dash for the frontier. After all, both the King of Spain and the Austrian Emperor had stressed that they could not help him until he and his family were in a place of safety. Once they were, the foreign powers would at least be given the opportunity of proving that they were not using the French royal family's present confinement merely as an excuse for doing nothing as the Queen suspected. The time chosen for the dangerous attempt was the night of 19 June 1791.

Escape from the Tuileries was not to be easy. For weeks past it had been expected that an attempt would be made. When a rumour got about that the Comte de Provence had already gone abroad to join the Comte d'Artois, a mob surrounded the Luxembourg, demanding that he show himself if he were there, and forced him to drive about the streets in a carriage accompanied by market-women who cheekily kissed him and fondled him. His two maiden aunts, Adélaïde and Victoire, daughters of Louis XV, had succeeded in escaping across the frontier with passports for Rome. They had been held for a time in Burgundy before being allowed to proceed, and crowds had besieged the Tuileries calling for their recall and insisting that a deputation be admitted to the palace to ensure that they had not taken the Dauphin with them. Since then the palace had been patrolled by hundreds of National Guardsmen in addition to those who closely watched the movements of the King and Queen. Sentinels stood at each garden gate and at intervals along the river terrace; 600 *sectionnaires* watched all the approaches. Several of the palace servants were paid informers, and no one could enter or leave the apartments which had been allocated to the royal family without the production of a stamped pass. As well as being difficult, escape would be expensive; and Louis had little money of his own readily available, while the Queen could not sell her jewels without arousing suspicion. But fortunately there was a man in Paris with both the means and the inclination to help them, a man of courage and re-source. This was Hans Axel, Count von Fersen.

Fersen, a tall, amusing, strikingly handsome man of thirty-six, was the son of the distinguished Swedish soldier and politician, Frederik Axel von Fersen. After a rigorous education in Sweden, Germany and Italy, he had entered the French military service and had served as aide-de-camp to General Rochambeau in America, being promoted *colonel propriétaire* of the *Royal-Suédois* regiment in 1785. Since then he had been appointed King Gustavus III's special

representative at the French Court. He had grown fond of the King
and was devoted to the Queen, 'an angel', as he described her in a
letter to his sister, a woman both brave and sensitive. He was, he
added, doing all he could to console her in her misfortune. Needless
to say, it was rumoured that they had become lovers. Perhaps they
had. Certainly Fersen was very attractive to women and much
attracted by them: he already had one devoted lover in Paris,
Eleonora Sullivan, a voluptuous Italian woman, once a circus acrobat
and courtesan, now the wife of an Anglo-American millionaire and
the mistress of a Scottish one.

Fersen, as generous as he was debonair, offered to lend the King
and Queen all the money he had; and if this sum, 600,000 *livres*,
proved insufficient for their purposes, he undertook to borrow the
rest. He also took it upon himself to provide a four-wheeled covered
carriage which would be commodious enough to carry the two royal
children and their aunt Elisabeth as well as the King and Queen; for
Louis and Marie Antoinette were both determined that the family
should not be parted. This carriage, a sumptuous berlin with dark
green and yellow bodywork, paler yellow wheels and white velvet
upholstery, ordered in the name of a friend of Fersen, Baroness von
Korff, was kept in the courtyard of Fersen's hotel so that it should
become a familiar sight to the citizens of Paris. It was occasionally
to be seen, drawn by six horses, driven as fast as it would go – which
was disappointingly slowly – along the Vincennes road so that Fersen could test its reliability.

On the night of the escape from Paris the berlin was to be taken
first to the courtyard of the house of Eleonora Sullivan's rich
Scottish lover, then to an agreed spot just beyond the customs post
on the road outside the Porte Saint-Martin. Three of the King's
former bodyguard were to wait there with it, dressed in yellow
liveries which Fersen had bought at a sale of the effects of an
émigré prince. Fersen himself, dressed as a cabman, was to drive the
royal family to the rendezvous in a hired carriage. Once he had got
them, suitably disguised, into the carriage Fersen foresaw no difficulties. The berlin to which they would be transferred outside the
Porte Saint-Martin would rattle off under cover of darkness through
Châlons. Ponte de Sommeville, Saint-Ménéhould, Clermont,

Varennes, Dun and Stenay towards the north-east frontier where troops of the Marquis de Bouillé, whose headquarters were at Metz, had been asked to provide an escort on the last stages of the journey. But the great difficulty would be in spiriting the family out of the palace.

The first problem arose when a woman who worked in the palace as a cleaner and who was known to spy for her lover, a convinced republican, decided to postpone the holiday which she had been due to take. The proposed flight would have to be put off until she had gone. The new date set was the night of Monday 20 June.

At ten o'clock that night the Queen woke her children, dressed the Dauphin in a girl's frock and pulled a wide-brimmed bonnet down over his eyes. 'He looked so beautiful,' his sister recalled, 'but was so sleepy that he could not stand and did not know what was happening. I asked him what he thought we were going to do, and he answered, "I suppose to act in a play since we have got these funny clothes on." ' His mother then led him and his sister downstairs to rooms which had until recently been occupied by the King's First Gentleman who had emigrated. Since his departure the door of these lodgings had been left unguarded. The Queen unlocked it. The children's governess, the Duchesse de Tourzel, crept out with her two charges to find Fersen waiting for them, whip in hand, playing the part of a hackney-coachman to perfection, so the Duchess thought, whistling, gossiping with a passer-by, taking occasional pinches of snuff. When she and the children came out he hurried them away to the waiting carriage while the Queen went back into the palace and eventually to bed. Soon after eleven when all seemed quiet she got up again, put on a brown dress and a black hat with a heavy veil, and waited for the King to come to her bedroom where it had been arranged he would change into a brown suit and a dark green overcoat and cover his hair with a grey wig. Wearing similar clothes and such a wig, the Chevalier de Coigny, who looked rather like the King, had left the Tuileries for the past twelve nights at the same time each night. So it was hoped that when the King left on the night of the 20th he would be mistaken for the Chevalier. And so he was. He walked past a sentry who did not challenge him; and as Fersen emerged from the shadows to join him, he made for the line of carriages which was habitually drawn up in the courtyard for the use of those whose business detained them at the palace until late at night. He climbed into one of them with Fersen and found the children already inside. Soon afterwards the Queen, who had left the palace the same way as the children, joined him there.

The transfer took place safely beyond the Porte Saint-Martin; and before three o'clock next morning Baroness von Korff's berlin had reached Bondy. Inside sat the Baroness's two children (the Dauphin and his sister), their governess (the Queen), her steward (the King) and the Baroness herself (the Duchesse de Tourzel). Fersen wished them farewell at Bondy and galloped away to Belgium while the berlin, drawn by six fresh horses from the post-house, lumbered off for Claye and, through Meaux, towards Chaintrix and Châlons. 'Lafayette must be feeling most embarrassed by now,' the King remarked contentedly, looking at his watch.

Dawn came and there was no sign of any pursuit. 'When we've passed Châlons,' the King said, 'we shall be safe. We shall then find the first detachment of troops and after that we shall have nothing to fear.' Forty hussars under the young Duc de Choiseul had been sent out by the Marquis de Bouillé to meet them just beyond the town at the village of Pont de Sommeville. Once they got there they would be out of danger.

When the berlin clattered to a halt outside the post-house at Pont de Sommeville, however, there was no sign of the promised soldiers. Fersen had calculated its time of arrival as 'Tuesday at 2.30 at the latest'. But there had been delays on the way: a wheel had struck the wall of a narrow bridge, the traces had snapped and the horses fallen, and even where the road surfaces were good it had proved impossible to drive the heavily loaded vehicle at more than about seven miles an hour. It was not, therefore, until six o'clock in the evening that the royal family reached Pont de Sommeville. By then the Duc de Choiseul had become alarmed by angry peasants who disbelieved his story that he was 'in their village to escort pay for the army in the east' and who supposed that he had come instead to enforce the collection of overdue rents on behalf of a local landowner. Threatened by these peasants who brandished pitchforks and pointed muskets at the faces of his men, Choiseul decided to withdraw from the village into a nearby forest where he became lost in the darkness.

So, when the horses had been changed at the post-house, the berlin had to move off again unescorted to Sainte-Ménéhould. Here the King had expected to find a detachment of dragoons, but again he was disappointed, for their commander, who had been constantly questioned by suspicious villagers throughout the afternoon, had received a message from Choiseul at Pont de Sommeville that there was no likelihood of the royal party arriving that day and had consequently allowed his men to dismount and to go for a drink in a wine shop. On the appearance of the berlin he walked up to it, saluted and told the King in a low voice that the plans had misfired and that he would have to stay out of His Majesty's way for fear of increasing the suspicions of the villagers. The villagers, however, were by now quite sure as one of them said later, that 'something very odd was going on'. They had not been convinced by the dragoon captain's evasive excuses for his men's presence in Sainte-Ménéhould, they had seen him salute the occupants of the new, expensive carriage and had watched him as he whispered his brief message through the window before walking hurriedly away. It was decided, therefore, to call out the National Guard and to disarm the dragoons while they were still dismounted. Thus it was that, as the berlin continued on its way through the outskirts of the town, the King looked behind in vain for the escort that he had been promised.

In Paris the flight of the royal family had been discovered early in the morning of 21 June when one of the King's *valets de chambre* had woken in his truckle bed in the King's room. He had detached from his arm the cord by which the King roused him if he needed him in the night; he had opened the shutters, removed his bed and the screen that shielded it from the King's, opened the door for the Pages of the Bedchamber, and approached the drawn curtains of His Majesty's bed. 'Sire,' he had announced, bowing respectfully, 'it is seven o'clock.' He then drew the curtains and discovered the bed to be empty.

The Queen's bedroom and the children's were also found to be deserted. And soon the tocsin was ringing and crowds of people from all over Paris were surging round the Tuileries, at first in a mood of indignant anger, so one observer considered, then in one of taunting contempt. They pushed through the gates on which was hung a sign reading 'House to let', telling a worried postman who was trying to deliver letters to mark them, 'Gone away. Left no address'. They then streamed into the palace, examining the rooms with curiosity, insisting that the palace servants remove their livery but otherwise neither molesting anyone nor doing any damage. A cherry hawker sat with her basket on the eiderdown quilt of the Queen's bed. 'Now,' she said. 'Today, it's the nation's turn to be comfortable.'

Awakened in his house in the Rue de Bourbon, Lafayette leaped out of bed, hurriedly put on his uniform and big cockaded hat and rushed off towards the Pont Royal, followed by an angry crowd accusing him of having connived at the King's escape. On his way he met Bailly who, accompanied also by a shouting mob and dressed in a black overcoat with a tricolour ribbon across his shoulders, appeared 'nearly overcome with anxiety'. They stopped to talk above the roar of the crowd. 'Do you think,' Lafayette asked, 'that the King and his family will have to be arrested and brought back to Paris for the public good?' Bailly thought that they would but wondered who could give the orders. The Assembly were not due to meet until nine o'clock and something would have to be done before then.

'All right, I will take the responsibility upon myself,' Lafayette said and immediately began to dictate an order to an aide-de-camp:

The King having been removed by the enemies of the Revolution, the bearer is instructed to impart the fact to all good citizens, who are commanded in the name of their endangered country to take him out of their hands and to bring him back to the keeping of the National Assembly. The latter is about to assemble, but in the meantime I take upon myself all the responsibility of this order. Paris, June 21, 1791.

Lafayette signed the paper, adding beneath the date, 'This order extends to all the royal family', and soon horsemen were riding in all directions out of Paris to find them. One of the horsemen was Captain Bayon who took the road to Valenciennes. He galloped through Meaux and east for Châlons, but after six hours in the saddle he felt he must have a rest. So he reined in his horse at Chaintrix, sending a message on to Sainte-Ménéhould that every effort must be made to stop the royal family if they had taken that road to the frontier. When this message reached the post-house at Sainte-Ménéhould the suspicions of the young postmaster, Jean Baptiste Drouet, were confirmed. Drouet had thought that the governess of Baroness von Korff's two children looked just like the Queen whom he had seen once or twice when he had been in the army and was 'equally struck' by the resemblance of the steward to the face of the King printed on an *assignat* he had in his pocket. He had said as much to his wife, but she had not wanted him to get into trouble and had advised him to keep quiet. Now, feeling convinced that the woman *must* be the Queen, he and a friend galloped off in pursuit of the berlin through the Forêt d'Argonne on the road to Verdun.

Ten miles east of Sainte-Ménéhould is the little town of Clermont en Argonne. Here the berlin had stopped once again to change horses, and Drouet's postilions riding back from the post-house there to Sainte-Ménéhould had overheard a shout from the box of the berlin as it continued on its journey: 'Take the road to Varennes!' Passing Drouet on their way through the Forêt d'Argonne, the postilions told him what they had heard. So Drouet and his companion, who had been making for Metz by way of Verdun, turned north for Varennes. 'We went by a side road through the woods,' Drouet recorded, 'and reached Varennes at the same time as the berlin which was drawn up beside the houses at the top of the town. It was then about half past eleven and the night was very dark. But in order not to be recognized or suspected, we took off our cross belts and as we passed the carriage at a walk, I said in a loud voice, trying to pass ourselves off as merchants bound for a nearby fair, "Good Lord! We'll be very late getting to Grandpré. Perhaps we shan't get there at all with these tired-out horses." '

Having passed the berlin they rode flat out down the hill, through the cobbled streets and across the stone bridge to the house of the local *procurateur*, a grocer and chandler named Jean Baptiste Sauce.

Coming out into the street with a lantern in his hand, Sauce called out the National Guard who took up their positions beside an archway that spanned the main street by the church. Soon the lamps of the berlin appeared in the darkness, and Sauce walked out into the middle of the street shouting, 'Halt!' The berlin came on despite the order and, as the National Guardsmen appeared from behind the arch, bayonets fixed to their muskets, Sauce cried out again, 'Halt! Halt! One step more and we fire!' The horses clattered to a halt.

Sauce went up to the carriage, knocked on the door and asked to see the occupants' passport. The Duchesse de Tourzel passed it through the window. Sauce took it from her and went into a nearby inn to examine it in a better light than his lantern afforded. It was made out in the proper form for the Baroness von Korff and her party. Sauce began to think there must have been a mistake, but Drouet insisted. 'I tell you the King and Queen are in that carriage. I've seen them. If you let them go you'll be guilty of treason.'

So Sauce asked the travellers to alight. He led them into his small shop, a wooden building with bundles of candles and pots of brown sugar in the window, and took them up the narrow stairs to a bedroom where the two children lay down on the bed. The two ladies sat on rickety, straw-bottomed chairs, and the man who claimed to be the Baroness's steward walked up and down restlessly as they waited for the arrival of a judge, Jacques Destez, who had lived at Versailles for a number of years and had often set eyes on the King. He came into the room at last, looked in astonishment at the figure in the green overcoat and immediately knelt before him. 'Oh, Sire!' he said.

'Yes,' the King answered in immediate acknowledgment of this identification. 'I am, indeed, your King.'

Sauce was as impressed and overawed by their Majesties' presence in his bedroom as was Destez. Having listened to the King's explanations as to why he had left Paris, he told them respectfully that in the morning he would provide them with an escort to take them on their journey.

But before dawn Captain Bayon arrived, together with one of Lafayette's aides-de-camp, Jean Louis Romeuf, who brought with him a decree from the Assembly confirming Lafayette's order for the royal family's return to the Tuileries. They were both embarrassed. Romeuf averted his glance when he saw the Queen. Bayon stammered when he addressed the King: 'Sire, you know – all the people of Paris are, er . . . You will not go any further, Sire – the interests of the state . . . Sire . . .'

'Well, what is it you want?' the King asked him brusquely.

'Sire, a decree from the Assembly.'

'Where is it?'

'My companion has it.'

Romeuf held out the paper, looking at the floor. The King snatched it from him and, having read it, said, 'There is no longer a King in France.'

He handed it to the Queen who also read it, then gave it back to him. He placed it on the bed where the children were still lying down. But the Queen suddenly seized it and flung it on to the floor with the angry comment, 'I will not have my children contaminated.'

At these words the people standing in the threshold of the room began to murmur angrily 'as though she had profaned the most sacred thing in the world'.

The King seemed to be in his usual quandary as to what ought to be done. He asked Bayon and Romeuf if they might not wait until 'at least eleven o'clock, as though still hoping that de Bouillé's troops might arrive. But then, as the crowds in the street outside shouted more loudly than ever, 'They must go back! They must go back! To Paris! To Paris!', he began to realize that he had no alternative but to obey the Assembly's commands. The Duc de Choiseul, who had now ridden into the town with his hussars and had pushed his way into Sauce's shop, quietly urged him to make a dash for the frontier with his family: there were fresh horses ready in the street below as well as the hussars. There were also, though, as the King well knew, hundreds of armed men there, and hundreds more National Guardsmen were still converging on Varennes from the neighbouring towns and villages. So, after breakfast, during which Madame Sauce suggested that he must be crazy to consider giving up all the money the nation paid him, it was decided that the royal family would have to return to Paris.

Before leaving, the King begged to be left alone for a few minutes with his family. When the others had gone he persuaded Sauce to go down to the carriage, to make an excuse for entering it and to bring back a box from a secret receptacle whose position he described to him, giving him the keys. On Sauce's return he opened the box. Inside were papers which he and his wife and sister frantically tore into tiny pieces, heaping them up in a bowl while Sauce stood on guard at the door. No sooner had the King set them alight, however, than there was a loud knocking at the door. He hurriedly picked up the bowl and hurled both it and its contents out of the window. The people below chased the fluttering fragments but, although they later tried to fit the charred edges together, they could make nothing of the writing on them.

It was now half past seven in the morning. The royal family walked down the steps towards the carriage, on whose box the officers of the bodyguard had been sitting affecting imperturbability at the curses of the crowd who now let out repeated shouts of '*Vive la Nation!*' The King and Queen climbed in followed by the children and the Duchesse de Tourzel, and Choiseul closed the door. 'Don't leave us,' the Queen begged him, leaning out of the window; but the berlin jolted forward, and, as the mob surged after it, he was knocked to the ground.

The return journey to Paris was a dreadful ordeal. At Sainte-Ménéhould, the berlin, escorted now by a vast crowd of curious onlookers and by National Guards, some in uniform, others not, was halted while the mayor made a speech of admonition and rebuke. Later, an old quixotic nobleman, who rode up with the cross of St Louis on his breast to make the King an elaborate salute, was shot in the back as he rode away. The crowds increased, shouting insults and threats, spitting at the windows. Then near Pont à Binson, two members of the Assembly, Antoine Barnave and Jérôme Pétion, who had been sent out to meet the carriage, climbed into it, obliging the Queen to take the Dauphin on her knee. Pétion, soon to be Mayor of Paris, a good looking, though fat and vain and tiresomely garrulous man, afterwards gave a detailed account of the last stages of the journey. He described how anxious the Queen and Madame Elisabeth were to assure him that the King had had no intention of leaving the country, and how the King, whose linen was now very dirty, on several occasions offered him something to drink and poured it out for him, trying to make conversation. He began to talk about the English, their industry and keen commercial sense; but he uttered a few sentences only, then became embarrassed and blushed. Often 'the difficulty he found in expressing himself made him shy'.

We stayed for twelve whole hours in the carriage [Pétion continued] without once getting out. What surprised me particularly was that neither the Queen nor Madame Elisabeth nor Madame de Tourzel showed any sign of wanting to get out. The Dauphin made water two or three times. The King himself unbuttoned his breeches and made him pee into a big silver cup. Once Barnave held the cup. It has been said that the coach contained an English convenience. Perhaps it did; but I saw no sign of one.

As the hours passed, Pétion began to flatter himself that Madame Elisabeth was physically attracted by him. Their eyes 'met now and then with a kind of understanding'. He stretched out his arm and she placed hers over it. 'Our arms were interlaced,' he said, 'and mine touched her armpit. I felt a hurried movement of her heart and a warmth passing through her clothes . . . I noticed a certain abandon in her attitude . . . and I believe that if we had been alone she would have fallen into my arms and given herself up to the promptings of nature.'

Once a fight broke out among the people surrounding the carriage, and men carrying bayonets could be seen staring angrily at the Queen through the windows. 'Soon they started swearing at her. "Look at the bitch," they shouted. "It's no good her showing us her child. Everyone knows it isn't his." The Dauphin, frightened by the noise and the clank of arms, started to scream. The Queen soothed him, the tears pouring down her cheeks. Barnave and I spoke to the men, one of whom replied, "Don't worry. No harm will be done. We can promise you that. But the post of honour belongs to us." It turned out that the fight had been caused by a quarrel over precedence.'

So the journey continued in the insufferable heat. Clouds of dust rose from the wheels of the carriage and the clopping hooves of the horses, until at last, after five exhausting days of fruitless travelling, the royal family arrived back in Paris where the streets were lined with National Guards, their arms reversed as though for a funeral procession. The crowds were immense. Every window and roof in the Champs Elysées was filled with faces. People clambered on to gates and into the trees. But there was a strange silence broken only by shouts of '*Vive la Nation!*' Hundreds of official notices had been pasted to the walls of Paris reading: 'Whoever applauds the King shall be flogged. Whoever insults him shall be hanged.' The carriage stopped outside the Tuileries. The doors opened. The King climbed out. Still there was silence. But, so Pétion said, 'the Queen's appearance was greeted with violent expressions of disapproval, though the children were received with good humour and even with endearments.' They walked up the steps into the palace where a deputy approached the King and reprimanded him, like a schoolmaster speaking to a naughty pupil. 'Well, that was a fine way to behave! That comes of having such bad advisers. Now see what a mess you've got yourself into.' Then, as the man suddenly and unexpectedly burst into tears, the Marquis de Lafayette, having inspected the guards and ensured that there was no chance of further escape, came up to the King and asked formally for orders. 'I seem,' the King replied petulantly, 'to be more at your orders than you are at mine.'

THE DAYS OF THE TUILERIES

20 June and 10 August 1792

*'What a joy for these gentlemen
to be able to give orders
to their head clerk, the King of France'*

BARON NECKER

Before dying at the age of forty-two on 2 April 1791 in his house in the Chaussée d'Antin, the Comte de Mirabeau said sadly to Talleyrand, 'I carry away with me the last shreds of the monarchy.' After the flight of the royal family to Varennes and their enforced return to Paris, the French monarchy was, indeed, doomed. There were many deputies like Barnave who had been able to put his ideas to the Queen during their journey together back to the Tuileries, who still hoped that some sort of compromise with the Court was possible, who still believed that, although the Constituent Assembly had ordered Ministers to execute decrees without troubling to obtain the King's signature, the monarchy should still have a place in the new Constitution which would soon at long last be ready for his approval. But the *monarchiens*, while still quite numerous in the Assembly, were losing ground outside it. Sieyès continued to assert his belief in the monarchy; so did Bailly. But these heroes of the Revolution's early days, like several others, were now derided for their caution: the firebrands of 1789 were, in the words of Antoine de Rivarol, now coming forward as firemen. At the same time, ever sharper distinctions were being made between those who considered that the Revolution had gone far enough, who were content to observe that the prestige of the two once privileged orders was being usurped by the bourgeoisie, and those who were demanding the trial and punishment of the King, 'liberty for all', and further advances in the 'emancipation of the people'. The differences between these new revolutionaries and their more moderate bourgeois opponents were highlighted by numerous disturbances during the late winter and spring of 1791. One of the earliest and most serious of these took place at the end of February when over a thousand workers from the Faubourg Saint-Antoine, encouraged by members of the Cordeliers Club, marched upon the Château de Vincennes which was being converted into a prison for the reception, so it was alleged, of political prisoners. Accompanied by a battalion of the National Guard under the unwilling command of the brewer, Antoine Santerre – who had been forced to lead them as Lafayette had been compelled to lead the National Guard to Versailles seventeen months before – the *ouvriers* carried with them crowbars and

133

pickaxes, which had been used in the demolition of the Bastille, and vigorously set about the demolition of the château. Their work was interrupted by Lafayette who arrived on the scene with a large force of troops and who loudly and sternly rebuked Santerre in front of the assembled company. More than sixty prisoners were taken and were carried off to the Conciergerie as the rest of the *ouvriers* hooted and jeered at their captors.

As the weeks passed the rift between the workers, many of whom were now unemployed, and the more well-to-do citizens was deepened both by the Cordeliers, who sought to enlist the *ouvriers'* support for the advancement of revolutionary democracy, and by the readers and writers of such reactionary news-sheets and gossip-sheets as *Le Babillard* which constantly blamed the workers and unemployed for all the ills of France.

Citizens of every sort [*Le Babillard* declared in its issue of 6 July] are beginning to lose all patience with the workers. The National Guard, merchants, manufacturers, *les bourgeois, les artisans* alike all cry out against these people who are in the pay of sedition-mongers ... One hears everywhere that they ought to be swept out of the way by a blast of cannon fire.

Less than a fortnight after the publication of this issue of *Le Babillard*, there was a violent clash between the opposing parties which became known as a massacre. It occurred on Sunday, 17 July.

On the afternoon of that day a huge crowd of people assembled on the Champ de Mars. They had come to sign a republican petition drawn up by the leaders of the Cordeliers Club, a popular club in the Rue Dauphine with a subscription of only two *sous* a month, whose members had sworn to protect the people against abuses of authority. The petition was laid out on an altar which had been erected for the recent celebration of the second anniversary of the fall of the Bastille. As the signatories filed past, many writing their names with evident difficulty, some unable to write at all, two men, one a hairdresser, the other an *invalide* with a wooden leg, were discovered under the steps leading up to the platform. It was later supposed that they had hidden there to peep up the women's skirts, but at the time the cry went up that they intended to set fire to the altar of liberty, that they were spies for counter-revolutionaries. They were dragged out and hanged on the spot.

At the Hôtel de Ville, where reports were received of a potentially dangerous riot, it was decided that the time had come for a show of forceful authority. Martial law was declared; the National Guard were called out and, led by Bailly and Lafayette, marched off to the Champ de Mars behind a red flag. They were greeted by jeers, boos, catcalls, and, finally, by a volley of stones. Lafayette ordered a few shots to be fired in the air in retaliation. The crowd scattered for a few minutes but then drew together again to renew their shouting and stone-throwing. Lafayette called upon them to disperse, and when they showed no sign of being willing to do so, he gave the command, 'Fire!' In the ensuing volleys about fifty of the demonstrators were killed.

Order had been rapidly restored, but the split in the revolutionaries' ranks was now wider than ever. Lafayette lost his popularity with the citizens of Paris overnight, and Bailly's political career was ruined. Having been succeeded as Mayor of Paris by Jérôme Pétion, who was more acceptable to the *sans-culottes*, Bailly retired to write his memoirs in the provinces whence he was eventually to be dragged back to the capital for execution.

For the moment, however, the conservative revolutionaries had the upper hand and were determined to keep it. From the Hôtel de Ville and from the Assembly came a stream of orders authorizing the arrest of extremists including Camille Desmoulins and Santerre, both of whom went into hiding; newspapers that supported the *sans-culottes* were suppressed; martial law was kept in force. And the left-wing Jacobin Club, which had previously wielded such influence, almost disintegrated, most of its members seceding to form the more moderate Feuillant Club in protest against a petition to dethrone the King.

The members of the Feuillant Club were by far the largest of the political groups that made up the new Legislative Assembly which, elected on a restrictive middle-class franchise, met on 1 October 1791, soon after the long-awaited Constitution had at last been promulgated and been accepted and signed by the King. In this Assembly, from which all members of the Constituent Assembly were excluded, the clergy and nobility no longer had separate representation. A few nobles and clergy who held liberal views had been elected, but nearly all the deputies were middle class, many of them lawyers, as had been the case in the Third Estate in 1789. Yet, although the great majority of the Legislative Assembly held moderate opinions and were in favour of some sort of accommodation with the monarchy, the most gifted and rhetorically most powerful deputies were those who sat on their left, several of whom came from the Gironde and were therefore collectively to be known as Girondists. Prominent amongst these men, who were inclined to worship Rousseau and the Romans rather than God, were two lawyers from Bordeaux, Pierre Victurnien Vergniaud and Marguerite Élie Guadet. Closely associated with them was a lawyer from Normandy, François Buzot, and the unashamedly ambitious, impulsive, imaginative and rather affected editor of the *Patriote français*, Jacques Pierre Brissot.

Vergniaud, the son of a merchant, was a quiet, withdrawn and scholarly man of thirty-eight who sat for much of the time in what appeared to be abstracted reverie, but when he did rise to speak, his oratory was so compelling that he was elected the Assembly's President. Guadet, three years younger than Vergniaud, dark, thin, intense, with gleaming eyes and a sharp, sarcastic tongue, was an almost equally gifted orator. But overshadowing them both was Brissot.

Brissot, the son of an inn-keeper and the husband of a woman who had been a governess in the household of the Duc d'Orléans, was born at Chartres in 1754. His father, anxious that the boy should get on in the world, had ensured that he was given a good education which enabled him to enter a lawyer's office in Paris where, with that customary desire of the *bourgeois* to appear to be more highly born than he was, he called himself Brissot de Warville. Abandoning the law for letters, he became a prolific writer of books, treatises and pamphlets as well as newspaper articles, contributing to the *Mercure* and the *Courrier de l' Europe* before becoming editor of the *Patriote français*. The views he expressed had frequently landed him in trouble with the Government, and for a time he had been incarcerated in the Bastille, the keys of which were presented to him after its capture by the *Vainqueurs*. He had spent some time in exile in London and, as an agent of an anti-slavery society, had visited Philadelphia whence he had returned with his Quaker-like appearance and manner much intensified. Since he had spent more time abroad than most of his colleagues, he was considered to have an expert knowledge of foreign affairs, a reputation which led to him being appointed to the diplomatic committee of the Legislative Assembly. He soon became the acknowledged leader of this committee and consequently one of the principal arbiters of the foreign policy of France. His fervent advocacy of war as a means of saving the Revolution had a profound influence on the events which were now to unfold.

Although the Feuillants were opposed to war, there was wide support for it not only among other members of the Legislative Assembly but also in the country at large. Both in the provinces, where the flight of the King to Varennes had led to renewed disturbances such as those which had characterized the Great Fear, and in Paris, where members of the Assembly had been booed and insulted after granting an amnesty for political prisoners, there was a growing feeling that the fissures in society were becoming so deep that all the ground that had been gained would be lost unless a violent assault were made upon the enemies of the Revolution beyond the nation's frontiers.

To millions of peasants it seemed that the only real beneficiaries of the upheavals of 1789 were the middle classes. Several peasants had acquired sizeable parcels of land which had been thrown on to the market by the nationalization of the property of the Church, while many nobles, who had been compensated by the Assembly for the loss of their offices, had been enabled to extend their estates, but it was the wealthy bourgeoisie who had acquired by far the largest holdings. In fact, the expropriation of ecclesiastical property had tended to reinforce the class distinctions as reflected in land ownership rather than to break them down. At the same time the flight of

137

many landowners abroad had done nothing to alleviate the peasants' economic plight, since the *émigré* still made his demands upon them through his agents. 'We thought,' ran one of the numerous complaints addressed to the Assembly from country districts, 'that, after the decrees suppressing the feudal régime had been passed, we should be as free in our property as in our persons. Two years' experience has shown us that we are still slaves. We have no seigneur any more: he is at Coblenz. But he has left us his *fermiers* who badger and persecute us just as they did before the Revolution ... Unless you come to our help we are ruined!'

In several parts of the country unrest was still fostered by popular support for priests who, having refused to take the oath required by the Assembly, were being driven from their parishes. There were renewed riots as armed crowds forced open churches whose doors had been shut against recalcitrant *curés*. Prompted by the Left, the Assembly passed a decree depriving non-juring priests of the pensions that had been granted them and expelling them from all places where disturbances had occurred.

To this decree the King applied the veto which the new Constitution had granted him and of which he had not yet been deprived. He also exercised his right of veto when the Assembly, harangued again by the Girondins, passed another decree sentencing to a traitor's death and confiscating the property of all *émigrés* who had not returned to France by the end of the year.

Confronted by these vetoes the Girondins, believing that there would be large-scale desertions from the enemy ranks, called more loudly than ever for war against those who sheltered and armed the *émigrés* and who supported priests owing allegiance to the Pope rather than to the nation. Brissot, determined to force the King to give way to the Girondins' demands and to declare himself openly on the side of the militant Revolution, declared that France urgently needed war 'to purge her of the vices of despotism'. 'Do you wish at one blow to destroy the aristocracy, the refractory priests, the malcontents?' Brissot asked. 'Then destroy Coblenz [where an *émigré* army was being formed]. The head of the nation will then be obliged to reign in accordance with the Constitution.'

The cry was taken up by all Brissot's vociferous supporters, most of whom, as one of their colleagues admitted, were inclined to be intoxicated by their own words once they heard themselves applauded, frequently being carried away 'far beyond the limits of their own feelings, and, as they left the Assembly, blushing for what they had said'. Maximin Isnard, a wealthy ship-owner who had been elected to the Legislative Assembly for the department of the Var, told his fellow-deputies that caution was 'merely weakness. The bravest are the best and an excess of firmness is the safeguard of success. We must amputate the gangrened limb to save the rest of the body.' Outside the Assembly a female voice advocated violence in even stronger terms: 'Peace will set us back . . . We can be regenerated through blood alone'. This was the voice of Madame Roland.

Manon Roland was the intelligent, passionate daughter of a Parisian engraver. 'Her face was not conventionally beautiful,' wrote a man who came to know her well, 'but she was extremely attractive . . . She had a graceful figure and beautifully shaped hands. One suspected that she was witty even before she began to speak; and no woman spoke with more purity, grace and elegance.' Her own opinion of herself was equally high. 'My complexion,' she wrote in her memoirs, 'is of a dazzling colour. My mouth is rather large but it would be impossible to find a smile more sweet or disarming. Though my hands are not small they are very elegant because of their long slender fingers which suggest cleverness and grace. My teeth are white and well positioned. I enjoy perfect health. Such are the treasures with which nature has blessed me.' She might with truth have added that she was a thrifty, conscientious housekeeper and an excellent cook.

She had received little formal education but, being of a studious disposition, she had read a great deal ever since she had learned to read at all, and was extremely well informed. She was also opinionated, outspoken, snobbish, high-spirited and undiscerning, incapable of judging men, so fervently did she love and admire her friends and hate her enemies. At the age of twenty-seven she had married Jean-Marie Roland, an inspector of manufactures in Lyons, twenty years older than herself, a staid and righteous man, very conscious of his virtues, pedantic, energetic and ambitious. Manon

was quite as ambitious as her husband for whom she wrote newspaper articles which appeared under his name. Having corresponded
with Brissot, they came to Paris where they took cheap, fifth-floor
rooms in the Hôtel Britannique. From here Roland walked out one
day to join the Jacobin Club in the plain dark clothes he invariably
wore, a black hat covering the sparse, neatly brushed hairs on his
dome-shaped head. His wife sought out the company of the Girondins to whom she aired sentiments inspired by her study of Plutarch,
Voltaire and Rousseau, and made vehement attacks upon the Queen
whom she detested.

These attacks were echoed by two journalists of extraordinary
vituperative power, Jacques René Hébert and Jean Paul Marat.

The abusive and often obscene language that Hébert used in his
journal, *Le Père Duchesne*, was in marked contrast to his appearance
and manner. He was a small, polite man, 'fussy and effeminate', always neatly dressed and carefully scented, the husband of a former
nun. Born at Alençon where his father kept a goldsmith's shop, he
had come to Paris after the family had been ruined by a lawsuit and
had lived for a time in dire poverty, writing plays which manage-
ments declined to present and having to work as a box-office assistant at the Variétés, until his gift for scurrilous and ribald invective
brought him both a wide readership among the disaffected, who had
a taste for such language, and a large following in the Cordeliers
Club. He insulted the Queen, 'the Austrian bitch', her sister-in-law,
'Big-arse Babet', and the King, 'Monsieur Veto, the drunken drip',
with persistent and coarsely imaginative contempt.

Marat's targets, who were attacked with equal venom if less
scabrously in his paper *L'Ami du peuple*, were more diverse. Indeed,
suspecting almost everyone and constantly complaining, '*Nous
sommes trahis*', Marat attacked the Assembly, the Feuillants, the
royal family, the Ministers and municipality with fine impartiality.
'In order to ensure public tranquillity,' he once declared, 'two
hundred thousand heads must be cut off.' Dark and intense, with
high cheek bones and wide-set, greenish-yellow eyes, Marat seemed
incapable of keeping his body still. When he spoke he gestured

constantly with his strong, thin arms; when he read his wide mouth twitched convulsively. He claimed that he slept only two hours a night, devoted a further hour to 'eating, dressing and household affairs' and spent the rest of his time working. He was forty-nine, thirteen years older than Hébert, ten years older than Desmoulins, older indeed than Brissot and Vergniaud and all the leading Girondins. Moreover, in his own opinion, he was not only more experienced than they were but also far more wise and honest. 'When the Revolution came I immediately saw how the wind was blowing,' he wrote. 'And at last I began to breathe in the hope of seeing humanity avenged and myself installed in the place which I deserved.'

He came from Neuchâtel, but his father was Sardinian and his mother Swiss. He had studied medicine at Bordeaux and had become an expert on diseases of the eye, suffering himself from one which he managed to cure by his own treatment. He had practised as a doctor in London and Holland after leaving Paris and, following a visit to Scotland, had been recommended for an honorary degree at the University of St Andrews. Thereafter there is no reliable record of his activities, but he seems to have run heavily into debt and to have endeavoured to extricate himself from his difficulties by stealing some medals from a museum. On his return to France, vain, quarrelsome but undoubtedly ingenious, he had found himself again in demand as a fashionable physician whose writing-paper was adorned with an imaginary coat of arms. He had composed various scientific papers, on light, heat and electricity, which he had presented to the Académie des Sciences whose members, shocked by his contradictions of Newton, refused to admit him to their number, thus increasing the sense of persecution which haunted him and drove him to excess.

Abandoning medicine and science for politics on the eve of the Revolution, he became a prolific pamphleteer, attacking a variety of targets with more concern for wide-ranging insult than accurate aim. A visitor, Charles Barbaroux, once called upon him to find him busy writing. 'He was in a hurry: the printer was calling for copy. You should have seen the casual way in which he composed his articles. Without knowing anything about some public man, he would ask the first person he met what he thought of him and write it down.

"I'll ruin the rascal," he would say.' In 1789 he founded the paper which, though he held the people as a whole in low esteem, he was to call *L'Ami du peuple*. Being perpetually in trouble with authority, warrants were more than once issued for his arrest. He was imprisoned for a time towards the end of 1789, but on a later occasion escaped by fleeing to London. After the day of the Champ du Mars his presses were seized and, accompanied by his kindly and devoted mistress, the former laundress, Simone Évrard, he went into hiding in the cellars and sewers of Paris where he contracted that painful and unpleasant skin disease known as prurigo. At the end of 1791 he again escaped to London, returning in April the following year to castigate the policies of the Girondins in the pages of the revived *L'Ami du peuple* and to denounce their call for war as being inspired not so much by anxiety for the future of the Revolution as for their own. He had taken to wearing ostentatiously grubby clothes with open shirts revealing a yellowish neck, and a red bandana soaked in cheap vinegar around his forehead and his greasy, matted hair to alleviate his headaches. On occasions the smell that emanated from him was nauseous. Men would recoil from him, sickened as much by his physical presence, by the 'open sores, often running, that pitted his terrible countenance', as by the ferocity of his political opinions. But no one doubted his courage or his importance as a propagandist of the Left.

Marat's suspicions of the '*propagandistes de guerre*' were shared by certain members of the Jacobin Club, one of whom declared, 'We should be betrayed, thus defeated. Or else, were we to be the victors, the triumphant general would become the enemy of the people.' These were not popular views, though. The Feuillants still feared war, but what influence the Feuillants had once enjoyed had now been largely dissipated and most of their leaders had been dispersed. Barnave had retired to Grenoble whence, like Bailly, he was to be brought back for execution. The revolutionary careers of his closest associates were also virtually over: Adrien Duport was soon to be arrested and to die in exile in Switzerland; Alexandre de Lameth left to join the army; so did his brother, Théodore.

Thus the cries for war became more insistent. The respected and profoundly boring mathematician and philosopher, the Marquis de Condorcet, who sat in the Assembly as one of the deputies for Paris and who, while aligning himself with no political group, had already spoken in favour of a republic, now lent his great influence to the war party. So did the King's War Minister, the Comte de Narbonne, the only one of his Ministers who enjoyed any respect in the Assembly. And so did the Queen who had long since come to the view that the Constitution which the King had been required to accept was 'monstrous' and that their 'only source of help [lay] with the foreign powers'. 'At whatever price,' she told the Austrian Ambassador, 'they must come to our aid.' 'It is for the Emperor to put an end to the disturbances of the French Revolution,' she added in a letter to her brother Leopold who had succeeded to the Austrian throne on the death of Joseph II. 'Compromise has become impossible. Everything has been overturned by force and force alone can repair the damage.'

The King was, predictably, in two minds. His brothers, both of whom were now in exile, had told him that he must not accept the Constitution; that if he did so they would take it that he had been forced to do so and that they were, therefore, no longer bound by his commands. They strongly advocated war and, like their sister Elisabeth, urged Austria to invade France. For the moment the Emperor Leopold hung back from taking such a step. By the Declaration of Pillnitz of August 1791 he and the King of Prussia had announced that they regarded the situation of King Louis XVI as 'an object of interest to all the sovereigns of Europe', and that they were willing to restore a monarchical system in France. The Declaration was, however, nullified by the proviso that the intervention would not take place without the cooperation of the other powers; and, while some might have agreed to this, others, including Britain, would not.

The King's indecision was brought to an end in March 1792. In that month, which saw the death of the Emperor Leopold and the accession of his son, the young, impetuous and adventurous Francis II, the King dismissed Narbonne who had been intriguing against His Majesty's favourite Minister, de Molleville. The dismissal of

Narbonne caused uproar in the Assembly where Vergniaud rose to condemn it on behalf of the Girondins and to threaten the Court at the Tuileries in the most violent terms. 'Terror and dread have often sallied forth from that place,' he cried. 'Let them today enter it in the name of the law. Let all those who now live there know that the King alone is inviolable, that the law will, without distinction of persons, overtake all the guilty sheltered there, and that there is not a single head which, once convicted of crime, can escape its blade.'

Overawed by such assaults as these, the King's Ministers resigned. The Girondins in the Assembly could not replace them as the provision in the Constitution that none of its members could serve in the Government was still in force. So men closely involved with the Girondins were chosen instead. Jean Roland became Minister of the Interior and moved from his shabby rooms in the Hôtel Brittanique to the palatial *hôtel particulier* of Calonne where his wife presided over an increasingly influential salon. And Charles François Dumouriez, a brave, vain, pushing and dashing lieutenant-general, and in Madame Roland's opinion 'a very witty rake', who had successively attached himself to whichever political party seemed most likely to advance his career, became Minister for Foreign Affairs. A few weeks later the King felt compelled to give way to the demands for war which were now almost universal. He appeared before the Assembly looking tired and abstracted. Necker's daughter, Madame de Staël, described the scene in her memoirs:

I was present at the sitting in which Louis was forced to a measure which was painful to him for many reasons. His features were not expressive of his thoughts ... a combination of resignation and dignity suppressed every sign of his true feelings. On entering the Assembly he looked to the right and left with that sort of vacant curiosity which is not unusual with persons who are so short-sighted that their eyes appear to be of no use to them. He proposed war in the same tone of voice that he might have used in proposing the least important decree imaginable.

'Gentlemen,' he said, 'you have just heard the result of the negotiations in which I have been engaged with the Court of Vienna. The conclusions of the report have been unanimously approved by my Council. I have adopted them myself. They are conformable with the wish the National Assembly has several times expressed and with the sentiments communicated to me by a great number of citizens in different parts of the Kingdom. All would rather have war than see the dignity of the French people insulted any longer ... Having done my best to maintain peace, as I was in duty bound to do, I have now come – in conformity with the terms of the constitution – to propose war to the National Assembly.'

The proposal was loudly applauded. There were shouts of '*Vive le Roi!*' from all sides. And soon France was at war with Prussia as well as with Austria.

The French army, with a strength of less than 140,000, was in no fit state to fight the combined forces of these enemies. Over 3,000 officers had left their regiments since a new oath of loyalty, omitting the King's name, had been required of them after the flight of the royal family to Varennes. Many of those that remained exercised little authority over their men. Mutinies were common, equipment defective, ammunition in short supply. The troops and insubordinate volunteers marched towards the enemy in their wooden sabots and blue jackets without enthusiasm or confidence, and were soon retreating in confusion, throwing away their arms, and crying out, 'We are betrayed! *Sauve qui peut!*' General Théobald Dillon, an officer of Irish descent, whose corps had advanced on Tournai, was murdered during the precipitate withdrawal to Lille; General Rochambeau offered to hand in his resignation; the Duc de Biron was reported to have had to rescind an order for a bayonet charge when his men voted against it; the Marquis de Lafayette, refusing to comply with the ill-considered plans of Dumouriez, eventually returned to Paris in the hope of restoring order by a *coup d'état*.

The disastrous beginning of the war had led to the most violent demonstrations in the capital: rumours of counter-revolution were rife, the King and Queen were accused of conspiring with the enemy and an 'Austrian Committee' at the Tuileries was supposed to be betraying military intelligence to Vienna. The Legislative Assembly, concerned by these rumours and disturbances and by repeated reports from the provinces that recalcitrant priests were stirring up trouble amongst their parishioners, passed a series of decrees directed against the forces of counter-revolution: refractory priests denounced by twenty citizens were to be deported to Guiana; priests responsible for fomenting disturbances were to be deported on the denunciation of a single citizen; the King's 6,000-strong Household Guard, which had been authorized by the Constitution, was dismissed; and 20,000 National Guardsmen from the provinces were summoned to a camp just outside Paris.

The King accepted the decree disbanding the Household Guard, but he vetoed both those concerning recalcitrant priests and that authorizing the formation of the *fédérés* camp near Paris. And in protest against these vetoes, Jean Roland, urged on by his wife who had become the guiding force of the ministry, publicly condemned the King's action, reading out the sharply worded condemnation in His Majesty's presence and reminding him that he would have to choose between the Revolution and its opponents. The King, already exasperated by the rudeness of Roland who insisted on appearing at Court with laces in his shoes instead of the prescribed buckles, responded by dismissing most of his Ministers and replacing them with more amenable Feuillants.

Feelings in Paris now rose higher than ever and divisions between and within the political parties grew more and more deep. On the Right there were those who considered that royal authority should be restored even if this meant the defeat of the French army; yet there were also those who, like the Marquis de Ferrières, could 'never condone the introduction of a foreign army in France' and who were seized 'by a feeling of horror for those who could contemplate such a crime'. On the Left the arguments and quarrels between factions were quite as bitter: Girondins angrily accusing those members of the Jacobin Club who had condemned the war of being agents of counter-revolution; Jacobins with even greater vehemence accusing Girondins of being in the pay of the Court; Marat bringing down fire and brimstone on both their houses and urging soldiers to massacre their officers.

While Jacobins, Girondins and Feuillants squabbled fiercely with each other and among themselves, and journalists, supporting one faction or another or condemning them all, became ever more intemperate, popular leaders of the *sans-culottes* decided upon independent action. They urged the assemblies of the forty-eight *sections* into which Paris had now been divided for administrative purposes to admit 'passive' citizens – that is to say those who did not have votes – as well as 'active' ones – those who paid a minimum of three days' wages in direct taxation – into their meetings, to distribute pikes to citizens who did not have the right to carry firearms (a privilege still reserved to the National Guard) and to join together in another demonstration against the Court.

The day chosen for this demonstration was 20 June 1792, the third anniversary of the Tennis-Court Oath when, as part of the celebrations, a tree symbolizing Liberty was to be planted in the Tuileries gardens. It had originally been planned that the tree should be carried by an unarmed deputation, but the leaders of the *sans-culottes* and the radical *sections* were determined that the peaceful celebrations must be transformed into a violent popular uprising. They met to discuss means of making it so. Among them were Antoine Santerre, the brewer; Louis Legendre, one of the founders of the Cordeliers Club, an ill-educated butcher who had an enormously powerful voice and was extremely proud of his 'explosions of feeling'; Claude Lazowski, a factory inspector; and Rossignol, a jeweller's assistant. They decided that as many people as could be assembled in the eastern *faubourgs* of the city, women as well as men, should march upon the Hôtel de Ville and then to the Assembly with petitions against the royal veto and the dismissal of Roland and his colleagues. They should then make their way to the Tuileries. There should be no difficulty in collecting a good crowd, they thought, as the citizens of Paris had economic as well as political grievances: inflation was soaring and the price of certain foods had increased so enormously that there had been riots in several *sections*. Grocers' shops had been invaded by angry women demanding sugar at twenty-five *sous* a pound, instead of the three *livres* they were being asked to pay.

Early on the morning of the appointed day about 8,000 people, National Guardsmen, shopkeepers, artisans, market porters, working women and their children, began their march. Armed with muskets, pikes, pitchforks and scythes, sharp pieces of iron fastened to the end of stout bludgeons, they swarmed towards the Assembly. When information reached the Manège that there were as many as 8,000 of them, one of the deputies stood up to exclaim, 'Eight thousand! And we are only seven hundred and forty-five. We must adjourn immediately.'

As cries of 'Order! Order!' echoed round the hall, and a deputy of the Right leaped up to remind the Assembly that while there might well be 8,000 citizens on the march in Paris there were a further 24,000,000 Frenchmen to be considered elsewhere, a group of leading demonstrators bearing a petition burst through the doors. The deputies rose to their feet in indignation as the President put on his hat and required them to wait outside. To the deputies' apparent surprise, the petitioners then withdrew; whereupon the mollified Assembly consented to admit them again and to allow the thousands of demonstrators to march peacefully through the hall.

In they came, therefore, led by men carrying huge tables upon which had been pinned the Declaration of Rights and around which danced women and children singing the *Ça ira*. To cheers from the public galleries, they marched across the floor waving flags, shouting slogans, displaying banners inscribed with such watchwords as 'The Constitution or death,' brandishing ragged trousers to cries of '*Vivent les sans-culottes!*' and a calf's heart fixed to a pike with the inscription, 'The heart of an aristocrat'. For three hours the demonstration continued, while the deputies both of Right and Left sat in subdued and anxious silence. As the last of the citizens marched out of the hall, Santerre presented the deputies with a flag, then went off to the Tuileries where a vast crowd had assembled in the courtyards, shouting 'Sanction the decrees! Down with the veto! Down with the priests!' '*Rappel des ministres patriots! Tremblez tyrans! Voici les sans-culottes!*'

It was now about four o'clock in the afternoon. There were large numbers of troops on duty but they made no move to disperse the demonstrators who, finding the Porte Royale, a side entrance to the palace, unlocked, pushed it open, mounted the stairs, dragging up a cannon with them and hacking down doors with hatchets. They discovered the King in an anteroom whose door they smashed down with their pikes.

For some time past he had been in a state of utter despondency.

For ten days together [recorded the Queen's maid, Madame Campan] he did not utter a word even to his family, except at a game of backgammon which he played with Madame Elisabeth after dinner when he merely pronounced the words which are necessary to play that game. The Queen roused him from this state, so ruinous in a crisis, by throwing herself at his feet, and sometimes by employing images calculated to terrify him, at others expressions of her affection for him. She also urged him to remember what he owed to his family, and went so far as to say that if they must perish at least let them do so with honour and not wait to be strangled to death on the floor of their own apartment.

When the demonstrators rushed in upon him, however, he had recovered from his morose and silent depression and showed himself to the armed intruders with remarkable composure. 'Here I am,' he said, standing still in front of them. Madame Elisabeth was with him, her arms thrown round his shoulders as though pleading for protection. But the Queen, for whom his sister was at first mistaken, had been taken away with the children to the Council Room by a courtier who barricaded them in with furniture.

The King was persuaded to move to another, larger room to listen while a petition, which Legendre had brought with him, was read in his presence. He was asked to stand on a bench; several other benches and a table were set before him, while guards and attendants hurried into the room to stand on either side of him. The demonstrators crowded in front of him, shouting in unison with the people in the courts below, 'No aristocrats! No veto! No priests!'

With his booming voice Legendre quietened them by reading the petition, each sentence of which was punctuated by shouts of agreement from his companions and by cries of '*Long live the Nation! Vive la Nation!*'

'Yes, *vive la Nation!*' said the King when Legendre had finished. 'The nation has no better friend than me.'

'Prove it then!' someone shouted, proferring a red cap on the end of a pike. 'Put this on.'

The King seemed embarrassed rather than intimidated. He took the cap which had recently been introduced by the Girondins as an emblem of revolutionary fervour, and tried to put it on, but it was too small and fell off. A man picked it up, stretched it over his knee, and handed it back to the King who managed to get it over the back of his head. Another man now thrust a bottle of wine at him, asking him to toast his visitors.

'People of Paris,' the King said, obediently taking the bottle and putting the neck to his lips, though someone warned him it might be poisoned. 'I drink to your health and to that of the French nation.'

He would not, however, withdraw his veto of the Assembly's decrees, and he was still standing firm in his refusal when a delegation of deputies arrived, followed some time later by the Mayor of Paris, Jérôme Pétion, who made the improbable excuse that he had only just heard of the royal family's plight. Finding that the King's friendly but determined manner had earned the respect of many people in the room, Pétion advised the demonstrators to leave 'for fear lest enemies of the nation' might question their 'respectable intentions'. So the crowd slowly filed out of the room; and when they had all gone the King fell down into a chair looking exhausted, the red cap still on his head until, suddenly becoming aware of it, he snatched it off and threw it on to the floor.

His behaviour that day brought about an immediate reaction in favour of the monarchy. Numerous resolutions came in from the provinces, denouncing the insult to the royal family, and in Paris a petition protesting against the demonstration at the Tuileries was signed by over 20,000 people. Pétion was suspended for a time from his functions. So was Louis Manuel, the former tutor of a banker's son who was now a leading member of the Paris Commune. Hundreds of young men from the western *sections* volunteered for guard duty at the Tuileries, while royalist members of the National Guard attacked anyone suspected of republican tendencies whom they came upon walking in the Tuileries gardens. And when Lafayette made a speech condemning the events of 20 June in the Assembly he was loudly applauded, and not only by the Feuillants.

But the reaction was short-lived. The court did not take proper advantage of it, the Queen, in particular, being wary of accepting help from those whom she considered untrustworthy or dislikeable.

'She was more intent upon appearing to advantage in the midst of the peril,' Lafayette later remarked with some bitterness, 'than in averting it. As for my relations with the King, he always gave me his esteem, but never his confidence.' 'Better to perish,' the Queen herself said, 'than to be saved by M. de Lafayette.' Agreeing in their turn to anathematize Lafayette as a 'scoundrel, a traitor, an enemy of the nation', the Left temporarily buried their differences in face of the common enemy. By 13 July Pétion had been restored as Mayor; Manuel was also back in office, and the Legislative Assembly, as concerned by the threats of the Austrians as by the activities of the *sans-culottes*, declared '*La patrie en danger*'. A state of emergency was proclaimed, and all Frenchmen capable of bearing arms were called up for national service. The King was forced to agree to the establishment of a military camp at Soissons and to the *fédérés* being allowed to pass through Paris in order to attend the now customary celebrations on 14 July.

In the provinces, local authorities which had been authorizing the disarming of suspects ever since the military disasters had seemed to presage an Austrian invasion, extended their campaign against refractory priests, disregarding the royal veto by ordering arrests, and in some places appearing to condone murders. In Paris also the Revolution was evidently approaching a crisis as the war news worsened. In several streets and squares platforms draped with tri-colours were erected to serve as places of recruitment for men answering the call to arms. And, as the alarm guns thundered from the Pont Neuf and the Arsenal, municipal officials, wearing tri-colour sashes over their shoulders and escorted by troops of cavalry, marched from street to street and square to square to spread abroad the Assembly's proclamation, '*La patrie en danger*'.

The celebration of 14 July that year was a sadly different affair from that of 1790. In the Champ de Mars eighty-three tents had been erected representing the eighty-three departments of France, and beside each was a poplar from which fluttered a tricolour. In the centre of the circle described by these tents was a large marquee in which the Assembly and the King were to gather; another large marquee had been put up for the administrative bodies of Paris. The area resembled a military encampment rather than the scene of a festival. On one side was a memorial to those many French soldiers who had died in the recent fighting; on the other, a tall tree, called the Tree of Feudalism, was bedecked with titles of nobility, escutcheons, armorial bearings, crowns, blue ribbons, cardinals' caps, St Peter's Keys and other symbols of aristocracy, royalty and the papacy, to which the King was to be asked to set fire.

The King, with his sister, wife and children, stood on a balcony to watch the parade of soldiers and *fédérés* pass by. He looked quite calm but his wife seemed almost in tears and had, so one observer thought, already been weeping. As the royal family waited, a huge crowd of people pushed their way into the Champ de Mars beneath them, shouting 'Pétion for ever!' They were followed by columns of *fédérés*, marching along casually, arm in arm; by a group of men bearing a model of the Bastille; by the operators of a printing press which was put down from time to time so that sheets of patriotic songs could be produced and distributed to the bystanders; by the National Guard and regiments of the line; and finally by the members of the Assembly.

When the procession had passed beneath him, the King went forward as required to the 'altar of the nation' – a truncated column placed at the top of the tiers of seats which had been constructed for the first festival – where he was expected to swear an oath of loyalty. Although surrounded by troops he had difficulty in making his way through the dense crowds of people; and the Queen, watching his progress with the aid of a glass, was frightened that he would be crushed to death or assassinated. She had had a thickly padded undergarment made for him which she hoped would resist the first thrust of a dagger, but she had not expected these suffocating crowds of people. She saw him stumble on a step by the altar and screamed as the confusion around him increased.

He took the oath, and was then escorted to the Tree of Feudalism which he was required to burn down. He protested at this indignity, and ordered the soldiers of his escort to take him away to the École Militaire. They marched off shouting '*Vive le Roi!*' A few voices in the crowds took up the cry and an occasional murmur of sympathy could be heard, but most spectators watched him in silence. To Madame de Staël he looked like a martyr. To others, he was a strangely pitiable figure who seemed, contrasted with the appearance of the people around him, to belong to another age, with his clothes 'embroidered in the ancient Court fashion' and his carefully dressed and powdered hair. He disappeared from view and was thereafter rarely glimpsed by the people until the day of his death.

As the King resumed his sad life at the Tuileries, the news from the front grew more alarming and demands for more decisive measures to meet the crisis became insistent. The Commune had already decreed that all citizens who possessed pikes should be enlisted as National Guardsmen, and soon the Assembly felt obliged to permit their general distribution. Gradually the distinction between 'active' and 'passive' citizens was being lost, the National Guard becoming less a bourgeois body than a force of the *sans-culottes*.

Towards the end of the month it became known in Paris that a manifesto, drafted by Count Fersen helped by an *émigré*, the Marquis de Limon, and signed at Coblentz by the Duke of Brunswick, commander of the enemy army, had threatened Paris with 'total destruction' if the royal family were not respected and protected, or if the Tuileries were again invaded. The manifesto had also declared that any National Guard who resisted the Austro-Prussian advance would be treated as an irregular, shot out of hand and have his home demolished. It was the provocation for which the King's enemies had been waiting. The *fédérés*, who had refused to leave Paris for Soissons after 14 July until some decisive action had been taken, and who had been entertained while they remained by various of the city *sections*, marched about the city shouting, 'Citizens to arms!' A contingent of five hundred of them from Marseilles, who had put down a royalist insurrection in Arles, sang as they marched through the streets the stirring words of a song which had been written at Strasbourg for the Army of the Rhine by Rouget de Lisle, an officer of engineers. These *fédérés* from Marseilles—patriotic heroes, in the opinion of some citizens, to others, like the French Guards officer, General Thiébault, 'an infernal gang of assassins' –

'sing this song with the greatest fervour', reported the *Chronique de Paris*, 'and the passage where, waving their hats and brandishing their swords, they all sing together "*Aux armes, citoyens*" is truly thrilling ... They often sing at the Palais Royal – sometimes in the theatre between two plays.'

The Assembly, hesitant and still for the most part innately conservative, was losing control of Paris to these *fédérés* and to the radical city *sections*, nearly all of which had now admitted 'passive' citizens to their committees and had enrolled volunteers for the defence of Paris. The *section* known as *Bon Conseil* which had enrolled 300 men – two thirds of them artisans and most of the rest, apart from two surgeons' apprentices and two architects, shopkeepers and clerks – voted at a crowded meeting no longer to recognize the King and to march on the Assembly and thence on the Tuileries on Sunday, 5 August. The section *Quinze-Vingts* also voted for an armed march on the Assembly and the Tuileries on the 5th and asked all the other *sections* of Paris to come with them. By no means averse to such a march but anxious not to be found on the wrong side on Monday morning, Pétion persuaded the *Quinze-Vingts* to delay it until the 10th so as to give the Assembly time to dethrone the King themselves.

The *Quinze-Vingts* and the other *sections* agreed to wait; but on 6 August a vast crowd of *fédérés* and *sectionnaires* gathered in the Champ de Mars to demand the King's abdication. And since the Assembly still took no action, the *sections*, organized by the Jacobins, decided to act independently in accordance with their previous threats.

On the night of 9 August their delegates arrived at the Hôtel de Ville, announced that the Commune was summarily disbanded and replaced it with an Insurrectionary Commune of their own in which there were twice as many artisans as lawyers. Protests were answered with the claim, 'When the people place themselves in a state of insurrection, they withdraw all power from other authorities and assume it themselves.' The royalist commander of the National Guard, Mandat de Grancy, was arrested, executed and replaced by Antoine Santerre, while plans were laid to keep Pétion a prisoner in his own room in case he should take it upon himself to interfere.

Early the next day, a day of almost tropical heat, the march of some 20,000 armed people on the Tuileries began.

The main defenders of the palace were 900 Swiss Guards whose ammunition was severely limited. They were supported by about 2,000 National Guardsmen but these were suspected to be in sympathy with the marching citizens rather than the King to whom it was suggested that, if he went out to show himself to the National Guard, they might feel more inclined to protect him. He took the advice and went down into the courts. He had refused to put on the padded waistcoat which he had worn on 14 July, maintaining that, while such protection was acceptable against the dagger of an assassin, there was 'something cowardly' in wearing it when reviewing men who might be required to fight in his defence. As he appeared, untidily dressed in a purple suit, a sword at his side, his hair powdered on one side only, there were some shouts of '*Vive le Roi!*' but these were not so loud as cries of 'Down with the veto!' 'I can see him now as he passed along our front,' a National Guardsman wrote. 'He was silent and careworn and, with his swaying walk, he seemed to say to us, "All is lost." ' An officer by his side advised him not to proceed with the review of the men drawn up in the courts and gardens, but to go over instead towards the battalion posted on the Pont Tournant. He agreed to do so, but while walking past the terrace of the Feuillants, which was crowded with people shouting insults and abuse, he was mortified to see this battalion followed by another move off with the evident intention of joining the demonstrators in the Place du Carrousel. Already several of the gunners had turned their cannon round to face towards the palace and had had to be disarmed; and, confronted by this further desertion, the King seemed to lose the last vestiges of hope. Mme Campan was watching him from a window of the palace. She saw 'some of the gunners quit their posts, go up to the King and thrust their fists in his face. He went as pale as a corpse . . . The Queen later told me that the King had shown no energy, that this sort of review had done more harm than good.'

From inside the palace the shouts from the direction of the Place du Carrousel could now be heard quite clearly. The marching citizens, who were accompanied by about 400 Marseillaise and smaller

numbers of *fédérés* from other provincial cities, were far from being
'*la dernière plèbe*' of Hippolyte Taine's description. From the
casualty lists it appears that they came from nearly all the *sections* of
Paris and, while there were few professional men – a surgeon, an
architect and a drawing-master are mentioned – many of them seem
to have been shopkeepers, small traders, manufacturers and master
craftsmen. Far less than half were wage-earners. There were musicians, journeymen cabinet-makers and journeymen goldsmiths,
domestic servants, clerks, jewellers, water-carriers, master glaziers
and master locksmiths, gauze-workers and carters.

As they marched towards the Tuileries, Lucille Desmoulins
anxiously waited for news in her lodging-house. She had spent an
almost sleepless night listening apprehensively to the sound of the
tocsin, her beloved husband's head resting for a time on her
shoulder.

> We got up [she recorded, remembering every detail of the events of
> that day]. We had breakfast. Camille went off assuring me that he would
> not expose himself. Ten o'clock, eleven o'clock passed without our
> hearing a word. We picked up some of yesterday's papers, sat on the sofa
> in the drawing-room and tried to read . . . I thought I heard the sound of
> cannon-fire . . . Jeanette, Camille's cook, was bleating like a goat. We
> heard shouting and weeping in the street. We thought Paris would be
> running with blood . . . People were crying, 'To arms!'

At the approach of the marching citizens, the King sent an urgent
message to the Assembly asking them to send a delegation to the
Tuileries for his protection. This request elicited no response but,
soon after it had been sent, Pierre Roederer, the *procureur général
syndic* of the Department of Paris, a body strongly opposed to the
Jacobins, arrived at the palace in the hope, shared by the Girondins,
that bloodshed might be averted and the Legislative Assembly
afforded some chance of regaining control of the situation if the
royal family were persuaded to throw themselves upon the protection of the deputies. Roederer was shown up to the room where
the King and Queen and several Ministers were anxiously discussing
their predicament. Roederer told them that the National Guard at
the gates were talking cheerfully to the people who had already

begun to pour into the courtyard and he urged the royal family to hurry over to the Assembly.

The Queen strongly opposed such a move. It would be disgraceful, she said, to seek the protection of men who had behaved so badly towards them; she would rather be nailed to the walls of the palace. 'Madame,' Roederer answered her, 'you endanger the lives of your husband and children. Think of the responsibility which you take upon yourself.' The argument grew more and more vehement as the King turned indecisively first to his wife, then to the others who urged him to leave. At last he made up his mind to go. '*Marchons*,' he said, raising his hand as though to silence the disputants.

He then walked round the circle formed by the members of the Court [Roederer recorded]. I did not notice that he spoke to anyone in particular; I just heard him say, 'I am going to the National Assembly.' Two files of guards arrived and we walked out of the Palace through one apartment after another. When we were going through the *Oeil-de-boeuf* the King removed the head-dress of the National Guardsman who was marching on his right, and put his own hat, which had a white feather in it, on the man's head in its place. The man looked surprised, then, after a moment's hesitation, took the hat off his head and put it under his arm.

When we reached the colonnade at the bottom of the great staircase the King asked, 'What is going to happen to all the people we have left behind?' 'Sire,' I replied. 'The demonstrators from the *faubourgs* will soon be here ... Our numbers are not sufficient. There is no one with the authority to resist even the crowds in the Place du Carrousel.'

When we were under the tree opposite the cafe on the terrace of the Feuillants, we walked through the leaves which had fallen in the night and had been swept up by the gardener into heaps. We sank up to our knees in them. 'What a lot of leaves!' said the King. 'They have begun to fall very early this year.' Manuel had written in a newspaper that the King would not last beyond the fall of the leaves. One of my colleagues told me that the Dauphin amused himself by kicking up the leaves on to the legs of the person in front of him.

As they crossed the garden numerous gentlemen of the court ran out after them, followed by palace servants. Roederer tried to prevent them, begging them to realize that their presence would not only annoy the Assembly but would excite the rage of the populace; that they might even cause the King and Queen to be murdered. Only a few paid heed to him; the rest came on, getting as close as they could to the Swiss bodyguard, increasing the press and confusion of people now surging around the royal family. So dense did the throng become, indeed, that a soldier had to pick the Dauphin up and carry him over his head, and at the sight of what she took to be the child's kidnapping the Queen, who could not reach him, shrieked in terror.

When they arrived at the gate which opened on to the passage leading up to the Assembly, a National Guardsman came up to the King and said to him in a strong Provençal accent, 'Don't be afraid, Sir. We are all decent people but we just don't want to be betrayed any more. Be a good citizen, Sir, and get rid of those Holy Joes you keep in the Palace. Don't forget. It's high time to do as I say.' The King, so Roederer commented, replied good-naturedly.

The doors of the Assembly were opened and the royal family walked inside. 'I come,' the King said to them, 'to prevent a great crime, and I think, gentlemen, that I cannot be safer than in your midst.' Vergniaud replied that he could rely on the protection of the National Assembly who had sworn to die in defence of the properly constituted authorities. The King then sat down beside the President; but, following the objections of François Chabot, a former friar who was one of the leaders of the Cordeliers Club, that his presence there would affect the freedom of debate, he and his family – 'their heads lowered like whipped dogs', according to a deputy from the Aude – were removed to the shorthand-writers' box, a small room scarcely ten feet square beneath the gallery and separated from the main hall of the Manège by an iron railing. This railing was removed so that they could more easily take shelter in the midst of the Assembly, should it be necessary for them to do so, the King himself pulling out several bars. They had not been in the box long when the sound of musketry and cannon fire could be heard from the direction of the palace and a few stray balls flew through the open windows of the hall. 'I assure you,' shouted the King, 'that I have ordered the Swiss to be forbidden to fire.' The sounds of firing grew louder, however, and a delegation of twenty deputies was sent to try to stop the fighting. No sooner had they left on their vain mission than a band of armed citizens began battering on the doors of the hall, demanding admittance. 'We are stormed!' shouted one deputy as others rushed to hold the door; and the President, making the gesture which custom required of him on such occasions, put on his hat.

The door was soon forced and a crowd of *sans-culottes* stormed into the hall, demanding that the deputies 'swear in the nation's name to maintain liberty and equality' with all their power or to die at their posts.

No one answered at first [reported one deputy, Michel Azéma, to friends in Carcassonne]. Then all the deputies … shouted … unanimously and simultaneously, 'I do swear!' … The roll was called at once, and on the rostrum each in turn pronounced the … charming oath … indicated by the *sans-culottes* … Meanwhile, fierce fighting was going on at the Tuileries.

Here the *fédérés* from Marseilles and Finistère, at the head of the long column of demonstrators, had advanced towards the palace steps, calling out friendly greetings.

Every effort was made to persuade the Swiss to leave their position and join us [reported Pierre-François Desbouillons, a clerk from Brest who commanded the Finistère *fédérés*]. No one intended to do anything other than disarm them. But they steadfastly refused to give way to our urgent pleas to come over to our side. One of them decided to come over by himself to talk to the National Guard and was descending the steps when men who were no doubt paid to start the conflict tried to stab him. He rejoined his comrades at once. Everyone was still conferring. A musket shot had been fired but this had not yet started the fighting. The Swiss commanders persisted in saying they could not leave their posts without an order from the King. 'Then you all want to die,' someone said to them. 'Yes,' they replied, 'we shall all certainly die rather than abandon our posts without orders from the King.'

The area around the bottom of the steps was now filled with citizens, most of whom were armed only with sabres. In the milling about one of the Swiss commanders was slightly cut; and this immediately resulted in the citizens being fired on.

Crying out, '*Trahison! Trahison!*' the citizens and *fédérés* fled in confusion while the Swiss came down the steps in good order, discharging their muskets, then running towards the cannon which had been negligently left in the courtyard and opening fire with shot. At this moment the King's order not to fire reached them. They immediately abandoned the guns and marched off in the direction of the terrace of the Feuillants. Other companies of the Swiss were still in the palace, however. The King's order did not reach them; and they were still there when the Marseillais, together with some Breton *fédérés*, rallied and renewed the attack, repeating their shouts of '*Trahison! Trahison! Mort aux traîtres!*' Wild with fury, they dashed across the courtyard under heavy fire, reached the steps and, followed by crowds of *sans-culottes*, streamed into the palace. The Swiss, having almost exhausted their ammunition, surrendered, throwing down their arms, but they were shown no mercy. The mob poured into the palace, cutting down everyone they found, ushers, pages, doorkeepers, cooks, maidservants as well as soldiers, and the Dauphin's sub-governor. They threw the bodies out of the windows, impaled heads on pikes, looted the rooms, smashed furniture and windows, pocketed jewellery and ornaments and scattered papers over the floors. Fugitives who tried to escape were struck down as they ran across the garden and hacked down under the trees and beside the fountains. Some clambered up the monuments but were prodded down with pikes and bayonets by the assailants who, forbearing to fire for fear lest they injure the marble, stabbed them as they fell at their feet. One witness saw 'some very young boys playing with human heads'; another heard 'an honest artisan' remark, 'Ah, Monsieur. Providence has been very good to me. I killed three of the Swiss with my own hands.'

I ran from place to place [recorded one of the royal servants], and finding the apartments and staircases already strewed with dead bodies, I took the resolution of jumping from one of the windows in the Queen's room on to the terrace . . . I got to my feet and ran away to the Dauphin's garden gate where some Marseillais, who had just butchered several of the Swiss, were stripping them. One of them came up to me with a bloody sword in his hand, saying, 'Hello, citizen! Without arms! Here take this and help us to kill.' But luckily another Marseillais seized it and, being dressed in a plain coat, I managed to make my escape. Some of the Swiss who were pursued took refuge in an adjoining stable. I concealed myself in the same place. They were soon cut to pieces close to me. On hearing their cries the master of the house ran up and [he took me back to his house with him] . . . Presently a body of armed men came in to see if any of the Swiss were hiding there. After a fruitless search these men, their hands red with blood, stopped and calmly related to each other accounts of the murders which they had committed. I remained in the house until four o'clock in the afternoon, having before my eyes a view of all the horrors that were being perpetrated. Some of the men were still continuing the slaughter; others were cutting off the heads of those already slain; while the women, lost to all sense of shame, were committing the most indecent mutilations on the dead bodies from which they tore pieces of flesh and carried them off in triumph. Towards evening I took the road to Versailles and crossed the Pont Louis Seize which was covered with the naked carcasses of men already in a state of putrefaction from the intense heat of the weather.

Over 500 of the Swiss guards had been slaughtered in the grounds of the palace or on its steps, and a further sixty who were escorted under guard to the Insurrectionary Commune at the Hôtel de Ville were massacred when they got there. Of the besiegers about ninety *fédérés* and almost 300 citizens from the sections, three of them women, had also been killed.

At the Manège the King and the royal family were still in the shorthand-writers' box listening to the agitated debate of those few deputies who had been courageous enough to be present that day. At nightfall they were all escorted to a convent where they were given beds. In the morning they were taken back to the box where all that day and the next they listened to the continuing debates of the Assembly which, 'under the orders of the galleries', as one contemporary put it, 'feeling the eyes of the Insurrectionary Committee always upon them', voted for the suspension of the King from his functions, the establishment of a provisional council of six Ministers, the imposition of all the decrees upon which the royal veto had been imposed, the summoning of a National Convention which was to be elected on the basis of universal manhood suffrage, and the imprisonment of the King. The deputies at first decided that he should be held in the Luxembourg, the house from which the Comte de Provence had fled in June the year before, but it was later decreed, at the insistence of the Insurrectionary Commune, that he should be confined in the Temple which had formerly been occupied by the Comte d'Artois and which could be more securely guarded.

The atmosphere in Paris was now suddenly transformed as ambassadors were withdrawn by their governments, the salons closed their doors, and aristocrats, who, though stripped of their titles, had previously been left in peace provided they were not suspected of being counter-revolutionaries, thought it as well to leave their houses and go into hiding. Some tried to escape from Paris but found the gates shut and carriage-horses commandeered by the Insurrectionary Commune for the army. Several were arrested and, with their families and various conservative deputies, were thrown into prison where they waited apprehensively for the next stage in the Revolution's development. And in prison they heard with alarm that, while five of the six Ministers appointed to the provincial government were Girondins, the Ministry of Justice had gone to an ugly, sensual lawyer of commanding personality who was more powerful than any of them, Georges Jacques Danton.

THE DAYS OF THE
SEPTEMBER MASSACRES
AND THE
EXECUTION OF THE KING

2–7 September 1792 and 21 January 1793

*'The people of Paris administer their own justice
and I am their prisoner'*

PÉTION

Like most of the other leading revolutionaries, Danton came from a respectable middle-class provincial family. His father, who died when he was three, was a lawyer; one of his uncles a canon at Troyes. He was born near Troyes, at the little town of Arcis-sur-Aube, on 28 October 1759, and from his earliest years his character seems to have been as carefree and lively as the sparkling wines of the district. His grandfather was a farmer and it was in the country where most of his days were spent and where the accidents, which marred his features for life, took place. His scarred and twisted lip, so it was said, was the result of his being gored by an angry bull when he was sucking the teat of a cow; his squashed nose was also the consequence of an encounter with a bull; the scars on his cheeks and eyelids were caused by the hooves of a herd of pigs. The skin around them was badly disfigured by smallpox.

Quite undeterred by these misfortunes and deformities, the young Danton continued to enjoy life, to make friends easily, to do well at his school at Troyes where his oratorian masters provided the lazy but clever boy with a wider and more liberal education than he could have expected at many another establishment. This enabled him to read and enjoy the English books which, as well as the classics of the Enlightenment, including scores of volumes of Voltaire and Rousseau, were to fill the shelves of his sitting-room in Paris.

He arrived in Paris when he was twenty-one to enter a lawyer's office and, having obtained a legal degree from the University of Rheims and borrowed a good deal of money from, among others, the father of the girl he intended to marry – the daughter of a prosperous restaurateur – he bought the remunerative office of *avocat aux Conseils du Roi*. Thus, at the age of twenty-seven, he established himself in a far more promising position than so many of his impecunious contemporaries who, coming up from the provinces to swell the ranks of an overcrowded profession and finding success in it difficult to achieve without money, took to ill-paid journalism and other literary pursuits while idly hoping for, or actively working for, the overthrow of an order that so circumscribed their talents and ambition.

Danton, who at this time chose to call himself d'Anton, did not share their disgruntlement, though he joined in their discussions at the Café Procope. He seems to have worked conscientiously, earning over 20,000 *livres* a year according to a friend, and taking on any cases that came his way without too scrupulous a regard for the justice of his clients' claims. While preparations were being made for the election of the Estates General in 1789, for example, d'Anton was busy defending a landowner who had arbitrarily enclosed an area of common land adjoining his estate. With a satisfactory income, and helped by the generous dowry of his attractive wife, he moved into a comfortable and well-furnished apartment in the Rue des Cordeliers. Here the d'Antons and their two sons were living contentedly when the Estates General met.

He had played no part in the selection of deputies, not having been chosen as an Elector of the Cordeliers District. But once it became clear that French society was, indeed, upon the verge of upheaval he realized that he must throw himself into the struggle if he were to survive as a successful lawyer. He did so with a fervour that astonished those who knew him at home in the Rue des Cordeliers, at the tables of the Café Procope and in the courts where he pleaded his cases.

I saw my colleague, Danton, whom I had always known as a man of sound judgement, gentle character, modest and silent [wrote a fellow lawyer who came across him in the Cordeliers District the day before the attack on the Bastille]. Imagine my surprise at seeing him standing on a table, declaiming wildly, calling the citizens to arms to repel 15,000 brigands assembled at Montmartre and an army of 30,000 poised to sack Paris and slaughter its inhabitants . . . I went up to him to ask what all the fuss was about as I had just come from Versailles and everything was perfectly calm and orderly there. He replied that I did not understand anything, that the people had risen against despotism. 'Join us,' he said. 'The throne is overturned and your old position lost.'

If Danton had ever been the gentle, modest and silent man that this colleague of his describes, he was certainly not so now and was never to be again. His loud, harsh voice was to be heard everywhere in the District, and became as familiar as his bulky frame and his scarred and pock-marked face. He spoke with a controlled vehemence, a mastery of improvisation and a wonderful command of vivid language and dramatic gesture, the words tumbling out of his mouth so fast, and on occasions so ambiguously, that it was difficult to remember afterwards what he had said, or to gather exactly what he had meant. But it was impossible not to admire the skill of his passionate delivery. He soon became one of the leading figures among the revolutionaries of the troublesome Cordeliers District; and, though he preferred to work through others rather than to appear to have assumed such power within it, he gained a dominating influence over the Cordeliers Club. He was also appointed commander of the Cordeliers battalion of the National Guard.

In his attempts to gain recognition for his talents on a wider stage, however, Danton was not so successful. He was not elected to the Legislative Assembly, and it was not until the end of 1791 that, after repeated attempts, he managed to obtain a minor post as assistant *procureur* in the Paris Commune. The trouble was that his motives were frequently in question; he was accused at various times of working for the Duc d'Orléans, for Mirabeau, and – like Mirabeau – for the Court. It was even rumoured that he was deeply involved with a gang of forgers. Madame Roland, who did not like him and who evidently found his overt sexuality disturbing, said that he once boasted to her that, since the Revolution began, he had managed to acquire a fortune of one and a half million *livres*. And another witness recorded that at a dinner party Danton, who was drunk, had shocked his fellow-guests by declaring that the Revolution ought to be treated like a battle in which the victors shared the loot; that the time had come for them to enjoy splendid houses and fine food, 'handsome clothes and the women of their dreams'. Certainly, in 1791 Danton, who loved the pleasures of life, began spending money on such a scale and buying land so extensively in Champagne that it was impossible to believe that his resources were derived, as he claimed they were, from the compensation he received for the loss of his office as *avocat aux Conseils du Roi*. It seems now more than likely that he was, indeed, like Mirabeau for a time in the pay of the Court; that – as Mirabeau had done – he made violently effective speeches on issues which were not fundamental to the royalist cause but which established his radical credentials; and that he chose to attack Lafayette, for instance, in the way that he did because Lafayette was disliked by both the *sans-culottes* and by the Court. If the Revolution failed, he could then retire to a country life in Champagne with his pockets well lined; if it succeeded, he had not lost the opportunity of guiding its future and of establishing in France that more equitable society which it would be unjust to him to suppose he did not in his heart desire. On the eve of the attack on the Tuileries he went home to Arcis-sur-Aube to settle some private business and to arrange for pensions to be paid to his mother and his former nurse in case the attack led to his downfall. Soon afterwards his immediate fears were allayed. The *journée* of 10 August succeeded in its purpose, and Danton, recognized as a man with unique influence in the *sections*, became Minister of Justice.

He was, in fact, far more than that: he was 'the vehement tribune of the people', the 'Mirabeau of the mob', the 'voice of the Revolution', indispensable to the Girondins, as one of their supporters admitted, the one man whose oratory and intelligence could save them from their enemies. It was he alone among the new Ministers who exercised a commanding influence in the Insurrectionary Commune which was a far more powerful body than the Girondin Government itself; it was he who guided the policies of the Ministries of Foreign Affairs and of War as well as those of the Ministry of Justice; it was among his friends in the Cordeliers Club that were found many of the emissaries who were sent out into the provinces to reconcile the people to the new administration in Paris and to justify the events of 10 August.

In Paris there was widespread fear that royalist conspirators, ecclesiastical spies and other counter-revolutionaries might combine to ensure that the lives lost on that day would be sacrificed in vain. And there were insistent demands that the army must be purged of officers who might desert to the enemy – as Lafayette did on 17 August – and that all the other enemies of the Revolution must be rounded up and punished. Vigilance Committees were established in the *sections*; internal passports were suspended; hundreds of suspects, including many recalcitrant priests, were arrested and imprisoned. The call for more violent measures became irresistible when news reached Paris towards the end of the month that the frontier fortress of Longwy had fallen after so weak and brief a resistance that treachery seemed unquestionable. With Verdun now in danger and with reports received of a conservative uprising in La Vendée, Danton insisted in the Assembly that the time had come 'to tell the people that they must throw themselves upon their enemies *en masse*'. He proposed that all men fit for military service should be called up and sent to the front, that house to house searches should be carried out in a hunt for both arms and men in hiding. 'The tocsin that will ring will be no mere signal for alarm; it will sound the charge against the enemies of the nation,' he declared in the most passionate and most often quoted of all his speeches. 'To deflect them, Messieurs, we need boldness, and again boldness and always boldness; and France will then be saved.' As though echoing his words, recruiting posters appeared that day on the walls of the city under the call, 'To arms, citizens! The enemy is at our gates.'

From those who feared that this might actually be so there were now repeated cries for the extermination of all those dangerous opponents of the Revolution within the gates as well as those outside them. In support of these demands, Marat in his *L'Ami du peuple*, Hébert in *Le Père Duchesne*, Louis Fréron in *L'Orateur du peuple* and other propagandists advocated in their newspapers an attack on the prisoners being held in the Paris gaols. These gaols were overcrowded; they were ill supervised by corrupt warders, nearly all of whom could be bribed; escapes from them were common; within their walls worked forgers producing those streams of false *assignats* which were held responsible for rising prices and soaring inflation. Through their unlocked doors, it was suggested, there would flood a horde of counter-revolutionaries, together with criminals in their pay, who would fall upon the families of volunteers once their homes had been left unprotected. 'Let the blood of the traitors flow,' cried Marat. 'That is the only way to save the country.'

An organized attack upon the prisons had therefore been expected by the authorities for some time. The day after the march on the Tuileries two police officers warned Santerre as commander of the Paris National Guard that a plan was 'afoot to enter all the prisons of Paris, take out all the prisoners and give them prompt justice'. Since then several other warnings had been received, and the nervous, panicky atmosphere in Paris had been intensified by pamphlets, scattered all over the city, headed, *The Great Treason of Louis Capet* [the King], and revealing the 'discovery of a plot for assassinating all good citizens during the night between the 2nd and 3rd of this month'. So neither the police nor the National Guard were much surprised when on the fine afternoon of Sunday, 2 September a party of recalcitrant priests who were being taken in six hackney coaches to the prison known as L'Abbaye by an escort of *fédérés* from Brittany, Avignon and Marseilles, were attacked by a mob between the Rue Dauphine and the Carrefour Bussy. The leader of the mob rushed up to one of the carriages and plunged his sabre twice through the open window. As the passers-by gasped in horror, he waved the reddened blade at them and shouted, 'So, this frightens you, does it, you cowards? You must get used to the sight of death!' He then slashed at the prisoners again, cutting open the face of one, the shoulder of another, and slicing off the hand of a fourth who endeavoured to protect his head. Others of the mob then joined in the attack, as did some of the *fédérés*; and soon blood was dripping from all the carriages as the horses dragged them on their way to the doors of the prison. Here another mob was waiting; and when those prisoners who had escaped unscathed or only slightly wounded tried to escape inside, nearly all of them were cut down and killed before they could reach safety.

The same afternoon another small gang of armed men burst into the garden of the Carmelite Convent off the Rue de Vaugirard where about 150 priests, who had been held prisoner for the past fortnight, were gathered under guard, several of them reading their office. The men advanced upon them, calling out for the Archbishop of Arles. One of the priests went forward to meet them, demanding a fair trial for himself and his fellow-prisoners. A shot was fired and his shoulder was smashed. The Archbishop, after praying for a moment on his knees, then went towards the men himself. 'I am the man you are looking for,' he said, and was immediately struck across the face with a sword. As he fell to the ground a pike was plunged through his chest. At that moment an officer of the National Guard appeared and managed to get the priests away to the nearby church where they gave each other absolution. While they were saying prayers for the dying, the armed gang broke through the door and dragged the priests out in pairs to slaughter them in the garden. After several had been killed a man with an air of authority arrived at the church calling out, 'Don't kill them so quickly. We are meant to try them.' Thereafter each priest was summoned before a makeshift tribunal before being executed. He was asked if he was now prepared to take the constitutional oath and when he said that he was not – as all of them did – he was taken away to be killed. Some bodies were removed in carts, the rest thrown down a well from which their broken skeletons were recovered seventy years later.

These murders were the first of numerous other massacres which took place in the prisons of Paris over the next five days. At the seminary of St Firmin in the Rue Saint-Victor where other refractory priests were held; at La Grande and La Petite Force where men and women convicted of civil offences were incarcerated; at Les Bernardins whose prisoners were mainly men condemned to the galleys; at La Salpêtrière, a house of correction for female offenders; at Bicêtre, a prison hospital for the poor and the mad, as well as at Le Châtelet, the prison for common criminals – indeed in all the prisons of Paris except the Sainte-Pélagie, which was for debtors, and the Saint-Lazare, for prostitutes – gangs of citizens, later to be known as *septembriseurs*, broke in armed with swords, pikes, hatchets and iron bars and set about their work, resting from time to time to drink wine or eat the meals which their women brought to them 'to sustain them, so they said, in their hard labours'.

A prisoner at the Abbaye, Jourgniac de Saint-Méard, recorded how those whose cells had not yet been broken into heard with horror the screams of the victims and waited in terror for their turn to come:

The most important matter that employed our thoughts was to consider what posture we should put ourselves into when dragged to the place of slaughter in order to suffer death with the least pain. Occasionally we asked some of our companions to go to the turret window to watch the attitude of the victims. They came back to say that those who tried to protect themselves with their hands suffered the longest as the blows of the blades were thus weakened before they reached the head; that some of the victims actually lost their hands and arms before their bodies fell; and that those who put their hands behind their backs obviously suffered less pain. We, therefore, recognized the advantages of this last posture and advised each other to adopt it when it came to be our turn to be butchered.

As at the Carmes most murders were preceded by a rough form of trial. The prisoners were dragged into rooms lit by torches and candles to face groups of judges sitting round tables littered with papers, prison registers, bottles, pipes and jars of tobacco. In one room the judges included men with bare arms covered in blood or tattooed with the symbols of their respective trades, men with swords at their sides, wearing red woollen caps and butchers' aprons. In another several of the judges seemed drunk and the others half asleep. At the Abbaye the president of the self-styled court was that hero of the *sans-culottes*, Stanislas Maillard, who had played so prominent a rôle both in the storming of the Bastille and the women's march on Versailles.

Jourgniac de Saint-Méard described how he was dragged into the corridor where Maillard held his court by three men, two of whom grabbed hold of his wrists, the other of his collar. An old man, whose trial had just ended, was being killed outside the door. Saint-Méard, warned that 'one lie meant death', was asked why he had been arrested. While replying, some of the people in the crowded room distracted the attention of the judges by pushing papers in front of them and whispering in their ears. Then, after he had produced written evidence in his defence, Saint-Méard's trial was interrupted again by the appearance of a priest who, following the briefest interrogation, was taken away to be stabbed to death. There was a further interruption when a gaoler rushed into the room to say that a prisoner was trying to escape up a chimney. Maillard told the gaoler to fire shots up the chimney and that, if the prisoner got away, he himself would be killed in his place. When shots failed to dislodge the fugitive, a pile of straw was set alight beneath him and when the man fell down, almost suffocated by the smoke, he was killed as he lay on the hearth. Saint-Méard's trial was once more resumed, and, to his astonishment, his honest plea that, although he had been a confirmed royalist until 10 August, he had never played any part in public affairs, was unanimously accepted by the tribunal and he was allowed to depart. Greeted by cries of '*Vive la Nation!*' by the people outside, he was escorted to his home by men carrying torches who refused any payment for their services.

Saint-Méard's experiences were not uncommon. Others described how men, who seemed quite prepared to murder them at one moment, were at the next hugging them enthusiastically and declining all rewards for seeing them safely home. One assassin, refusing an offer of recompense, wept with emotion as he restored a father to his children. 'The nation pays us for killing,' said another who also refused a reward, 'but not for saving lives.'

Several prisoners were saved by compassionate men who risked their own lives to help them, as were both the Duchesse de Tourzel and her daughter. The Duchess herself recorded how kind were some of the people among the crowds who witnessed the massacres with apparent approval; how, when she was told to climb on to a pile of corpses to swear an oath of loyalty to the nation, several people came forward to protect her; and how, when asked to attend to a fellow-prisoner, the young wife of one of the King's gentlemen of the bedchamber, an onlooker who supposed a medallion the girl wore round her neck was stamped with a portrait of the King or Queen, whispered to the Duchess to remove it and hide it in her pocket. Saint-Méard said that when he admitted during his trial that he had been an officer in the King's army, someone gently trod on his toe as a warning not to say too much.

Yet most murders were committed with appalling ferocity. At the Conciergerie, which contained prisoners awaiting trial in the Palais de Justice, a gang of assassins, bursting into the courtyard which was separated from the Rue de la Barillerie by fine gilded wrought iron railings, battered down the doors behind which the prisoners had tried to barricade themselves and, sparing some, hacked others to pieces until the mangled remains of 378 of the 488 prisoners held there were piled up in heaps in the Cour du Mai. Having killed numerous prisoners in their cells, a party of assassins mounted the stairs to the courtroom where several Swiss Guards were on trial. At their approach the guards threw themselves under the benches while their commander, Major Bachmann, rose to his feet and marched forward resolutely to the bar. The presiding judge, formidable enough in his black robes and plumed hat, held up his hand to halt the intruders whom he commanded to 'respect the law'. They obeyed him and retreated. Bachmann was then sentenced to death and that afternoon was carried away in one of the carts to execution.

One prisoner who did not escape the assassins' blades was Marie Gredeler, a young woman who kept an umbrella and walking-stick depository in the courtyard of the Palais Royal. Charged with having mutilated her lover, she was herself mutilated, her breasts were cut off, her feet were nailed to the ground and a bonfire was set alight between her spreadeagled legs.

As the heaps of corpses mounted, carts drawn by horses from the King's stables were obtained to take them away to the Montrouge quarries. Women helped to load them, breaking off occasionally to dance the Carmagnole, then stood laughing on the slippery flesh, 'like washerwomen on their dirty linen', some with ears pinned to their dresses.

The carts were full of men and women who had just been slaughtered and whose limbs were still flexible because they had not had time to grow cold, so that legs and arms and heads nodded and dangled on either side of the carts [wrote a working girl, Marie-Victoire Monnard, who watched them being dragged away] ... I can still remember those drunken men and remember in particular one very skinny one, very pale with a sharp pointed nose. The monster went to speak to another man and said, 'Do you see that rotten old priest on the pile over there?' He then went and hauled the priest to his feet, but the body, still warm, could not stand up straight. The drunken man held it up, hitting it across the face and shouting, 'I had enough trouble killing the old brute.'

Equally revolting scenes were enacted elsewhere; and, while some stories can be attributed to the propaganda of the Revolution's enemies, others no less horrifying appear to be well attested. Men were reported by reliable witnesses to have been seen drinking, eating and smoking amidst the carnage, using for tables and chairs the naked bodies of their victims whose clothes had been removed as one of the recognized perquisites of the assassins.

'They were out of breath,' one observer reported, 'and they asked for wine to drink: "Wine or death!" The Civil Commissioner of the *section* gave them vouchers for twenty-four pints addressed to a neighbouring wine merchant. These they soon drank, and contemplated with drunken satisfaction the corpses scattered in the court.'

'Do you want to see the heart of an aristocrat?' asked one assassin, opening up a corpse, tearing out the heart, squeezing some blood into a glass, drinking part, and offering the rest to those who would drink with him. 'Drink this, if you want to save your father's life,' commanded another, handing a pot of 'aristocrats' blood' to the daughter of a former Governor of the Invalides. She put it to her lips so that her father could be spared. Women were said to have drawn up benches to watch the murders in comfort and to have cheered and clapped as at a cock fight.

Another witness, a lawyer, saw 'a group of butchers, tired out and no longer able to lift their arms', drinking brandy with which gunpowder had been mixed 'to aggravate their fury'. They were 'sitting in a circle round the corpses'. 'A woman with a basket full of bread rolls came past. They took them from her and soaked each piece in the blood of their quivering victims.'

The Queen's emotional friend, the Princesse de Lamballe, who had been held in La Petite Force, was one of the most savagely treated victims. She had been stripped and raped; her breasts had been cut off; the rest of her body mutilated; and 'exposed to the insults of the populace'. 'In this state it remained more than two hours,' one report records. 'When any blood gushing from its wounds stained the skin, some men, placed there for the purpose, immediately washed it off, to make the spectators take more particular notice of its whiteness. I must not venture to describe the excesses of barbarity and lustful indecency with which this corpse was defiled. I shall only say that a cannon was charged with one of the legs.' A man was later accused of having cut off her genitals which he impaled upon a pike and of having ripped out her heart which he ate 'after having roasted it on a cooking-stove in a wineshop'. Her head was stuck on another pike and carried away to a nearby café where, placed upon a counter, the customers were asked to drink to the Princess's death. It was then replaced upon the pike and, its blonde hair billowing around the neck, was paraded beneath the Queen's window at the Temple. The head of the Comte de Montmorin, the King's former Foreign Minister, was carried, similarly impaled, to the Assembly.

In all about 1,200 prisoners were massacred, almost half the entire prison population of Paris. Thirty-seven of them were women. Of the rest, less than a third were priests, nobles or political prisoners; most were ordinary criminals, thieves, vagrants and forgers. The assassins appear to have been relatively few in number, perhaps no more than 150 or 200 in all. Some were criminals themselves, but most appear to have been the kind of citizens, butchers, shopkeepers, artisans, *gendarmes* and young National Guardsmen from whom the radical *sections* drew their enthusiastic support. Many of them, returning to work when the massacres were over, seem to have considered that they had performed a necessary public service in saving the nation from its enemies, and that they were fully entitled to the payments of twenty-four *livres* which were made to them by agents, it was supposed, of the Commune. Such was the regard in which they were held, in fact, that men who claimed to be of their company displayed swords and axes, stained with blood, to groups of customers in their local wine-shops. Later, when *septembriseur* became an insulting rather than flattering epithet, these men excused themselves by explaining that they had dipped their weapons in butchers' buckets and pretended to be assassins in order to make an impression upon their neighbours and girl-friends. .

The authorities undoubtedly did little to prevent the massacres. Indeed, the *septembriseurs* were given some sort of sanction not only by Marat who advocated their actions but also by Jaen-Nicolas Billaud-Varenne, a deputy-commissioner of the Commune, who made a tour of the prisons, encouraging the assassins by telling them, 'You are slaying your enemies! You are doing your duty!' And certainly, if not given active encouragement in their murders, the assassins were never forcefully ordered to put an end to them. When a party of them arrived at the Hôtel de Ville to tell the Mayor that they had 'dispatched those rascals' and to ask him what should be done with eighty more with whom they had not yet dealt, Pétion merely replied, 'I am not the person to whom you should apply', and then gave orders for wine to be offered them. Santerre, whose ambiguous orders to the National Guard were disregarded, was equally ineffective. So was the Assembly which did little more than make half-hearted attempts to limit the atrocities by sending various deputies to talk to the assassins. And after it was all over there were those, even among the moderates, who could find excuses for what had been done. Jean-Marie Roland, while admitting that the events were no doubt better hidden by a veil, added, 'But I know that the People, terrible as its vengeance is, has yet tempered it with a kind of justice.' Parisians as a whole were, perhaps, able to persuade themselves that, dreadful as the massacres were, they had been necessary.

Many of them were quite unaware that they were taking place, for in those days Parisians neither knew nor very much cared what was going on outside their own particular districts. And many of those who did discover what was happening seem to have been taken by surprise. One of these was Philippe Morice who was walking home from the theatre on the night of 2 September:

I had just reached the Rue de Seine when I noticed an unusual light and heard a great clamour which seemed to come from the direction of the Rue Sainte-Marguerite. I went up to a group of women gathered on the corner of the street and asked them what all the noise was about.

'Where on earth *does* this bloke come from?' one of the women asked, looking at her neighbour. 'Do you mean to say you don't know that they're taking care of the goods in the prisons? Look! Look down there in the gutter.'

The gutter ran with blood. They were butchering the poor creatures in the Abbaye. Their cries were mingled with the yells of the executioners, and the light which I had observed came from bonfires which the murderers had lit to illuminate their exploits.

Another man who heard the screams of the victims comforted his shocked wife in words quoted by Baron Thiébault: 'This is a very terrible business. But they are our deadly enemies, and those who are delivering the country from them are saving your life and the lives of our dear children.'

Similar sentiments were expressed by a young apprentice semps-tress:

> Like everyone else, I was shaking with fear lest these royalists be allowed to escape from their prison and come and kill me because I had no holy pictures to show them ... While shuddering with horror, we looked upon the action as almost justified; while it was going on, we went about our own affairs, just as on any ordinary day.

Such attitudes were encouraged by the Commune which sent out to all the *départements* of France a letter which read:

> The Commune of Paris takes the first opportunity of informing its brethren of all the *départements* that some of the fierce conspirators de-tained in its prisons have been put to death by the people, who regarded this act of justice as indispensable, in order to restrain by intimidation the thousands of traitors hidden within its walls at the moment when it was marching against the enemy. And we do not doubt that the whole nation, after the long sequence of treachery which has brought it to the edge of the abyss, will be anxious to adopt this most necessary method of public security; and that all Frenchmen will exclaim, with the people of Paris, 'We are marching against the foe, but we will not leave these brigands behind us to cut the throats of our children and of our wives.'

Among the signatories of this letter, which led to massacres in several provincial prisons, including those at Meaux and Rheims, was Marat who, unlike most others who put their names to it, never dis-claimed responsibility for what had happened in Paris when it became politic to do so.

Danton's attitude to the massacre, however, was, as usual, ambigu-ous. Madame Roland, who said that the Revolution had now be-come 'hideous' to her, alleged that Danton answered the protests of a humane prison inspector with the impatient outburst, 'I don't give a damn for the prisoners. Let them look after themselves as best they can.' Later, according to the Duc de Chartres, he claimed to have actually been responsible for organizing the murders which were intended to put a river of blood between the 'youth of Paris' and the *émigrés*. 'It often happens,' he added 'especially in time of revo-lution, that one has to applaud actions that one would not have wanted or dared to perform one's self.' As always with Danton, though, one cannot be sure. He was preoccupied with the defence of France against the foreign enemy and may well have lamented the murders but have been reluctant to jeopardize his influence over the *sans-culottes* by making what may well have proved futile attempts to prevent them. Certainly he helped to protect certain men, including Charles Lameth and Duport, whom the more uncompromising of his colleagues wished to arrest or execute. And certainly, also, this violent, passionate, impulsive but never sustainedly cruel man did his best to prevent prisoners in gaols outside Paris being brought to the capital as long as the massacres lasted.

Within a fortnight of the murder of the last of the prisoners, Danton's anxieties about the French army were for the moment dispelled. For on 20 September 1792 at Valmy in the Argonne the well-trained Prussian army of Frederick William II, officered by veterans of the King's uncle, Frederick the Great, had faltered, halted, then turned aside, demoralized by the French artillery of the old order and the massed forces of the new. Johann Wolfgang von Goethe had witnessed the engagement through the thin patches of a drifting mist and afterwards recorded how 'the greatest consternation' had spread throughout the German army:

In the morning we had been talking of roasting and eating the French ... Now people avoided each other's eyes and the only words uttered were curses. In the gathering darkness we sat in a circle. We did not even have a fire as we usually had. Almost everyone remained silent ... then someone asked me what I thought of the events of the day ... So I simply said, 'At this place, on this day there has begun a new era in the history of the world; and you can all claim to have been present at its birth.'

'You'll see how these little cocks will strut now,' wrote one dispirited Prussian after this devastating cannonade at Valmy. 'We have lost more than a battle.'

*

While the French cannon were thundering at Valmy, the newly elected members of the National Convention assembled in the Manège in Paris. The delegates from the provinces, where, though the suffrage had been widened, voting had not been heavy, were for the most part the same kind of men who had been elected to previous assemblies. Among them were one or two workers; there were also a few former nobles, including the Duc d'Orléans who now chose to call himself Philippe Egalité, and nearly fifty clergy; but most of them were from middle-class backgrounds, lawyers as before predominating. They were inclined to support the Girondins and to deplore the *septembriseurs*.

In Paris, however, where the electoral assembly had been moved to the premises of the Jacobin Club, the mood of the electorate was more ardently revolutionary and care was taken to ensure that as many conservatives as possible were prevented from voting. All who had joined the Feuillant Club, for example, were deprived of the franchise, as were those who had inscribed their names upon the long petition that had been drawn up in June in protest against the invasion of the Tuileries. The result was that every Parisian candidate elected, with one single exception, was a supporter of the Jacobins.

The revolutionary atmosphere in Paris was maintained by admonitory posters and placards pasted to the walls of streets and squares, several of whose names had been changed in celebration of the death of the *ancien régime*; by the spread of *tutoiement* in conversation and the gradual abandonment of *Monsieur* in favour of *Citoyen*; by the professional classes' widespread rejection of the elaborate clothes and powdered hair of the *ancien régime* for the simple carelessness of the artisan; by their disinclination to raise their hats in greeting any more and by their wives' unwillingness to be seen wearing jewellery or using a fan which did not depict some hero or heroic event of the Revolution; by the choice of Christian names for babies which would reflect the radical nature of the age into which they had been born; and by the repudiation of surnames that carried with them regrettable echoes of the past.

One of the first acts of the Convention was to declare the monarchy abolished. This was followed by a decree that 22 September

1792 marked the beginning of Year I of the French Republic. But it soon became clear that the Convention would agree harmoniously on little else. The Girondins lost no time in mounting violent and repeated attacks on the Jacobins who, occupying the highest seats in the hall, became known as Montagnards or the Mountain. The Montagnards, deeply suspicious of the Girondins whom they believed capable of any political alliance to maintain their powerful but not impregnable position in the Convention and their control over the ministerial posts, responded no less abusively. Between them the independent members of what became known as the Plain sat, for much of the time, in brooding silence, watching and waiting.

The Girondins might well have maintained their supremacy had they taken more care to cultivate the Plain, had they not emphasized the political gulf that now separated Paris from the provinces, and had they not endeavoured to discredit the capital and its Commune in the eyes of the rest of the country. But, as it was, the Girondins succeeded only in alienating the Parisians when they might have profited by the revulsion that so many of them felt against the September Massacres – for which Vergniaud unreservedly blamed the Jacobins – and in antagonizing several members of the Plain as well as the followers of Danton whom Jean Roland, out of jealousy, and Manon Roland, from both distrust and personal distaste, vilified with increasing vehemence.

Discord in the Convention was deepened by the shadow of the King. The Girondins, who tried unsuccessfully to avert a judicial trial, would have chosen to spare him. So, it seems, would Danton who cautiously stated his belief that, without being convinced that the King was 'entirely blameless', it would be 'useful to get him out of the situation' in which he had placed himself. But, according to Théodore Lameth, who risked his life by returning to Paris from England in the hope of saving the King's life, Danton added privately, 'All the same, if I have to give up all hope for him, I warn you that, since I don't want my head to fall with his, I shall join those who condemn him.' And so in the end Danton did condemn him, declaring unequivocally, 'The only place to strike Kings is on the head.'

Most of the Montagnards had voiced such sentiments from the

beginning. Louis de Saint-Just, a hard, unsmiling, remorseless, dislikeable, clever young man from Blérancourt, spoke for many of
them when, his long fair hair dancing on his shoulders, he demanded the trial and execution of the King as an enemy of the
people. Such demands gathered even wider support when a large
iron box, containing compromising documents, was discovered in
the Tuileries. On 11 December Louis Capet as he was now
generally called – though Capet, so he protested, was not his
name: 'it was the surname of one of my ancestors' – was sent for by
the Convention to answer the charge of 'having committed various
crimes to re-establish tyranny on the ruins of liberty'.

The King and Queen and their children had now been incarcerated
in the Temple, behind a succession of locked doors, for four
months. The rooms, at first oppressively hot, had become cold and
damp, and the wind, blowing down the antiquated chimneys, filled
them with smoke. Most of the guards were unfriendly and sometimes rude, scrawling graffiti on the walls, rattling their keys 'in a
terrible manner' and insolently puffing their pipes in their captives'
faces. One of them, Louis Turgy, a former kitchen-boy at Versailles, less hostile than the others, recorded the 'extremely stringent'
precautions which were always observed at the Temple:

> This is the way in which my service had to be carried on. Before
> dinner, as before every meal, I had to go to the Council Chamber and ask
> for two of the officers to come, who themselves laid the dishes, and tasted
> the food to make sure there was nothing hidden in it ... They ac-
> companied me to the dining-room, and only allowed me to lay the table
> when they had examined it above and below. I had to unfold the cloth and
> the napkins in front of them. They cut each roll of bread in half, and
> searched the inside with a fork, or even with their fingers.

The King rose at six o'clock, shaved, had his hair rolled and was
helped to dress by his manservant, Jean-Baptiste Cléry, then, after
saying his prayers on his knees for five or six minutes, he spent most
of the morning reading or giving lessons to his son, getting him to
colour maps or to recite passages from Corneille and Racine. Before

dinner at two o'clock he was allowed out for a walk with his family during which, so Cléry said, 'the artillerymen or guard danced and sang; their songs were always revolutionary, and sometimes also obscene'. After dinner the Dauphin and his sister went into an ante-chamber to play at battledore and shuttle-cock or a game with a board, a flattened bowl and wooden pins called Siam, while the King played piquet or *tric-trac* with his wife and sister before lying down for an hour or so on his bed, snoring loudly in his sleep.

On the King's waking he would make me sit by him while I taught his son to write [Cléry recorded]. The copies I set were chosen by His Majesty from the works of Montesquieu and other celebrated authors . . . In the evening, the family sat round a table, while the Queen read to them from books of history, or other works proper to instruct and amuse her children . . . Madame Elisabeth took the book in her turn, and in this manner they read till eight o'clock. I then gave the Prince his supper in Madame Elisabeth's chamber during which the family looked on, and the King took pleasure in diverting the children by making them guess riddles in a collection of the *Mercures de France* which he found in the library.

After the Dauphin had supped, I undressed him, and the Queen heard him say his prayers. He said one in particular for the Princesse de Lamballe, and in another he begged God to protect the life of his governess. When the Municipal Officers were too near, the Prince, of his own accord, had the precaution to say these two prayers in a low voice . . . After his own supper at nine o'clock the King went for a moment to the Queen's chamber, shook hands with her and his sister for the night, and kissed his children. Then going to his own apartment he retired to the turret-room where he sat reading till midnight.

Nearly every week he read as many as twelve books, mostly history and travel and works of devotion, spending 'four hours a day on Latin authors'. The time passed very slowly.

For the Queen, too, the days were long. She spent hours on end knitting, making tapestries or embroidering chair covers which she would put down from time to time to give a lesson to her daughter or play with the Scottish terrier that the Princesse de Lamballe had given her. She called the dog Odin, a name that Hans Axel Fersen had given to a dog of his. She was still a young woman – her thirty-seventh birthday had been spent within these grey stone walls – but she looked much older; she had become painfully thin and her hair was now quite grey and in places streaked with white.

She said goodbye to her husband, kissing him fondly, when he went to face his accusers in the Convention. He behaved there with dignity, answering the questions that were put to him with calm brevity. He was allowed counsel and chose the elderly Chrétien de Lamoignon de Malesherbes, a blunt though kind and generous-hearted lawyer who had once been Master of the Household and now bravely answered his former master's call by returning from his retirement in Switzerland to defend him. 'I have,' Malesherbes said, 'been twice before called to be counsel for him who was my master, in times when that duty was coveted by everyone. I owe him the same service now that it is a duty which many people deem dangerous.' The King also asked to be defended by Gui-Jean-Baptiste Target, but Target excused himself on the grounds that he had not practised law since 1785 and that he was, in any case, far too fat; so the King's defence was entrusted instead to François Tronchet and Romain de Sèze.

Few members of the Convention were prepared to listen sympathetically to propositions of the King's innocence. But while leading Montagnards emphatically demanded the death penalty once the King's guilt was shown, there were several Girondins who, for reasons of expediency, argued that his life should be spared. 'No republican will ever be brought to believe that, in order to set twenty-five million men free, one man must die,' protested Brissot, 'that, in order to destroy the office of King, the man who fills it must be killed.' Supporting Brissot, Rabaut Saint-Étienne, one of the Secretaries of the Convention, suggested that 'Louis dead [would be] more dangerous to the people's freedom than Louis living in prison.' Such arguments, however, not shared by all the Gironde – which was never a homogeneous party – were derided by the *sans-culottes* in the streets of Paris where thousands of armed men marched intimidatingly past the houses and lodgings of the deputies, and where cheers went up for men like Saint-Just who demanded the execution of the King and of all men like him. 'What charming freedom we now enjoy in Paris,' commented Madame Roland caustically.

The verdict as to the King's guilt was never in doubt; indeed, it was given unanimously. But the Girondins still hoped that they might save his life, first by proposing that the matter of his punishment should be referred for ratification to the people of France as a whole and, when this had been condemned by their opponents as a mere political manoeuvre, by recommending a stay of execution. All the devices of the Girondins were, however, in vain. They aroused suspicions that they were royalists at heart, and increased the dislike in which they were already held by the Parisian *sans-culottes* without saving the King. A majority of over fifty deputies voted for death, and a majority of more than seventy subsequently voted against a stay of execution. The sitting of the Convention, during which the first vote was taken, lasted seventy-two hours. The spectators, amongst whom could be seen various friends of the Duc d'Orléans, 'ate ices and oranges and drank liqueurs', so the deputy, Sébastien Mercier, recorded. 'The uppermost galleries, kept open for the common people, were filled with foreigners and people from all walks of life. They drank wine and brandy as if they were in some low, smoke-filled tavern. At all the cafes in the neighbourhood bets were being laid on the outcome.'

Figures, rendered all the more sombre by the dim light, advanced one by one into the Tribune [Mercier continued his description of that night-long session]. In slow and sepulchral tones voices recorded the verdict, 'Death!' Face after face passed by . . . Some men calculated whether they had time to have a meal before giving their vote. Others fell asleep and had to be woken up to give their opinion. Of all that I saw that night no idea can be given.

The King accepted the verdict calmly, and remained quite composed when he was aroused from his sleep before dawn on 20 January 1793 to be told that he was to be executed the next day. He said goodbye to his family that evening. They all cried so loudly that 'their lamentations could be heard outside the tower'. He too wept, so his daughter recorded, 'but not on account of his own death. He told my mother the story of his trial . . . Then he gave my brother some good religious advice and told him in particular to forgive the people who had ordered his execution. He gave his blessing to my brother and me. My mother was very anxious for us to spend the night with my father, but he did not want us to as he needed to be quiet. My mother asked if she could come back to him the next morning. He agreed to this at first, but after he had gone he asked the guards to take care we did not come down again as it upset him too much.'

He ate his supper alone. Then Cléry helped him to undress and was about to brush his hair when he said, 'No, it's not worth while.'

The next morning he was woken at five o'clock, and after attending Mass and receiving Communion, he heard the clatter of drums. The Irish-born priest, Henry Essex Edgeworth, Elisabeth's former confessor whom he had asked to be with him at the end, said that his own blood froze in his veins at the sound of the hollow rhythmic tapping. But Louis retained his composure, remarking in a matter-of-fact tone, 'I expect it's the National Guard beginning to assemble.' Soon afterwards a company of National Guardsmen arrived at the Temple, accompanied by Santerre, by commissioners from the Commune and by Jacques Roux, a man who had once been a priest and was now one of the leaders of the *Enragés*, the extremist faction which, well to the left of the Montagnards, demanded among other comprehensive reforms the common ownership of goods and the strictest economic controls.

The King, who had been sitting by the porcelain stove in his room to keep warm, opened the door to them, so Edgeworth wrote, 'and they said that it was time to go. "I am occupied for a moment," he said to them in an authoritative tone, "wait for me here; I shall be with you in a minute." He shut the door, and coming to me knelt in front of me. "It is finished," he said. "Give me your last blessing, and pray God that He will uphold me to the end." In a moment or two he rose, and leaving the cabinet walked towards the group of men who were in the bedroom. Their faces showed the most complete assurance, and they all remained covered. Seeing this, the King asked for his hat. Cléry, with tears running down his face, hurried to look for it.'

Louis turned to Roux with a parcel containing a few personal belongings and his will which he asked him to give 'to the Queen'. 'To my wife,' he added, hastily amending the words.

'I have not come here to do your errands,' Roux roughly replied. 'I am here to take you to the scaffold.'

'That is so,' said Louis, offering the parcel to another man who accepted it.

Outside a light rain had begun to fall from a grey sky. There was a large green carriage waiting, and beyond it stretched line upon line of National Guardsmen and citizens with muskets and pikes on their shoulders. The King walked towards the carriage, 'turning once or twice towards the tower, as if to say a last goodbye,' so Edgeworth thought, 'to all that he held dear in this world. His every movement showed that he was calling up all his reserves of strength and courage.' The journey to the scaffold, which had been erected in the Place de Louis XV, renamed the Place de la Révolution and, since then, the Place de la Concorde, was a slow one. Edgeworth, the 'Citizen Minister of Religion', as the authorities referred to him, sat next to the King; two gendarmes sat opposite. Edgeworth offered Louis his breviary and at the King's request pointed out to him the most suitable psalms which they recited alternately. In front of the carriage marched a number of drummers, in order, so Edgeworth supposed, to 'prevent any shouts being heard that might be raised in the King's favour'.

At about half-past nine the carriage arrived at the Place de la Révolution where Louis saw the platform which had been set up between the promenade of the Champs Élysées and the pedestal from which the statue of his grandfather, who had laid out the square, had been removed. On the platform stood Charles Sanson, the city's executioner, whose father had preceded him in the office and whose son was to follow him. Above Sanson loomed the instrument of execution, the guillotine.

The guillotine took its name from Dr Joseph Ignace Guillotin, who was elected a member of the Constituent Assembly in 1789. A kindly man, he had suggested that all those convicted of a capital offence should have the right to be decapitated, a privilege hitherto reserved for nobles, and that the method of decapitation should be a machine which would render the process as quick and painless as possible. Such a machine had been known in Germany and Italy, as well as in Yorkshire in England where it was known as the Halifax gibbet, and in Scotland where it was called 'the Maiden'. In France it was adopted as the official method of execution by the penal code which became law in October 1791. Several machines were thereafter made for the various departments of France by a German contractor who produced them under the direction of the Secretary to the Academy of Surgeons. Those supplied to the department of Paris were tested on dead bodies from the hospital of Bicêtre. One of them was erected in the Place de Grève for the execution of the highwayman, Pelletier, and proved so efficacious that the people were 'disappointed', in the words of the *Chronique de Paris*. They had seen nothing. The whole thing was over too quickly. They went away complaining. The same machine was now to be used on the dethroned King.

Louis climbed down from the carriage. Three guards approached him and began to remove his clothes. He shook them off, undoing the buttons of his brown greatcoat himself, taking off his hat and removing his shirt and collar. The guards then pinioned his arms, and again Louis protested. 'What are you doing?' he asked, quickly drawing his hands back. 'Binding your hands,' one of them answered. 'Binding me!' exclaimed the King indignantly, looking appealingly at Edgeworth. 'Sire,' Edgeworth said, 'I see in this last outrage only one more resemblance between Your Majesty and the God who is about to be your recompense.' So Louis submitted while the guards tied his arms behind his back and cut his hair, leaving the neck bare above his white waistcoat.

Having arrived at the top of the scaffold Louis walked across it with a firm step, making a sign to the drummers who for a moment stopped tapping while he addressed the crowd in a loud voice. 'I forgive those who are guilty of my death, and I pray God that the blood which you are about to shed may never be required of France. I only sanctioned upon compulsion the Civil Constitution of the Clergy.' But his next words were lost as an officer on horseback shouted a command to the fifteen drummers who immediately resumed the beating of their drums. Sanson and his assistants then guided Louis to the plank of the guillotine where he lay face downwards. Sanson pulled the rope. The blade rushed down between the upright posts. Cléry heard his master scream for 'his head did not fall at the first stroke, his neck being so fat'.

When it had finally been severed, Edgeworth saw the youngest of the guards, who looked about eighteen, pick up the head by the roughly cut hair and walk about the scaffold showing it to the people, accompanying 'this monstrous ceremony with the most atrocious and indecent gestures'. Edgeworth, who was on his knees on the platform, was spattered with blood before rising and hurrying off towards the crowd into which, since he was wearing the lay dress that all priests were by now required to adopt, he soon disappeared.

The people were silent for a moment, as though stunned by the shock of the spectacle. Then they began to cry, '*Vive la Nation!*' '*Vive la République!*' The voices multiplied, and soon 'every hat was in the air'. The guard of cavalry waved their helmets on the points of their sabres and, so a doctor who was present said, crowds of people rushed forward to dip their handkerchiefs or pieces of paper in the blood spilled on the scaffold 'to have a reminder of this memorable event'. One of them put a drop of it to his lips, remarking to a companion that it tasted 'shockingly bitter'.

THE DAYS OF THE *ENRAGÉS*
AND THE *HÉBERTISTS*

28 May–2 June and 4–5 September 1793

*'It is to be feared that the Revolution, like Saturn, will end
by devouring its own children'*

VERGNIAUD

I   *Louis XVI. A regal portrait by Callet of the King who, in the words of Mme de la Tour du Pin, was, in fact, 'stout, about five foot six or seven inches tall . . . and with the worst possible bearing'*

2 *Marie-Antoinette as a young mother. Her first child was born, after more than eight years of marriage, in 1778*

3 *Versailles in 1722*

4 *A painting by Debucourt exhibited at the Salon in 1785. It depicts Louis XVI on a cold February day in 1784 giving money to a poor family in a cottage near Versailles (to which he had been conducted by a peasant who had approached him, not recognizing him as he was wearing a heavy cloak and had become separated from his suite)*

5 *Debucourt's painting of market people celebrating in Les Halles on the birth of the Dauphin in 1781*

6   *A caricature satirizing the inequality of taxation in France and representing an elderly
peasant carrying on his back a bishop and a nobleman*

7

The duc d'Orléans and the marquis de Lafayette carry aloft Jacques Necker, who treads underfoot symbols of enslavement while holding triumphantly the crown of France in one hand and a cap of liberty in the other

8   *The opening ceremony of the Estates General at Versailles on 5 May 1789. (The clergy are on the King's right, the nobility on his left, the Third Estate at the back of the hall and spectators crowding behind the pillars)*

9 *The Abbé Sieyès*   10 *Camille Desmoulins*

11 *J. L. David's painting of the deputies taking the oath in the tennis court at Versailles on 20 June 1789*

12 *Troops encamped on the Champs de Mars on 14 July 1789*

13 *The storming of the Bastille on 14 July 1789*

14 Mirabeau, sketch by David

15 *Jean-Sylvain Bailly, the astronomer and Parisian deputy, who was elected Mayor of Paris and who received the King upon his arrival at the Hôtel de Ville on 17 July 1789*

16 *The King arriving at the Hôtel de Ville*

17 *A contemporary print depicting 'the departure of the heroines of Paris for Versailles on 5 October 1789'*

18 *The arrival of the women at Versailles*

19 The celebrations on the first anniversary of the fall of the Bastille, 14 July 1790

20 *During subsequent celebrations the mood was far less joyful: on this occasion in 1792 the King was obliged to condone the burning of a Tree of Feudalism bedecked with symbols of royalty, aristocracy and the papacy*

21 *The mob looting a nobleman's house*

22 *Pierre-Victurnien Vergniaud*

23 *The King is apprehended in Sauce's house in Varennes*

24 *The King announces the declaration of war to the acclaim of the deputies*

25 *The attack on the Tuileries on 10 August 1792*

26 *'The Victory of Equality, or the Plots Baffled.' An allegory of the* journée *of 10 August* 1792

27 'La Femme du Sans Culotte'

28 'Sans Culottes du 10 Août et An 1er de la République Française.'

29 *A revolutionary committee during the Terror*

Danton au 10 août

30 *Georges Jacques Danton*

32 *The trial of Louis XVI in the National Convention, 26 December 1792*

33 *The execution of the King on the Place de la Révolution on 21 January 1793*

34 *J. L. David's celebrated 'Marat'. (The paper in his left hand reads: 'Du 13 Juillet 1793 Marie Anne Charlotte Corday au Citoyen Marat. Il suffit que je sois bien malheureuse pour avoir Droit à votre bienveillance.')*

35 *A contemporary print fancifully depicting Charlotte Corday, knife in hand, after the murder of Marat*

37 *Arrest of Robespierre*

36 *Robespierre. A sketch by David on which is inscribed 'Eyes green, complexion pale, green striped nankeen jacket, blue waistcoat with blue stripes, white cravat striped with red'*

38 *Antoine-Quentin Fouquier-Tinville, 'a man with very thick black hair, small round iridescent eyes, a low forehead, pale complexion, pock-marked nose, thin close-shaven lips and a chin expressive of mockery'*

39 *The Trial of Fouquier-Tinville*

40 David's sketch of Marie-Antoinette on her way to execution. Her hair had been cut by Henri Sanson's son who was acting as deputy for his father. (She was thirty-seven but looked far older)

41 The execution of Marie-Antoinette on 16 October 1793

42 *The interior of Frascati's during the days of the Directory*

43 *A Bonapartist print depicting the 'brave Grenadiers' protecting their hero in the Orangery at Saint-Cloud on 19 Brumaire as some deputies escape through the windows*

44 *David's painting of Napoleon's coronation in 1804 (detail)*

The courts of Europe reacted to Louis XVI's execution with protestations of outrage. Already perturbed by the Convention's announcement that military occupation would be followed by the sequestration of noble and ecclesiastical property, the abolition of feudalism and the introduction of French paper currency, they were now still more alarmed by Danton's declaration of France's right to expand to her 'natural frontiers' – the sea, the Rhine, the Alps and the Pyrenees. And, provoked by the 'heinous crime' of regicide, monarchial Europe coalesced to crush the Revolution. But, as diplomatic relations were severed, the French revolutionaries met protests with defiance. 'The kings in alliance try to intimidate us,' cried Danton challengingly. 'We hurl at their feet, as a gage of battle, the French King's head.' Accepting the inevitability of conflict with the country's traditional rival, the Convention declared war on England at the beginning of February; it also declared war on Holland, then on Spain, so that within a few weeks almost every major power in Europe was ranged against 'the assassins of Paris'.

The Convention's faith in the irresistibility of the Revolution's forces did not at first seem misplaced. After that decisive day at Valmy, the French armies – living off the land and therefore moving fast – had occupied Savoy and Nice, possessions of the King of Sardinia. General Custine had penetrated into Germany as far as Mainz and advanced towards Frankfurt. Dumouriez had entered Belgium, defeated the Austrians at Jemappes and advanced to Brussels, Liège and Antwerp. Encouraged by the disorganization of their enemies and by Russia's preoccupation with the dismemberment of Poland, the Convention, decreeing 'war on castles, peace for cottages', had offered *fraternité et secours à tous les peuples qui voudront recouvrer leur liberté*.

Yet now that the enemies of France had increased, now that new frontiers and coasts had to be watched, and more money found, the deputies were faced with problems that dissipated their earlier confidence. And as their armies faltered, the sharply rising cost of living, the fall in the value of *assignats* and the shortages of food all caused unrest and disturbances at home. For a time the Montagnards and the more moderate Girondins came together to form a united front, not only against counter-revolutionaries but also against the violent

sans-culottes and those extremists known as *Enragés* who were
intent upon exploiting the discontent in order to impose upon the
Convention a more radical programme, including the fixing of
prices and the requisition of food supplies. Jacques Roux, the fiery
ex-priest, played a leading part in these insurrectionary activities of
the *Enragés*. So did Jean Varlet, a postal worker. And both of them
planned a series of *journées* as the military situation worsened, as
Custine fell back from the Rhineland and Dumouriez, abandoning
plans for an invasion of Holland and retreating through the
Austrian Netherlands, was defeated first at Neerwinden, then at
Louvain. Having failed in an attempt to persuade his men to march
on Paris to restore order and the monarchy, Dumouriez finally
deserted to the Austrians, like Lafayette, taking with him the Duc
d'Orléans's son, the Duc de Chartres, and several officers of his
staff.

The problems of the Convention were now exacerbated by the
spread of the ferocious civil war in the Vendée where tens of
thousands of peasants, having risen in arms against mobilization
and the new revolutionary order, massacred republicans, scattered
the forces of the National Guard and advanced on Rochefort with
the declared intention of opening it to a British invasion fleet.
Elsewhere in France, also, peasants were protesting violently against
mobilization, refusing to comply with the Convention's decrees,
harbouring recalcitrant priests and attacking republican municipalities. Troops had to be dispatched to Brittany; while in Bordeaux
and Nantes, Lyons and Marseilles there were furious quarrels and
outbreaks of fighting between different groups of revolutionaries,
which led many to wish that there had been no Revolution at all.

The Convention responded to the crises by issuing a series of
emergency decrees designed to shore up the crumbling edifice of the
executive government. Rebels captured bearing arms were to be
executed; so were *émigrés* who returned to France. Foreigners were
to be closely watched by new *comités de surveillance*; priests denounced by six citizens were to be deported. And in early March the
establishment of a Revolutionary Tribunal was proposed to deal
judicially with those whom the *Enragés* and the *sans-culottes* might
otherwise have persecuted arbitrarily. This proposal aroused mur-

murs of protest from various moderates in the Convention, one of whom was brave enough to shout the word, '*Septembre.*' At this Danton, already profoundly distressed by the recent death of his wife over whose grave he had bellowed in unbearable grief, turned upon the man who had spoken and in 'thunderous tones' rebuked him: 'Since someone here has *dared* to recall those bloody days . . . I say that if a Revolutionary Tribunal had then existed, the people who have been so cruelly reproached for them would not have stained them with blood. Let us profit by the mistakes of our predecessors. Let us be terrible so that we can prevent the people from being terrible.'

So, despite the objections of Vergniaud, who said that they would be 'laying the foundations of an Inquisition a thousand times more fearful than that of Spain', the deputies agreed to the creation of a Revolutionary Tribunal, before which so many of them were later to appear. A month later, as the news from the front grew more alarming and the threat to France of being overrun by foreign troops was added to that of the spread of civil war, the Convention also set up a Committee of Public Safety which, with Danton, at first the most powerful of its nine members, was gradually to arrogate to itself the authority of a supremely omnipotent cabinet.

In Paris there were increasingly insistent demands from the Left to punish the Girondin leaders whose reputation had been tarnished by the treachery of their supporter, General Dumouriez, and by their campaign to gain control of provincial municipalities and to turn them against the political dominance of Paris. The Committee of Public Safety responded to these demands by ordering the seizure of the Rolands' papers; and, when these were found to contain little of a compromising nature, Camille Desmoulins produced a pamphlet, *L'histoire des Brissotins*, which, having listed various concocted charges, called upon the Convention to 'vomit the Girondins from its belly'. But the Girondins refused to be intimidated, seeming to Danton to be 'bent on their own destruction'. Danton, the one man who could have saved them, went to see some of their leaders with an offer of compromise. 'Let bygones be bygones,' he said to them, only too well aware that his own friendly relations with Dumouriez laid himself open to just such attacks as were being made upon them and that he might need their support as much as they needed his.

'Let it be war,' retorted Guadet challengingly, brushing Danton's overtures aside, 'and let one side perish!'

'You want war, then, Guadet, do you?' Danton answered, provoked into fury. 'Then you shall have death.'

Soon afterwards in the Convention both he and the Girondins came under open attack for their association with Dumouriez. 'His lips were curled in that expression of contempt which was peculiar to him. He inspired a sort of terror. His glance expressed both disdain and rage.' Suddenly he leaped to his feet to deflect attention from himself and Dumouriez by turning furiously on the Girondins.

'Citizens of the Mountain,' Danton exclaimed, waving a fist which the Abbé Kerenavent described as resembling 'that of a street porter', 'I must begin by paying you homage. You are the true friends of the welfare of the people. Your judgement has been clearer than mine . . . I was wrong. I now abandon moderation because prudence has its limits . . . I am now convinced that no truce is possible between the Mountain, the patriots who wanted the King's death, and these cowards who slandered us throughout France in the hope of saving him . . . No more terms with them! I have returned to the fortress of Reason. I will have it armed with the artillery of Truth in order to blow these enemies to dust!'

He continued for some time in the same vein, his great voice resounding round the walls, while the Montagnards cheered and Marat shouted his encouragement.

Yet the Girondins still refused to compromise and responded to the attacks made upon them by the Left by arraigning Marat, now President of the Jacobin Club, before the Revolutionary Tribunal.

Ever since his election to the Convention as one of the deputies for Paris, Marat had been one of the Girondins' most persistent critics. An English visitor to Paris, Dr John Moore, who listened to him speaking, described how the 'little man' appeared to be both detested and feared not only by them but also by most of the Montagnards:

He has a cadaverous complexion and a countenance exceedingly expressive of his disposition ... The man's audacity is equal to anything, but what I thought full as wonderful was the degree of patience, and even approbation, with which he was heard ... So far from ever having the appearance of fear or of deference, he seems to me always to contemplate the Assembly from the tribune either with eyes of menace or contempt. He speaks in a hollow, croaking voice, with affected solemnity ... Marat has carried his calumnies to such a length that even the party which he wishes to support seem to be ashamed of him, and he is shunned and apparently detested by everyone else. When he enters the hall of the Assembly he is avoided on all sides, and when he seats himself those near him generally rise and change their places. He stood a considerable time yesterday near the tribune, watching an opportunity to speak. I saw him at one time address himself to Louvet and in doing so he attempted to lay his hand on Louvet's shoulder. Louvet instantly started back with looks of aversion, as one would do from the touch of a noxious reptile, exclaiming, '*Ne me touchez pas.*'

Yet, while shunned in the Convention, Marat was highly regarded by the extremists outside it; and, as the Girondins might have foreseen, he was immediately acquitted upon his appearance before the Revolutionary Tribunal. He was carried back in triumph by a mob of cheering women and *sans-culottes* to the Convention whose meeting hall had by now been transferred from the Manège to the Court's former theatre at the Tuileries. The doors burst open and Marat, smiling sardonically, a wreath of oak leaves round his forehead, was borne shoulder high before the deputies. 'Citizen President,' announced a man with an axe, 'we bring you the worthy Marat. Marat has always been the friend of the people, and the people will always be the friends of Marat. If Marat's head must fall, our heads will fall first.' As the people in the public galleries roared their approval and several deputies left their seats in disgust, permission was sought for Marat's escort to parade him about the theatre. 'I will consult the Assembly,' the President replied. But not waiting for him to do so, the mob rushed in shouting Marat's name, milling about the floor and occupying the vacated seats. Marat was returned to his place with the Montagnards; then, mounting the rostrum, he made a speech, praising his own pure heart and vilifying

197

his accusers, before being borne off again in triumph to the Jacobin Club.

The Girondins now compounded their mistake in having Marat summoned before the Revolutionary Tribunal by dismissing the popular demands for the control of corn prices – thus allowing the Jacobins, who endorsed the demands, to gain further favour with the *sans-culottes*. They then attempted to overthrow the Commune by issuing orders for the arrests of Hébert – now its deputy *procureur* – of the *Enragé*, Varlet and of four others of the Girondins' most vexatious opponents. 'I declare to you, in the name of the whole of France,' threatened Maximin Isnard when the Commune protested against this Girondin counter-attack, 'that if these extremists are allowed to have their way and the principle of national representation suffers, Paris will be annihilated; and men will soon be searching the banks of the Seine to see if the city had ever existed.'

The *Enragés* and *sans-culottes* in the Paris *sections*, with the rather nervous complaisance of most of the Jacobins and with the active help of some of them, now decided to take action to destroy the Girondins once and for all. On 27 May a mob burst through the doors of the Convention, demanded and obtained the release of Hébert, Varlet and the other prisoners, as well as the abolition of a Girondin-dominated Commission of Twelve which had recently been established to investigate the behaviour of the Commune and the troublesome *sections*. The next day the Commission of Twelve was re-established by the Girondins, but the prisoners remained free and the *sans-culottes* prepared another *journée*.

On the evening of that day, 28 May, a new Insurrectionary Committee was formed with Varlet one of its members. A militia of 30,000 *sans-culottes* was raised; a petition was prepared demanding the permanent abolition of the Commission of Twelve and the arrest of the Girondin leaders. Command of the National Guard was entrusted to François Hanriot, a former clerk, beadle, footman and brandy seller, one of the *sans-culottes* who took part in the assault on the Tuileries on 10 August 1792, 'a coarse and irascible man who never opened his lips without bawling,' according to a police report, 'and remarkable for a harsh and grimacing countenance.'

Danton and the Committee of Public Safety did not intervene, but the Convention as a whole, even a majority of its Jacobin members, were reluctant to accede to the Insurrectionary Committee's demands for the arrest of the Girondins, fearing that this might result in the collapse of the entire Convention. When, therefore, the petition was presented on 31 May, the demonstrators were told that the Commission of Twelve would be abolished, as they had demanded, but that the proposed arrest of the Girondins would be referred to the Committee of Public Safety.

The crowd went home dissatisfied and determined to make further protests. That day was a Friday and many of those who would have otherwise joined in the march on the Convention were unwilling to lose a day's wages in order to do so. So the Insurrectionary Committee decided to march again on Sunday when all the workers would be free to come with them.

On that Sunday, 2 June, to the sound of drum beats, the roar of the alarm-gun, and the peal of the tocsin, which Marat had rung with his own hand in the tower of the Hôtel de Ville the day before, the Convention was once again surrounded by shouting demonstrators, by tens of thousands of armed men from the *sections* and by the battalions of Hanriot's National Guard supported by sixty cannon. A delegation of their leaders entered the theatre to 'demand for the last time justice against the guilty'.

At these words Jean-Denis Lanjuinais, one of the Montagnards' bravest and most outspoken opponents, a former professor of ecclesiastical law at Rennes, rose to protest against 'this disgraceful intimidation of the country's elected representatives'. To threats and catcalls from the galleries, to shouts of 'Down! Down! He wants to start a civil war!' from a group of Montagnards, Lanjuinais stood his ground, insisting, 'So long as one is allowed to speak freely here, I will not let the character of representative of the people be degraded in my person! So far you have done nothing; you have permitted everything; you have given way to all that was required of you. An insurrectional committee meets. It prepares a revolt. It appoints commanders to lead it. And you do *nothing* to prevent it.'

Failing in their attempts to shout him down, several Montagnards rushed up to the rostrum and tried to drag Lanjuinais off it. But he clung on tenaciously until, some semblance of order having at last been restored by the President, Lanjuinais brought his protests to an end by proposing that the revolutionary authorities which had illegally established themselves in Paris should be dissolved. While a deputy of the Left was asking just how he suggested that this should be done, the members of the Insurrectionary Committee again stormed into the theatre, repeating their demands more forcefully than ever.

One deputy now suggested, as a compromise, that the Girondins, whose arrest the armed crowds outside were demanding, should all voluntarily resign their functions. Some agreed to do so, but others, including Lanjuinais, refused. 'If the Convention compels me to resign, I will submit,' said Charles Barbaroux, a deputy from Marseilles, supporting Lanjuinais. 'But how can I resign my powers when a great number of people write to me and assure me that I have used them well and press me to continue to use them? I have sworn to die at my post, and I will keep my oath.'

During the course of the debate a number of deputies had tried to leave the theatre, but had been prevented. Some had been roughly man-handled, and one of them had returned to display in indignation his torn clothes. It was then suggested that, to prove that they were still free, the entire Convention should leave the theatre in a body. The deputies of the Right and the Plain all stood up and began to file out of the doors led by their handsome, debonair President, Hérault de Séchelles, an elegant and independently minded man who derided the fashion for dressing carelessly and who, questioned about his political affiliations, replied that he belonged 'to the party that snapped its fingers at the others'.

The Montagnards remained at first in their places but, reproached for not daring to share the common danger, they, too, rose to their feet and followed the others outside on to the Carrousel.

Here Hanriot, wearing a hat bedecked with plumes, was sitting in the saddle at the head of his National Guard. 'What do the people want?' Hérault de Séchelles asked him. 'The Convention is concerned only with their welfare.'

'Hérault,' Hanriot replied brusquely, 'the people have not come here to listen to idle talk.' They had come, he said, to demand that the guilty Girondins should be arrested.

'Seize this rebel,' Hérault de Séchelles commanded the National Guard, who merely looked at him as Hanriot backed his horse and bellowed at his artillerymen, 'Gunners, to your cannon!' The deputies quickly turned away. They tried to find some other avenue of escape, but the National Guard stood firm, some of them shouting, 'Down with the Right! Long live the Montagnards! To the guillotine with the Girondins! Long live Marat!'

Marat himself, surrounded by a group of admiring boys, shouted to Hérault de Séchelles, 'I can call on you and your followers to return to the posts which you have abandoned like cowards.' Reluctant as he was to take Marat's advice, the President realized that he really had no alternative but to retreat. So, while the crowds jeered and insulted them, he led the deputies back into the building where they continued to discuss the fate of the proscribed deputies. The Right refused to vote on the issue, protesting that they were no longer free agents, but the Montagnards ignored their protests. A decree was passed ordering the arrest of twenty-two leading Girondins. Their names, among them many of those who had dominated the earlier days of the Revolution, were read out by Marat, slowly and with evident relish.

By taking the initiative and running all the risks, the *Enragés* and *sans-culottes* had given the Jacobins the opportunity to assume control of Paris and vigorously to prosecute the war which the Girondins had provoked. But few of the demands of these forceful demonstrators from the Paris *sections* had yet been met, and the Jacobins on the Committee of Public Safety were now faced with the problem of restraining them as well as of suppressing the Insurrectionary Committee without arousing their enmity. The Committee of Public Safety had also now to find some way of preventing a reaction in favour of the Girondins – over seventy of whom had signed a protest against the Jacobin *coup d'état* – and of putting a stop to their campaign in the provinces where they were inciting people to protest against this fresh proof of Parisian terrorism and urging them to rise up against the Jacobin dictators in the capital and to impose *fédéralisme* on France.

During the next few weeks the federalist revolt in the provinces continued to spread until no less than sixty *départements* were infected and the rebels were in possession of several towns in the Loire valley. General Paoli established control of Corsica; parts of Normandy were in uproar; and civil war, such as that fought in the Vendée, raged round Lyons, Marseilles and Toulon. Some of the movement's leaders hoped to see France divided into a number of more or less independent republics bound together by not too restrictive federal ties. Others were merely anxious to regain for their communities the independence and privileges of which the Revolution had deprived them. But all were strong in their condemnation of the Parisians' intimidation of an elected national assembly.

The Committee of Public Safety attempted to quieten the protests and subdue the uprisings by making various economic concessions to the peasants and by drawing up a new constitution which – though it never came into operation and was perhaps not intended to – would demonstrate the good intentions of the central government by establishing the principle of universal suffrage and proclaiming the duty of society to provide work for those who could work, help for those who could not, and education for all. The federalist revolt failed, however, not because of these palliatives but because it lacked both unity of direction and the fervour of its opponents, and because, so long as there was still a real threat of foreign invasion, *fédéralisme* seemed an issue that must give way to national salvation.

The war was, indeed, the issue upon which all others turned. The Austrians had followed up their victory over Dumouriez by advancing towards the frontier fortresses of Condé and Valenciennes, both of which fell that summer. Custine was retreating before the Prussians; Spanish armies were threatening to cross the western frontier both north and south of the Pyrenees; the Sardinians were poised to retake Savoy. British troops began to lay siege to Dunkirk. At Lyons, the second most important city in France, royalists had assumed control and were busy executing the republicans whom they had displaced, and at Toulon counter-revolutionaries were soon to hand over arsenal, town and fleet to the British admiral, Lord Hood who, without the discharge of a single broadside, took under his command twenty-six of France's sixty-one frigates.

The crisis appeared quite beyond the control of the original Committee of Public Safety, and Danton's attempts to save France by diplomatic negotiations both with foreign powers and federalist leaders were by now utterly discredited. He and several others were thrown off the Committee; and on 27 July a new member joined it, a man who for long had played a dominant role in the affairs of the Jacobins and was now to dominate the Revolution itself.

Maximilien Robespierre was a small, thin, dogmatic man of thirty-two with thick, carefully brushed and powdered hair and a slightly pock-marked skin of a deathly greenish pallor. His grey eyes, too, had a greenish tint; and green was the shade he most often favoured in the choice of the clothes he wore with such attention to their immaculate neatness and precision of cut. He seemed extremely nervous and highly strung: he walked very fast on high-heeled shoes; a convulsive tic occasionally distorted the livid, pitted skin between his prominent cheekbones and the corners of his long thin lips; he bit his nails; he had a habit of sharply pushing his tinted spectacles up from his short-sighted eyes on to his bonily bulging brow. He rarely laughed and when he did so the sound seemed forced from him, hollow and dry. He appeared to be unremittingly conscious of his own virtues.

He came from Arras where he was born on 6 May 1758, the son of a lawyer who was himself the son and grandson of lawyers. In fact the Derobespierres, as their name was then written, had been well-known attorneys, notaries and barristers in north-eastern France for several generations, though Maximilien's father had at first been intended for the Church. After spending some time as a novice at an abbey in Ponthieu, however, François Robespierre had decided that he had 'no inclination for a religious life' and, having studied law at Douai University, he joined his father's practice. Unfortunately he had little inclination for the respectable life of an Arras lawyer either. He shamed his family by falling in love with the daughter of a brewer and by marrying her when she discovered herself to be pregnant. Maximilien was the first of the five children of this marriage.

Maximilien's early years were fairly happy ones. His mother was kind and gentle, and his father, whose restless, unhappy nature was soothed by her devotion, prospered as a barrister. But then the death of his fifth child was quickly followed by that of the mother, and his father, overwhelmed by grief, sank into what Maximilien's sister called his 'odd behaviour again'. He took to drink and neglected his practice. Eventually, abandoning the children to the care of his sisters and his father-in-law, he left Arras and not long afterwards died in Germany.

At the time of his father's departure Maximilien was eight years old. The cheerful, carefree little boy had now become quiet and grave. When he heard his mother spoken of, tears came into his eyes. He spent much of his time making lace, a craft which his mother had taught him, constructing models of farms and houses and churches, collecting pictures, showing the fruit of his careful labours to his younger sisters, anxious for their approval and praise. He was kind to these sisters. But if he joined in their games it was usually to tell them how they ought to be played; and when they asked him for one of his pet pigeons he refused to give it to them for fear that they might not look after it properly. In the end he relented. They left its cage out in a storm one night and it died. Between his tears, so Charlotte said, he poured reproaches upon the culprits for their carelessness.

At school he was a model pupil, attentive, hard-working and intelligent. And at the age of eleven he was awarded a scholarship to the famous Collège Louis-le-Grand in Paris. Before leaving he gave his sisters all his toys. He would not give them the pigeons, though, entrusting these to someone more responsible.

In Paris his own responsibility was never in doubt. He was not one of the university's brightest students, but there was scarcely another more conscientious, more thorough, more determined to succeed, readier to return to subjects which he felt he had not fully mastered or in which his examination results had proved disappointing.

He seems to have been a solitary student who made no intimate friends and was apparently content to spend most of his time alone in the private room with which his scholarship provided him. He was not much liked, his contemporaries resenting in particular his practice of reporting their misdemeanours to their masters. 'He was a melancholy boy,' one of them recalled. 'I do not remember ever having seen him laugh.' Even then he was excessively neat in his dress, and spent the little pocket money that was allowed him on lace cuffs and shoe buckles and on having his hair curled at the barbers.

No one who knew him then pictured him as a revolutionary. He professed – and for several years continued to profess – his belief in the King as a 'young and wise monarch', part of whose 'august character' was a 'sacred passion for the happiness of the people'. And when the King and Queen passed by the gates of the Collège Louis-le-Grand in the summer of 1775 to be greeted by its masters and students, Maximilien Derobespierre was deputed to make the speech of welcome in Latin. He did so most respectfully, kneeling in the rain by the open door of the royal carriage while the King remained seated inside, shy and confused, not knowing what to say when the speech was finished, so saying nothing.

Yet the masters at the Collège Louis-le-Grand, who included Jean le Rond d'Alembert, a contributor to the *Encyclopédie*, were anxious to instil into their pupils not so much the glories of the Bourbon dynasty as the virtues of the Roman Republic and the principles of the *philosophes*. And Derobespierre was soon reading Rousseau's *Social Contrat* with profound attention and respect. He did not care for the agnosticism of Voltaire and clung to his belief in God and the immortality of the soul. But his former observances as a good practising Catholic were now abandoned for ever.

After nine years at the Collège Louis-le-Grand, Derobespierre began to specialize in legal studies, and in June 1780, at the age of twenty-three, he received his degree. He was awarded a leaving prize of 600 *livres*, the highest sum ever given to a graduate of Louis-le-Grand, and with this he endeavoured to establish himself in practice in Paris. But the weeks passed; no clients came to him; and within four months he was back in Arras. He rented a small house which he shared with his sister, the pretty and possessive Charlotte, and, like his father and grandfather before him, was admitted as a barrister to the Superior Council of Artois. Helped by a friend of the family who brought him his first brief, he soon established a reputation for himself as a clever, honest, fastidious young man, never greedy for large fees, anxious always to do his best for his clients, and, unlike Danton, avoiding cases in which he might be expected to propound or defend an unworthy cause.

But if he was recognized as a man who was not set upon making money, everyone who knew him realized how determined he was to make himself famous. Having won one well-publicized case, he persuaded his client to pay for the cost of having his pleadings printed. Reluctantly the client agreed, and the printed copies went off to professional colleagues, to relations and acquaintances, and to celebrated men he did not know, including Benjamin Franklin whom he addressed in his covering letter as 'the most brilliant scholar in the universe'.

It was, however, admiration for his gifts as a writer rather than for his skill as an advocate which he principally desired. And it was in the Academy of Arras, to which he was elected in 1783, that he sought to shine even more than in the courts of law. This Academy, like similar establishments in other provincial cities, was a kind of literary and scientific club whose members read papers to each other, debated the important questions of the day, and held intellectual competitions for the winners of which occasional prizes were awarded. Derobespierre soon made himself a leading member, and within three years of his election he was appointed its director with the responsibility of presiding over meetings and making official speeches on its behalf.

By this time he had seen his work in print once more. The Academy of Metz had offered prizes for the best essays submitted on the theme of whether or not a criminal's family should share his shame. Derobespierre had immediately put his eager mind to work, and had submitted an entry which had been awarded the second prize. He had spent the money he won in having an extended version of his essay printed and distributed in a booklet of sixty pages. He had also submitted an entry for a competition later set by the Academy of Amiens. This did not win a prize, but its author had had it printed and circulated all the same.

During his time as director of the Academy of Arras, when he was one of the three judges appointed to consider the entries, no prizes were awarded to any of the essays submitted in its competitions. They were, indeed, more likely to be rejected with some severe strictures upon their merits by the Academy director who, jealous as always of those whom he considered his rivals, pronounced upon one essay that it was as ill-organized as it was undeveloped; that it put forward nothing either new or useful; that it was 'badly written and badly presented'; that its only merit was that it was short.

Derobespierre's sister, Charlotte, described her brother's daily life and habits at this time in a light which softens the rather harsh and disagreeable portrait others have drawn of the dapper, little, ambitious, pushing lawyer, marching so quickly and so purposefully through the cobbled streets of Arras. According to Charlotte, he woke up early and was out of bed by seven o'clock, sometimes by six. He worked for an hour or two before getting dressed, an operation which was performed with the utmost care and attention. Before putting on his coat his hair was brushed, dressed and powdered by the barber who now came to the house every morning for this purpose. After a meagre breakfast of bread and milk, he set off for the law courts, returning in time for an almost equally meagre evening meal with which he drank a little wine, and that much watered. He seems to have been almost completely uninterested in food, living mainly on bread, fruit and coffee. He had a passion for pastry, but as this gave him indigestion he could not indulge himself, and he never appeared to enjoy anything else. A fellow-guest at a dinner party said that when eating he looked like a cat lapping vinegar. Whenever Charlotte asked him what he would like for a meal he replied that he did not care.

Still, she did not find him either difficult or morose. Admittedly he was usually reserved and quiet, withdrawing to an armchair in a corner whenever other people in the room began to gossip about their neighbours or produced a pack of cards. Charlotte remembered one evening when she and her brother had been out visiting friends. On the way home he started walking at an even faster pace than usual, leaving her trailing far behind him. By the time he arrived home he had forgotten that she had been with him. He let himself into the house and settled down to work in his study. 'I went into his study,' Charlotte said, 'and found him already in his dressing-gown, working very hard. He asked me with a look of some surprise where I had been to arrive back so late.'

In 1789 Robespierre, as he was beginning to call himself, was elected to the Estates General as one of the deputies for Artois. Although he was eventually to speak more than five hundred times during the life of the National Assembly and to gain wide respect as one of the shrewdest and most incorruptible men of the Left, he found it difficult at first to obtain a hearing. His voice was weak; his views unacceptable to most of his fellow-deputies; his rather self-righteous manner irritating; his habit of blinking his eyes and never looking directly at those to whom he spoke, disconcerting; his self-confidence not proof against the rowdy interruptions and catcalls with which speakers in those early days of the Assembly had to contend. 'Monsieur de Robespierre took the floor,' runs an account in the *Courrier* of one of his failures, 'but the Assembly having shown its impatience, the honourable member withdrew with tears in his eyes.' 'He was interrupted again,' according to another account describing a different occasion, 'and, at last . . . he left the rostrum. The President remonstrated with the Assembly that this conduct was not fair. Monsieur de Robespierre was invited to take the rostrum once more. He did so. But whatever excellent things he might have had to say, the rude opposition he had experienced had put him off his stroke.'

When the Assembly moved to Paris, however, Robespierre's voice was heard with greater respect and his sincerity unquestioningly admitted. 'That man will go far,' Mirabeau said of him. 'He believes what he says.' The public, too, admired him and listened to him attentively, and it was to them that his speeches were principally addressed. 'I was always looking beyond the narrow confines of the house of legislation,' he confessed. 'When I spoke to the body of representatives, my aim was above all to be heard by the nation and by humanity. I wanted to arouse, and to arouse for ever in the hearts of citizens the feeling of the dignity of man.' His only regret was that the Manège was not bigger; he would have preferred a debating chamber 'open to twelve thousand spectators'. For, 'under the eyes of so many witnesses neither corruption, intrigue nor perfidy would dare show themselves. Only the general will would be consulted. The voice of the nation alone would be heard'.

Robespierre's new fame and influence in the Assembly and at the Jacobin Club made no alteration in the extreme – it seemed to some ostentatious – simplicity of his life. He still dressed with excessive neatness and was often to be seen in a smart green striped nankeen coat, a blue striped waistcoat and a crisp cravat of red and white stripes. His hair seemed more neatly brushed and carefully powdered than ever. But once his appearance had been attended to, he seemed to have little use for the generous allowance of eighteen *livres* a day which the deputies had voted for themselves. He shared a small third-floor apartment in the Rue Saintonge with another bachelor, and appeared to take no respite from his work except for an occasional walk in the gardens of the Tuileries, where he fed the sparrows, or a visit to the theatre where – fortunately for him since there were so many of them – he 'liked declamatory tragedies'.

After the day of the Champ de Mars, when warrants had been issued for the arrest of several left-wing leaders, and various members of the Jacobin Club had gone into hiding, a master joiner, Maurice Duplay, who belonged to the Club, suggested that Robespierre would be safer with him than living so far away in the Rue Saintonge. So, after trying life with the Duplays for a few weeks, he moved his belongings and his beloved dog, Brount, from his apartment and settled in at 398 Rue Saint-Honoré with the Duplays who treated him as an honoured guest. Both the father and mother, as well as the three daughters who lived at home with them, tried 'to detect in Robespierre's eyes all his wishes,' so one visitor thought, 'in order to anticipate them immediately'. According to his sister, Robespierre was 'extremely sensitive to all this kind of thing'; and it was certainly obvious to everyone who came to the house and found the Duplays' distinguished guest sitting at the dining-table at which it was his practice always to say grace, that he greatly enjoyed the fussy attentions which were paid to him and that he was not in the least averse to having pictures of himself displayed in every room. One of the girls, Eleonore, a fat, plain girl of twenty-four, was particularly attentive. It was rumoured that they were engaged to be married, but his sister doubted this: 'Overwhelmed with business and work as my brother was, and entirely taken up with his career,' she asked, 'how could he think of love or marriage?' Indeed, Robespierre seemed to have as little interest in women as in food: some said he hated women.

There was certainly no doubt that he was preoccupied with his career. At the end of March 1790 he was elected President of the Jacobin Club and thereafter he was recognized as potentially its most influential member. He was largely instrumental in keeping it alive when so many of its members left to form the rival and more moderate Feuillant Club in protest against the petition for the King's dethronement. And he received further acclaim both inside and outside the Jacobin Club when the military disasters of 1792 seemed to justify his early opposition to the war in which, he predicted, France would 'be betrayed, thus defeated'. His strictures upon Brissot and the Girondins carried all the more weight because of these prescient warnings, and now that new military campaigns had to be fought and Danton appeared to be lost in his web of ineffective diplomacy, Robespierre came forward as the man of the hour. He possessed a truly Machiavellian skill, so one of his rivals said, 'in dividing men and sowing differences between them, of enticing others to test the ground for him and then either abandoning them or supporting them as prudence or ambition dictated'. Some held it against him that he was never to be seen when the Revolution needed a *journée* and men and women took to the streets. The Girondins, taking note of the fact that he played no part in that momentous day of 10 August when the *sans-culottes* attacked the Tuileries, accused him of having hidden in a cellar. And it was also remarked that on the day the King was guillotined he remained in his sparsely furnished room in the Rue Saint-Honoré; that he asked the Duplays to close the shutters and the gates; and that he replied, when asked by the

daughters why he required this to be done, 'Because there is something that is going to take place today that it is not seemly that you
should see.' As Marat observed, 'Robespierre avoids any group
where there is unrest. He grows pale at the sight of a sabre.' All
the same, in the summer of 1793 he was recognized as being the
potential saviour of revolutionary France. He was still an unin-
spiring orator, but there was something in his feline presence which
commanded respect and defied inattention.

Robespierre came slowly forward [recorded a man who heard him
speak at the Jacobin Club that year]. He was one of the few men who still
wore the clothes that had been in fashion before the Revolution. He
resembled a tailor of the *ancien régime* more than anything else ... His
delivery was slow and measured. His sentences were so long that every
time he stopped to raise his spectacles one supposed that he had finished,
but after looking slowly and intently over the audience in every part of
the room he would readjust his spectacles and then add some more phrases
to those sentences which were already of inordinate length ... It was
difficult to take one's own eyes off him.

Under Robespierre's persuasive leadership the Committee of
Public Safety began to prosecute the war against foreign enemies
and native rebels with effective vigour, but his Government had to
contend with powerful opponents inside Paris as well as beyond its
walls. The Insurrectionary Committee which had organized the
journées of 29 May to 2 June had been successfully dissolved as a
condition of the Government's offer to honour a promise of forty
sous a day as compensation for the *sans-culottes'* loss of wages during
the demonstrations. The *Enragés* who had been the guiding force
behind the Insurrectionary Committee were, however, still a
troublesome group. Both Varlet and Roux continued to castigate
the Government for its failure to attend to the needs of the poor,
for not stamping out speculation, and for declining to decree the
death penalty for hoarding.
'Why have you not climbed from the third to the ninth floor of
the houses of this revolutionary city?' Roux demanded, as he
harangued the Convention. 'You would have been moved by the
tears and sighs of an immense population without food and clothing,

brought to such distress and misery by speculation and hoarding, because the laws have been cruel to the poor, because they have been made only by the rich and for the rich ... You must not be afraid of the hatred of the rich – in other words, of the wicked. You must not be afraid to sacrifice political principle for the salvation of the people, which is the supreme law.'

Encouraged by the *Enragés*, crowds of people took the law into their own hands, protesting that while wages had increased, the cost of living had outpaced them, demanding cheaper wine, and a reduction in the cost of butter, which had more than doubled in price since 1790 and of soap, the price of which had almost quintupled. Grocers' and chandlers' shops were invaded and their owners forced to sell goods at what was considered a fair price. Worried by the spreading incidence of this *taxation populaire*, the Committee of Public Safety took action against Roux who was expelled from the Cordeliers Club, repeatedly mauled in the Jacobin press, and eventually disowned by his *section*. Yet, while Roux was successfully discredited and his influence irreparably damaged, other *Enragés* continued to attack the Committee of Public Safety, to demand price controls and more severe punishments for hoarders and counter-revolutionary suspects. Their influence was much increased after 13 July when a devoted adherent of the Girondins committed a murder.

This was Charlotte Corday, a tall, strong, mystical yet practical young woman from a noble but poor Norman family, a descendant of the dramatist, Corneille. She had been educated at a convent at Caen and had then gone to live with an aunt in whose house she studied Voltaire and Plutarch and those other authors whose works had exercised so profound an influence on the young Manon Roland. When, after the fall of the Girondins, several of their leaders fled to Normandy to advocate *fédéralisme*, she attended their meetings, fell under their influence, undertook to work for them in Paris and, without their knowledge, took it into her head to assassinate the man she held principally responsible for their fall, Jean Paul Marat.

On her arrival in Paris she took a room in the Hôtel de la Providence in the Rue des Vieux Augustins and wrote a letter to Marat: 'Citizen, I have just arrived from Caen. Your love for your native place doubtless makes you desirous of learning the events which have occurred in that part of the republic. I shall call at your house in about an hour. Have the goodness to receive me and give me a brief interview. I will put you in a condition to render great service to France.'

Marat refused to see her both on that occasion and when she called a second time with a promise to reveal important secrets and presenting herself as a victim of counter-revolutionary plots. But she persisted, calling for the third time at 30 Rue des Cordeliers on 13 July. She was 'dressed in a spotted négligé costume and wore a high hat with a black cockade and three rows of black braid,' according to Laurent Bas, who worked on *L'Ami du peuple* and was in Marat's office folding copies of the newspaper at the time. 'She descended from a hackney cab and asked to speak to Citizen Marat. She was carrying a fan in her hand. The *concierge* replied that he was not available at the moment. She said that this was the third time she had called and that it was most tiresome not to be admitted to him . . . Citizeness Marat then went to ask her brother if the person was to be admitted and Citizen Marat said she was.'

She came into the room with a sharp dinner-knife which she had bought the day before for two francs concealed in the bodice of her dress together with her baptismal certificate and a paper entitled '*Adresse aux Français*' which explained the political motives behind her intended deed. She found Marat lying in a high-walled copper bath wrapped in towels, for he could now only thus find relief from the pain and irritation of the skin disease which was slowly putrefying his flesh. She told him what was happening at Caen, giving him the names of men she said were working there against the Jacobins. He picked up a pen from the board upon which he had been writing and copied the names down, commenting, 'They shall soon all be guillotined.' At these words, Charlotte Corday took out her knife and plunged it into his chest, piercing the left lung and the aorta. At his cry of '*À moi, ma chère amie!*' his distraught mistress, Simone Évrard, rushed into the room and seeing the blood pouring from the wound, put her hand over it in an attempt to stop the flow. But Marat was already dead. His murderess calmly walked out of the room and, although she seems to have had no intention of escape,

Bas seized a chair and with it knocked her to the ground. She got up and he 'clutched her by the breasts, threw her down and struck her'. '*Je m'en fous!*' she cried. 'The deed is done; the monster is dead!'

To the jealous Robespierre's disgust, Marat was now the heroic martyr of the extreme Left. His coffin was followed by young girls in white dresses who strewed flowers upon it, by boys carrying branches of cypress, by deputations from the *sections*, and by Montagnards who displayed or affected the deepest sorrow. Some members of the Jacobin Club had his bust placed on a pedestal in the Convention; his heart was suspended in a porphry urn from the ceiling of the Cordeliers Club; his ashes were later given a place of honour in the Pantheon; his mistress, 'the widow Marat', was granted a pension. Streets, squares and no less than thirty-seven towns in various parts of France were renamed after him; poems and hymns were composed in his honour; in some schools children were told to make the sign of the cross when his name was mentioned. His portrait, 'Marat Assassinated', by a fellow-Montagnard, the ugly Jacques Louis David – who had voted for the death of the King, his former patron – was acknowledged to be one of the great masterpieces of the Revolution. The *Enragés* claimed him as their patron saint, founded newspapers with the titles which he had chosen for his own, and invoked his name in pressing their demands upon the government. And the Committee of Public Safety deemed it prudent to give way to some of these demands by introducing the death penalty for hoarders, allocating a large sum of money for the purchase of grain, and establishing warehouses in various parts of Paris for its storage.

The *Enragés* were not the only influential critics of the Committee of Public Safety. The Committee also had to contend with the followers of Danton, who, far from being a spent political force, had been elected President of the Convention a fortnight after losing his seat on the Committee of Public Safety. Perhaps in the hope that Robespierre would show himself incapable of exercising such a burdensome responsibility, Danton proposed that the Committee should now be given the omnipotence of a provisional Government of France backed by a grant of a hundred million *livres*. This proposal was rejected, but it was clear that the Dantonists were a strong and devious group whose activities could not be ignored.

Nor could the activities of another group which became known as the Hébertists after the editor of that extremist newspaper, *Le Père Duchesne*, which defamed the Queen and Madame Roland be ignored. Hébert, who considered himself ill-used by the Jacobin leadership which had failed to reward him for his help in the overthrow of the Girondins, presented himself to the Paris *sections* as the most eloquent supporter of radical proposals for the exemplary punishment of speculators, the round-up of suspects, stricter price controls, the purge of all noble officers still remaining in the army, and the trial of the Girondins and of the Queen.

Prodded and harassed by both Dantonists and Hébertists, the Committee of Public Safety became more zealous than ever in their conduct of the war against both foreign enemies and provincial rebels. General Custine was dismissed from his command, arraigned before the Revolutionary Tribunal and accused of having pitied Louis XVI, prevented the circulation of *Le Père Duchesne* in the army, denigrated Robespierre and Marat, 'surrounded himself with aristocratic officers and never had good republicans at his table'. He was sentenced to death and guillotined. General de Biron was also executed, while Pitt was execrated as 'the enemy of the human race'. The devastation of the Vendée was authorized; the federalist leaders were denounced as traitors, negotiations with them being abruptly terminated; troops were ordered to overthrow the royalist counterrevolutionaries in Lyons; the trial of the Queen was authorized; so was the arrest of all enemy aliens not resident in France on 14 July 1789. Then, following the election of Lazare Carnot to the Committee of Public Safety, the Convention called out the entire population of the country to fight for the Revolution in a *levée en masse.*

Carnot, the practical, unflaggingly energetic organizer of the Revolution's victory, had been a captain in the Engineers when elected to the National Assembly as a deputy for the Pas-de-Calais. Frequently employed as a military commissioner, he had displayed a remarkable talent for organization, exposition and detecting talent. Although still only a captain at forty, he was recognized as a brilliant soldier, capable of building an army of conscripts that could overcome the more carefully drilled and far more experienced forces of the old European powers. Carnot, of course, was well aware that general and total mobilization was not immediately practicable for it would be impossible either to train or equip so vast a host. The decree enforcing it was largely propagandist in intent. For the moment, therefore, only unmarried men and childless widowers between the ages of eighteen and twenty-five were recruited into the army. But the rest of the population, both male and female, were liable to be called up for any kind of work which was held to be conducive to the war effort, and funds were provided for the construction of armaments factories. A target was set for the manufacture of a thousand muskets a day.

From this moment until that when the enemy shall be driven from the territory of the French republic [ran a decree of 23 August], all the French people shall be in permanent requisition for the service of the armies. The young men will go forth to fight. The married men will forge the arms and transport the supplies. The women will make tents and clothes and act as nurses in the hospitals. The children will make lint from rags. The old men will be carried to the public places to excite the courage of the warriors, to preach hatred of kings and love of the republic.

Yet, vigorous and determined as Carnot, Robespierre and the other members of the Committee of Public Safety were now proving themselves to be, the Dantonists and Hébertists still loudly voiced the popular complaints which were exacerbated in the late summer by another bread shortage caused by a severe and lengthy drought. And at the beginning of September a march upon the Hôtel de Ville of workers demanding bread and higher wages was seized upon by Hébert as an opportunity to bring pressure to bear upon the Committee. He asked the workers to gather together the next day, 5 September, to march to the Convention.

The march took place as planned. Hundreds of demonstrators invaded the Convention, milling around the table upon which the stillborn Constitution lay enshrined in a case and gazing up at the canvases on either side of the President's seat which depicted the murders of Marat and of Lepeletier de Saint-Fargeau, an enormously rich former President of the Convention whose assassination had also been portrayed by David.

Demonstrators and Jacobin deputies vied with each other in the advocacy of radical policies and the expression of *sans-culotte* sentiments. A representative of the Commune, crying, 'No more quarter, no more mercy for traitors ... the day of justice and wrath has arrived', called for the immediate creation of a revolutionary army. Danton, endorsing a decree already passed for the arrest of suspects and the intensification of repression, aroused loud cheers as he paid 'homage' to the 'sublime people' and demanded that every citizen should be given a musket, that a minimum of a hundred million *livres* should be voted for the manufacture of armaments and that working men who could not afford to attend the meeting of their *sections* should be compensated for their loss of wages whenever they did so. A delegation from the Jacobin Club, in which Hébertists were now dominant, proposed that '*Terreur* be the order of the day'.

The Convention gave way to nearly all of the Hébertists' demands. On 6 September the extremist deputies, Billaud-Varenne and the equally ruthless Jean-Marie Collot d'Herbois, an actor and playwright, were both admitted to the Committee of Public Safety. Soon afterwards prices were fixed by the *maximum général*. And by the middle of the month arrangements had been made for the arrest of all 'suspects' by a law which at last established their identity and included among their number even those who were no more than passively opposed to the Revolution, or who had not been able to obtain 'certificates of good citizenship' from the notoriously prejudiced and corrupt Vigilance Committees of their *sections*. The guillotine was soon given much more work to do.

THE DAYS OF THE TERROR

October–December 1793 and March–July 1794

'*It is a falsehood to say that the Terror saved France,*
but it may be affirmed
that it crippled the Revolution'

LOUIS BLANC

The Queen was one of the first to suffer. At the beginning of July she had been told that she was to be parted from her son.

My mother was horrified by this cruel order [her daughter recorded] and refused to give him up. She defended his bed against the men who had come to take him away. But they insisted on taking him and threatened to use force and to send for the guard ... We got him up and when he was dressed my mother handed him over, crying over him, as if she knew she would never see him again. The poor little fellow kissed us all tenderly and departed in tears with the men ... My mother felt she had reached the depths of misery now ... and her misery was increased when she knew that the shoemaker [Antoine] Simon was in charge of him ... He cried for two whole days inconsolably and begged to see us ... We often went up into the tower. My brother went by every day and the only pleasure my mother had was to watch him pass by through a little window. Sometimes she waited there for hours to get a glimpse of her beloved child ... Every day we heard him and Simon singing the Carmagnole, the Marseillaise and many other horrid songs. Simon made him wear a red bonnet and a carmagnole jacket and forced him to sing at the windows so as to be heard by the guard and to blaspheme God and curse his family and the aristocrats. My mother fortunately did not hear all these horrors as she had been taken away [to the Conciergerie prison on the Île Saint Louis].

At the Conciergerie the Queen was kept in a small, damp cell containing three beds, one for herself, another for a female attendant and the third for two gendarmes who, so Count Fersen recorded, 'never left the cell even when the Queen had to satisfy the needs of nature'. She spent her time reading such books as *A History of Famous Shipwrecks*, crocheting pieces of thread which she picked from the cloth screens that lined the walls of the cell, or pacing about between the beds as she twisted the rings on her fingers. Towards the middle of September, after the failure of an attempt to release her, she was moved into an even smaller cell, a dark room, formerly the prison dispensary and still smelling of medicines, whose only light during the hours of darkness came from a lantern in the courtyard beyond the barred window. She spent three weeks here before being taken to her trial in the bare marble hall of the Paris *parlement* from which the tapestries and the carpet with its pattern of fleurs-de-lis had been removed. Here she was accused of a variety of crimes from conspiracy with her brother to incest with her son whom, it was alleged, she had taught to masturbate. When roughly called upon to answer these accusations, she replied, 'If I give no answer it is because nature itself refuses to accept such an accusation brought against a mother. I appeal to all the mothers here present.' There was an obvious wave of sympathy for her after this spirited response. But the President angrily threatened to clear the court; the processes of the trial were speeded up and she was found guilty and condemned to death. 'Having heard the sentence pronounced', the *Moniteur* reported, 'she left the court without addressing a further word to the judges or the public, no trace of emotion appearing on her face.'

On the morning of 16 October she dressed herself for the last time in a white piqué dress, white bonnet, black stockings and red prunella high-heeled shoes. Charles Sanson's son, Henri, came into the cell to tie her hands behind her back. Then, having removed her bonnet, he cut off her hair, which she had dressed with care for her trial the day before, and put it into his pocket. Outside, a tumbril was waiting. At the sight of it she began to tremble and had to have her hands untied so that she could relieve herself in a corner of the courtyard wall. But, once seated in the cart, she regained her composure. Pale and drawn, with sunken cheeks and weary eyes, 'the widow Capet', as the *Moniteur* referred to her, remained staring silently ahead of her throughout the long journey to the scaffold. Having climbed the steps she stumbled and trod on the executioner's foot. 'Monsieur,' she apologized as he cried out in pain, 'I beg your pardon. I did not do it on purpose.' They were the last words she spoke.

That same month Brissot, Vergniaud and nineteen other Girondin leaders were also put on trial. They defended themselves so skilfully that Hébert angrily complained, 'Need there be so much ceremony about shortening the lives of wretches already condemned by the people?' But they were, without exception, condemned to death. Four of them were in their twenties; their average age was forty. One of the older of them, Valazé, stabbed himself to death in court with a dagger which he had concealed under his coat; yet it was decreed that his corpse should nevertheless be carted next morning to the guillotine and there beheaded with the others.

The morning was fine and an immense crowd collected to see them pass through the streets on their way to the Place de la Révolution. The houses on either side were decorated as if for a festival with tricolours flying from the windows and coloured placards bearing such inscriptions as 'unity, liberty, equality, fraternity or death', for it had become dangerous, so one Parisian said, 'to be considered less revolutionary than your neighbour'. As the condemned men passed beneath these gaily decorated windows in the five slowly moving carts they sang the Marseillaise, so the chronicler of their careers, Alphonse de Lamartine, tells us; and, on reaching the scaffold, jumped out to embrace each other, shouting, '*Vive la République!*' Sillery, the oldest of them, was the first to die. He mounted the steps, bowed to the spectators with grave courtesy, and walked steadily to the guillotine. The others, too, died bravely. Vergniaud, who had thrown away the poison with which he had been provided the night before so that he could die with his friends, was the last to climb the steps. His head was cut off precisely thirty-one minutes after Sillery's.

During the next few weeks the blade of the guillotine fell and rose in what Thomas Carlyle was to call relentless systole-diastole. On 6 November, Philippe Egalité, the former Duc d'Orléans, who was brought back from Marseilles, was tried and condemned before the Revolutionary Tribunal. Accepting the verdict without protest, he merely asked for a stay of execution for twenty-four hours. The request was granted and 'in the interval he had a repast prepared with care, on which he feasted with more than usual avidity'. Distrusted and unlamented, he died with a smile on his lips, displaying no sign of fear. On 8 November Madame Roland was also condemned to death. She had been arrested at home at the beginning of June, separated from her weeping daughter and lodged in the prison of the Abbaye from which she was released when Brissot was sent there, re-arrested immediately and taken to the Sainte-Pélagie and thence to the Conciergerie. Without news of her fugitive husband to whom, despite his recent cantankerous jealousy, she was deeply attached, or of François Buzot, the Girondin, with whom she had fallen passionately in love, constantly worried about her daughter and dismayed by the collapse of all that she had worked for, she nevertheless retained her spirit and dignity to the end, gaining the admiration of her captors as well as of her fellow-prisoners. At her trial she responded bravely to the inquisitors who bullied her unmercifully, who insisted that she reply yes or no to their questions, accused her of loquacity when she attempted a more detailed answer, and told her that she was 'not there to be clever'. She sometimes wept when questions were asked about her private life and her relations with Girondins other than her husband, but she never broke down and refused to admit any guilt or to compromise her friends, declaring defiantly when sentence was passed upon her, 'You judge me worthy to share the fate of the great men whom you have assassinated. I shall endeavour to carry to the scaffold the courage they displayed.'

She succeeded in doing so. While the mob surrounded the cart, shouting, ' *À la guillotine! À la guillotine!*', she tried to comfort a frightened forger who sat beside her. And on arrival at the scaffold she asked the executioner to behead him first so that he would be spared the spectacle of her death. The executioner declined: it was against the rules. But she pleaded with him, and he gave way. When it was time for her to be bound to the plank, she looked up at the statue of Liberty, which had been erected in the Place de la Révolution in commemoration of the events of 10 August, and uttered her famous apostrophe, 'Oh Liberty, what crimes are committed in your name.'

Three days later the former Mayor of Paris, Jean-Sylvain Bailly, who had been arrested while staying with a friend at Melun, was escorted on foot to the Champ de Mars so that he might be executed on the spot of the massacre of 17 July 1791 for which he was held responsible. But on his arrival there a man, who had shaken a red flag in his face throughout the walk from the Conciergerie, shouted that the place which had been the scene of so many revolutionary celebrations should not be polluted by the former mayor's blood. So, while Bailly walked about the Champ de Mars, insulted by people who threw mud at him, kicked him and struck him with sticks, the guillotine was dismantled and carried off to a dunghill by the banks of the Seine where, surrounded by a howling mob, he was beheaded in sight of the quarter of Chaillot where he had once lived.

Later that month Barnave, who had retired to his birthplace at Grenoble and been arrested there, was also brought back to Paris after ten months' imprisonment for trial and execution. And so, day after day, the guillotinings continued. Unsuccessful generals suffered with fallen politicians, men convicted of publishing counter-revolutionary writings or of airing royalist opinions with deserters and traitors. Even the faded courtesan, Madame Du Barry, who had gone to live in the country with the Comte de Cossé-Brissac and had visited England in 1792 to try to raise money on her jewels, was dragged before the Revolutionary Tribunal. Accused of having dissipated the treasures of the state and worn 'mourning for the tyrant' in London, she was condemned and, screaming with fright, beheaded. She was followed to the scaffold by eight Carmelite nuns.

Throughout the autumn and winter of 1793 the Terror was maintained unabated. The Committee of Public Safety insisted that it was vitally necessary to stamp out the machinations of both royalists and federalists, hoping thereby to persuade the militant *sans-culottes* that they shared a common cause and the Convention that the omnipotence of the Committee was essential at a time of crisis in the Revolution's course. Nearly 3,000 executions took place in Paris; about 14,000 in the provinces. Countless people lived in constant fear of death and went to bed dreading the sound of a knock on the door in the middle of the night when most arrests took place.

'You have no more grounds for restraint against the enemies of the new order, and liberty must prevail at any price,' cried Saint-Just, who, like Robespierre, 'regarded all dissidents as criminals'. 'We must rule by iron those who cannot be ruled by justice . . . You must punish not merely traitors but the indifferent as well.' An even more violent Jacobin, Brichet, advised that the Law of Suspects should be interpreted so that all the well-to-do came within its scope: questions should be asked in every village about the means of the principal farmer; if he were rich he should be guillotined without further ado – he was 'bound to be a food-hoarder'. But it was not only the rich, or even mainly the rich, who suffered. The poor were executed with the well-to-do, women with men, the young with the old, some accused of 'starving the people', others of 'depraving public morals', one witness for 'not giving his testimony properly'. 'The whole of the country seemed one vast conflagration of revolt and vengeance,' wrote William Hazlitt in a passage characteristic of English writers of his time and temperament. 'The shrieks of death were blended with the yell of the assassin and the laughter of buffoons. Never were the finest affections more warmly excited or pierced with more cruel wounds. Whole families were led to the scaffold for no other crime than their relationship; sisters for shedding tears over the death of their brothers in the emigrant armies; wives for lamenting the fate of their husbands; innocent peasant girls for dancing with the Prussian soldiers; and a woman giving suck, and whose milk spouted in the face of her executioner at the fatal stroke, for merely saying as a group were being conducted to slaughter, "Here is much blood shed for a trifling cause." '

If such accounts must be considered overpitched, and if many families – in several parts of the country most families – lived through these months in undisturbed tranquillity, the *Liste Générale des Condamnés* provides numerous examples of the Terror's merciless severity:

Jean Baptiste Henry, aged eighteen, journeyman tailor, convicted of having sawed down a tree of liberty, executed 6 September 1793 ... Jean Julien, waggoner, having been sentenced to twelve years' hard labour, took it into his head to cry '*Vive le Roi*', brought back to the Tribunal and condemned to death ... Stephen Thomas Ogie Baulny, aged forty-six, convicted of having entrusted his son, aged fourteen, to a *garde du corps* in order that he might emigrate, condemned to death and executed the same day ... Henriette Françoise de Marboeuf, aged fifty-five, widow of the *ci-devant* Marquis de Marboeuf, convicted of having hoped for the arrival of the Austrians and Prussians and of keeping provisions for them, condemned to death and executed the same day ... François Bertrand, aged thirty-seven, publican at Leure in the department of the Côte-d'Or, convicted of having furnished to the defenders of the country sour wine injurious to health, condemned to death at Paris and executed the same day ... Marie Angelique Plaisant, sempstress at Douai, convicted of having exclaimed that she was an aristocrat and that she did not care 'a fig for the nation', condemned to death at Paris and executed the same day.

Hundreds of innocent people suffered with those whom the Revolutionary Tribunal had some cause to consider guilty, some of them through clerical and administrative errors, or even because their accusers chose not to spare them. Others were sentenced on the strength of denunciations by jealous or vindictive neighbours. One victim was fetched from prison to face a charge which had been brought against another prisoner with a similar name. Her protests were silenced by the prosecutor who said casually, 'Since she's here, we might just as well take her.' Another who had lost his temper while playing cards and, when reprimanded for behaving as no good patriot should, had shouted, 'Fuck good patriots!' was also brought before the Tribunal, condemned and executed.

The worst excesses were committed in the provinces where – although most *représentants en mission* were more concerned with enlisting recruits and collecting supplies than with punishment – in several towns the guillotine was kept constantly at work and those convicted of crimes against the Revolution were slaughtered whole-sale on the instructions of fanatical or savage representatives or of those who were frightened of being considered too weak. At Lyons where numerous rich men's houses were blown up, including those in Mansart's lovely Place Bellecour, Collot d'Herbois, who had been sent there as the Committee of Public Safety's agent, and Joseph Fouché, a frail former teacher who had become one of the most dreaded of the Jacobins, decided that the guillotine was too slow an instrument for their purpose and had over three hundred of their victims mown down by cannon fire. 'What a delicious moment!' reported an approving witness to a friend in Paris. 'How you would have enjoyed it! . . . What a sight! Worthy indeed of Liberty! . . . Wish *bon jour* to Robespierre.'

From Feurs, the representative himself reported, 'The butchery has been good.' At Toulon numerous victims were shot by order of Paul Barras, a tall, cunning former army officer of noble birth who was a cousin of the Marquis de Sade, and Louis Fréron, founder of the inflammatory journal, *L'Orateur du peuple*. At Nantes, where the Committee's agent was the thirty-six-year-old Jean-Baptiste Carrier, an obscure attorney before the Revolution, three thousand captives perished in an epidemic in the grossly overcrowded prisons and a further two thousand were towed out in barges into the middle of the Loire and drowned, some of them stripped naked and bound together in couples. The river became so choked with these barges that ships weighing anchor brought them up filled with the dead. Birds of prey hovered over the waters, gorging themselves with human flesh, and the fish became so contaminated that orders had to be given forbidding them to be caught. On occasions Carrier appeared to be insane as, raving endlessly about the need to 'kill and kill', and to 'butcher children without hesitation', he slashed at the air with his sword. Even in his calmer moments he was abusive and intolerant, answering all complaints and pleas for mercy with the threat that those who approached him would themselves be thrown into prison.

In the north the *représentant en mission* was Joseph le Bon, a former priest of twenty-nine, who fixed his headquarters at Arras. From Arras he travelled about the departments of the Somme and the Pas-de-Calais with his judges and guillotine, leaving a trail of blood in his wake, 'in a kind of fever', so his secretary reported, returning home to imitate the grimaces of the dying for the benefit of his wife. Assiduously attending all the executions he could, he addressed both victims and spectators from a nearby balcony, ordered bands to play the *Ça ira* as at a festival, and afterwards invited the executioner to dinner.

Under the direction of Jean Tallien, the son of the *maître d'hôtel* of the Marquis de Bercy, a young man of twenty-six who had worked as a lawyer's clerk and in a printer's office, even more cruel punishments were inflicted at Bordeaux.

The most terrible atrocities were committed there [according to the thin, little, awkward Girondin, Jean Baptiste Louvet]. A woman was charged with the heinous crime of having wept at the execution of her husband. She was consequently condemned to sit several hours under the suspended blade which shed upon her, drop by drop, the blood of the

deceased whose corpse was above her on the scaffold before she was released by death from her agony.

'The time has come which was foretold,' as Madame Roland had
said, 'when the people would ask for bread and be given corpses.'

In Paris thousands of people went out regularly to witness the
operations of what the deputy, J. A. B. Amar, called the 'red Mass'
performed on the 'great altar' of the 'holy guillotine'. They took
their seats around the scaffold with the *tricoteuses*, buying wine and
biscuits from hawkers while they waited for the show to begin. They
placed bets as to the order in which the *huissiers* from the Revolutionary Tribunal, who wore silver chains round their necks, would
decide the prisoners were to mount the scaffold, anticipating those
three thrilling sounds – the first thud as the victim was thrown on to
the plank, the second thud as the neck clamp was thrown into place,
and the swishing rattle as the heavy blade fell. Yet there were
thousands more who, like Madame Roland, had become 'sick of
blood'. Shops were shut and windows closed in the Rue Saint-
Honoré as the tumbrils passed by on their way to the Place de la
Révolution, some by those who had grown tired of the spectacle,
many by others who were disgusted by it. So, following complaints
from the residents of the Rue Saint-Honoré that the smell of stale
blood which rose from the stones of the nearby square was en-
dangering their health and depreciating the value of their property,
the guillotine was removed first to a site near the ruins of the Bastille, then to an open space near the Barrière du Trône Renversé, now
the Place de la Nation. But the people in these districts were as unwilling to have the guillotine in their midst as were those of the
Rue Saint-Honoré. The scaffold was therefore taken back once more
to the Place de la Révolution where Louis XVI had died.

While prisoners captured in the civil wars, suspected federalist
agents, counter-revolutionaries and those accused of currency mani-
pulation or food hoarding were all dispatched in the 'red Mass', a

campaign was simultaneously mounted against Christianity. For some time now the more ardent revolutionaries had been encouraging anti-clerical feelings among the people and endeavouring to endow the Revolution itself with the aura of a religion. They had condemned the celibacy of the clergy. They had joined with the Montagnard, Delacroix, in denouncing the action of a bishop who had prevented one of his *curés* from marrying as a 'blasphemy against the sovereignty of the people'. And they had even supported demands for the demolition of church belfries, 'which by their height above other buildings seem to contradict the principles of equality'. They had also welcomed the custom of giving babies names untainted with Christian associations, and of changing the names of streets, which were called after saints or festivals of the Church, to those of heroes, *journées* or symbols of the Revolution.

This campaign was initiated in the Nièvre where Fouché was Commissioner of the Republic. In September Fouché had had a visit from Pierre Chaumette, a former medical student born at Nevers, a young man of a rather strait-laced disposition and homosexual inclinations who had been one of the most eloquent speakers at the Cordeliers Club and an outspoken opponent of the Girondins. Inspired or encouraged by Chaumette, Fouché immediately instituted a programme of de-Christianization in the district for which he was held responsible. On 22 September in the church of Saint-Cyr at Nevers he preached a sermon attacking 'religious sophistry' and unveiled a bust of Brutus. Later, in his avowed determination to substitute the 'cult of the Republic' for 'the superstition and hypocrisy' of Christianity, he had ecclesiastical vestments burned, crucifixes and crosses destroyed, church ornaments and vessels confiscated and notices posted outside cemeteries to the effect that, 'Death is an eternal sleep.' Denouncing the celibacy of priests, he ordered them all either to marry, to adopt a child or look after an elderly person. He eventually succeeded in obtaining the resignation of the Bishop of Allier and some thirty of the clergy in his diocese.

On his return to Paris at the end of the month, Chaumette, supported by Hébert, demanded a similar programme of de-Christianization in the capital. His demands, while making a strong appeal to the anti-clericalists in the radical *sections*, were not at first received with much enthusiasm elsewhere. But the ground had to some extent been prepared for Chaumette's campaign by the Convention's resolve to replace the Gregorian calendar with one which would emphasize the Republic's association with Nature and Reason rather than with traditional Christianity. The dawn of the new era, Year one of the Republic, had already been declared as having begun with the abolition of the monarchy on 22 September 1792. That year, and all subsequent years, were now to be divided into twelve months of thirty days each, with the five days left at the end of the year to be known as *sans-culottides* and to be celebrated as festivals. The task of compiling the new calendar was entrusted to Philippe Fabre, who called himself Fabre d'Églantine, a former actor and – like so many other revolutionary figures – a not very successful writer who had once been Danton's secretary. He decided that the months, which were to be divided into three *décades* of ten days' each, should be named after the seasons: the first three, as autumnal seasons, were to be known as *Vendémiaire*, *Brumaire* and *Frimaire;* the next three, those of winter, as *Nivôse*, *Pluviôse* and *Ventôse;* the three of spring, as *Germinal*, *Floréal* and *Prairial;* and the three of summer as *Messidor*, *Thermidor* and *Fructidor*. In addition, Fabre suggested the names of saints in the calendar should be replaced by those of fruits, plants and flowers. Since religious holidays were abolished and Sundays were no longer a day of rest, these changes were naturally displeasing to the clergy, many of whom refused to celebrate Mass on the new Sabbath, as well as to the devout members of their flocks. Nor were they universally popular with the workers who now had to make do with a holiday every ten days instead of every seven. Directed by Hébert and Chaumette, and supported outside the Commune by Fabre d'Églantine, whose disdainful manner and affectation of a lorgnette exasperated Robespierre, the de-Christianization campaign nevertheless soon gained momentum in Paris. Religious monuments outside churches were destroyed; various religious ceremonies were suppressed; ecclesiastical plate and other treasures were seized in the name of the people; images of the madonna were replaced by busts of Marat; surplices were cut up to make bandages and soldiers' shirts; and it was henceforth forbidden to sell in the streets 'any kinds of superstitious jugglery such as holy napkins, St Veronica's handkerchiefs, Ecce Homos, crosses, Agnus Deis, rings of St Hubert or any medicinal waters or other adulterated drugs'. Theatres began to offer such plays as *L'Inauguration du Temple de la Vérité* in which a parody of the High Mass was performed.

Jean-Baptiste Gobel, Archbishop of Paris since 1791, a weak, rather absurd figure who had achieved favour with the Hébertists and atheists by adopting the dress of the *sans-culottes*, expressing anti-clerical opinions and opposing the celibacy of the clergy, was intimidated into coming before the Convention with his mitre in his hand and a red cap on his head, declaring, 'Born a man of the people, *curé* of Porentruy, sent by the clergy to the Estates General, then raised to the Archbishopric of Paris, I have never ceased to obey the people. I accepted the functions which the people formerly bestowed on me and now, in obedience to the wishes of the people, I have come here to resign them. I allowed myself to be made a bishop when the people wanted bishops. I cease to be one now when the people no longer want them.'

That same week, a few days before the Commune ordered the closure of all churches in the city, a grand Festival of Reason was celebrated in Nôtre Dame. A young actress was carried into the cathedral by four citizens to represent the Goddess of Reason. Clothed in white drapery with a blue cloak over her shoulders and a red cap of liberty crowning her long hair, she was accompanied by a troupe of girls also dressed in white with roses on their heads. She sat on an ivy-covered chair while speeches were made, songs were sung, and soldiers paraded about the aisles carrying busts of Marat, Lepeletier and other martyrs of the Revolution. Later another young woman, the wife of Momoro, a printer who was a prominent member of the Commune, played the principal part in a similar festival at Saint-Sulpice.

From Paris the de-Christianization movement spread all over France. Not only streets and squares but towns and villages confusingly changed their names. The bestowal on babies of revolutionary first names became more common in certain districts than those of saints. More and more cathedrals and churches were deprived of their ornaments, vessels and plate; some were converted into Temples of Reason, others closed. Many clergy resigned and a number married. One even had himself ritually divorced from his breviary. The rites and processions in which the clergy had played their parts were parodied by local revolutionaries wearing vestments and mitres, employing croziers as drum-majors' staffs, and making obeisances to the prettiest girl in the community who was paraded for the day as Goddess of Reason. In Paris people 'danced before the sanctuary, howling the *carmagnole*,' according to a contemporary witness, Sébastien Mercier. 'The men wore no breeches; and the necks and breasts of the women were bare. In their wild whirling they imitated those whirlwinds which, foreshadowing tempests, ravage and destroy all within their path. In the darkness of the sacristy they satisfied those abominable desires that had been aroused in them.'

A reaction, however, soon became apparent. Catholicism, deeply inbred, could not be eradicated. Priests who married were as likely to be scorned as those who had earlier taken the Constitutional oath. Numerous parishes demanded the reopening of their churches, the return of their bells and altar furniture, and the reintroduction of their festivals. Everywhere there were fears that local calamities were acts of God who was roused in anger by France's blasphemy and atheism. At Coulanges-la-Vineuse in the Yonne a hailstorm that threatened crops induced the frightened peasants to enter the church which the revolutionaries had closed, to sing hymns, ring bells and pray for forgiveness and mercy.

Concerned by the unrest and dissension which the ruthless policies of de-Christianization were arousing in France, and anxious to reassert its central authority over the extremist deputies who were fanatically pursuing these policies in the provinces, the Committee of Public Safety now initiated a series of decrees intended to bring provincial agents more securely under its control. Several of these agents were recalled to Paris, while others returned of their own accord in order to defend themselves against the accusations of Robespierre who forcefully condemned their atheistic measures as liable to benefit the counter-revolutionaries. Danton also returned to Paris to lend his support to Robespierre.

For some weeks Danton, who had fallen ill in the summer, had been living quietly in the country at Arcis-sur-Aube where he had bought more land. Here, his convalescence complete and in one of his intermittent moods of indolence, he was enjoying the pleasures of country life, fishing in the Aube, going out shooting with the *curé*, relishing his food and wine and making love to the attractive, sixteen-year-old girl he had married as his second wife. He had been pleased to be out of Paris when Marie Antoinette and the Girondins had been executed, and had, it was said, reacted furiously when a neighbour passed on to him the 'good news' of the death of his 'factious enemies'. 'You wretch!' he had exclaimed. 'You call that good news! . . . You call them *factious*! Aren't we all? We deserve death as much as the Girondins and we shall suffer the same fate one after the other.' He returned to the capital with evident reluctance. It was no longer safe for him to stay away. He must be where he could exercise some influence over events in which, whether he liked it or not, he was bound to be implicated.

Ever since he had been away the political scene in Paris had been growing ever more confused and ever more embittered by rivalries and accusations of corruption, some invented, others true. One deputy, who had also been out of Paris that autumn, returned in the middle of November to find the Convention so changed that his 'head swam' and he could 'scarcely recognize' any of his colleagues. 'In the place of the Mountain,' he wrote, 'I found a swarm of rival factions that dared not fight each other in the open but waged underground war.'

Danton immediately plunged into the war himself, counter-attacking Hébert whose assaults on the Dantonists had been growing in intensity, allying himself with Robespierre in his offensive against the *Enragés* in the Jacobin Club and roundly condemning the outrages of the militant atheists as though speaking on behalf of the Oratorian fathers who had taught him as a boy, and of both his beloved and religious wives. In the Convention it might have been Robespierre speaking when Danton called for the introduction of national religious festivals. 'If Greece had its Olympic Games,' he said, 'France too will celebrate its *jours sans-culottides*. The people will have festivals where they will offer up incense to the Supreme

Being, Nature's master, for it was never our intention to destroy religion so that atheism could take its place.'

Turning upon the Hébertists, he asked the Convention why they wasted their time on such creatures. 'The people are sick to death of them ... Perhaps the Terror once served a useful purpose, but it should not hurt innocent people. No one wants to see a person treated as a criminal just because he happens not to have enough revolutionary enthusiasm.'

Danton's open advocacy of toleration in religion and moderation in politics, his declared belief that the time had come to be 'sparing of human blood', and his support of the *Indulgents* appeared at first to be decisive. By the middle of December the Convention was persuaded to establish a Committee of Clemency whose members were to examine the lists of suspects recently thrown into prison. But Hébert and his colleagues counter-attacked vigorously. Collot d'Herbois hurried home from Lyons to speak with passionate fervour in the Jacobin Club. Hébert and Billaud-Varenne joined him there to second his condemnation of the Dantonists. Their supporters in the Convention succeeded in suppressing the Committee of Clemency, and soon afterwards most of the Hébertists who had been arrested on 20 December were released. By then, however, Robespierre had become convinced that Danton's reasons for supporting him in his quarrel with the Hébertists were not all that they seemed. Danton, he suspected, had wanted to exacerbate the quarrel so as to deprive the Committee of Public Safety of the support of the *sans-culottes* and thus, by dividing his enemies, to protect his friends and himself from their righteous animosity. Robespierre, therefore, determined to destroy both Hébertists and Dantonists alike.

The Hébertists were dealt with first. This did not prove difficult. Among their number were several men whose foreign origin enabled Robespierre to accuse them of complicity in a 'foreign plot'; and when they planned to stage a *journée* on the lines of the *Enragés'* demonstration outside the Convention in June 1793, they were able to enlist little enthusiasm in the *sections* and were deserted at the last moment by both Collot d'Herbois and Billaud-Varenne. The planned *journée* gave the Committee of Public Safety an excuse to act. On 14 March 1794 Hébert and his associates were all arrested, and less than a fortnight later eighteen of them were condemned to death. Hébert fainted repeatedly on his way to the guillotine.

By then the Committee of Public Safety had also decided to take action against the *Indulgents* among whom they included both Danton and Camille Desmoulins. Overcome by remorse at the part he had played in the downfall of the Girondins, Desmoulins had burst into tears when they were executed. He had since infuriated Robespierre by declaring in an obvious reference to him, 'Love of country cannot exist when there is neither pity nor love for one's fellow countrymen but only a soul dried up and withered by self-adulation.' The Committee had already imprisoned Fabre d'Églantine who had become entangled in some corrupt financial transactions.

Robespierre, while persuaded that Fabre's corruption was proof of his treason, would have chosen to spare Desmoulins of whom he was fond. He would also have spared Danton, but Danton had made dangerous enemies. Both Saint-Just and Billaud-Varenne constantly decried him as a traitor. 'A man is guilty of a crime against the Republic,' declared Saint-Just, 'when he takes pity on prisoners. He is guilty because he has no desire for virtue. He is guilty because he is opposed to the Terror.' At the same time, Marc-Guillaume Vadier, a vindictive lawyer, ardent Jacobin and influential member of the Committee of General Security which dealt with police matters, had boasted that his Committee would soon get that 'fat stuffed turbot', Danton. Hearing of Vadier's threat, Danton had responded with characteristically scatological force: if his own life were threatened he would become 'more cruel than any cannibal'; he would eat Vadier's brains and 'shit in his skull'. But Danton did not really believe that his life was in danger any more than he meant to be taken seriously when he threatened Vadier. He had always said that he was invulnerable, and, up till the very moment of his arrest, he supposed that Robespierre would stand by him and that Robespierre's reputation would save him.

Yet Robespierre, reluctant as he was to sacrifice him and well aware that Danton's death would leave him isolated, persuaded himself that the *Indulgents* were agents of counter-revolution and accepted the unwelcome fact that Danton would have to be arrested and tried with them. His attitude towards Danton had always been equivocal: there were times when he expressed his admiration for him and seemed even to like him. But Danton's patent sexuality and coarse masculinity disturbed him – as it disturbed Madame Roland – and often shocked him. Once, during a heated discussion, Robespierre had exasperated Danton by his constant references to 'Virtue'. 'I'll tell you what this Virtue you talk about really is,' Danton said to him mockingly, 'It's what I do to my wife every night!' The remark obviously rankled with Robespierre who recorded it in his notebook and afterwards commented, 'Danton derides the word Virtue as though it were a joke. How can a man with so little conception of morality ever be a champion of freedom?'

On 22 March he met Danton for the last time at a dinner party. 'Let us forget our private resentments,' Danton said to him during the course of the evening, 'and think only of the country, its needs and dangers.' For a moment Robespierre did not reply. Then he asked sardonically, 'I suppose a man of *your* moral principles would not think that anyone deserved punishment.' 'I suppose *you* would be annoyed,' Danton riposted, 'if none did.' 'Liberty,' said Robespierre coldly, 'cannot be secured unless criminals lose their heads.' Despite this exchange, Danton made as if to embrace Robespierre when he left. But Robespierre pulled away from him in distaste.

A few days later they saw each other at the Théâtre Français.

Robespierre was in a box [an observer who was also in the audience that night recorded]. Danton was in the front stalls. When the words 'Death to the tyrant!' were declaimed on the stage [the play being performed was the tragedy, *Epicharis and Nero*] Danton's friends burst into wild applause and standing up they turned towards Robespierre and shook their fists at him. Robespierre, pale and nervous, pushed his little clerk's face forward and then pulled it back in the way a snake reacts. He waved his little hand in a gesture indicative of both fright and menace.

The decision to arrest Danton was taken at a joint meeting of the Committees of Public Safety and General Security on the night of 30 March after Robespierrists had been nominated to all the important posts in the Commune which had been vacated by the defeated

Hébertists. Saint-Just, Robespierre's pale, handsome, cold-blooded disciple, the 'Angel of Death' – upon whose lucid brain and incisive pen his master had come to depend in times like these – produced a document denouncing Danton which he intended to read out in the Convention the next morning. It was objected that this was too risky a procedure, Danton being still so popular a character in the Convention, and that he and the other leading *Indulgents* would have to be arrested first, whereupon Saint-Just, displaying some emotion for once, petulantly tossed his hat into the fire. Robespierre agreed with Saint-Just that Danton ought to be denounced in the Convention before his arrest, but he did not press the point after Vadier said, 'You can run the danger of being guillotined if you like, but I'm not going to.'

The warrant for Danton's arrest was placed on the table and, one after the other, those present at the meeting took up a pen to sign it. Only two of them refused, Ruhl, an Alsatian who protested that he could not betray an old friendship, and Robert Lindet, the Committee of Public Safety's hard-working administrator of food supplies, who bluntly said that his job was to 'feed citizens not put patriots to death'. Carnot afterwards claimed that he warned his colleagues, 'We must consider the consequences well before we do this. A head like Danton's will drag down many others after it.' But he signed the paper with the rest. And so, in the early hours of the following morning, warrants were issued for the arrest of Danton together with several of his associates and some foreigners whose financial crimes would conveniently serve to muddy the issues and discredit the political prisoners.

Warned of his impending arrest, Danton had sat up all night by the fire in his study on the first floor of his house in the Cour du Commerce. He had rejected all suggestions that he should try to escape abroad. 'A man,' he said, 'cannot carry his country away with him on the soles of his shoes.' Nor would he consider fighting back at his accusers: that would 'only mean the shedding of more blood' and there had been 'far too much blood shed already'. He would 'rather be guillotined than guillotine'. Besides, he was 'sick of men', and had not himself been guiltless. 'It was at this time of year,' he lamented, 'that I had the Revolutionary Tribunal set up. I pray to God and men to forgive me for it.'

So, when he heard the sounds of the patrol in the cobbled street outside he stood up with weary resignation and went to put his arms round his wife who was weeping helplessly. 'They are coming to arrest me,' he told her. 'Don't be frightened.' He walked down into the street and was taken up the hill to the prison of the Luxembourg.

There were some protests in the Convention later that day when Danton's arrest was announced but Robespierre, now committed to his downfall, turned angrily upon Legendre who had had the temerity to suggest that the accused was a victim of personal spite and that, having saved France in September 1792 'ought to be allowed to explain himself before the Convention'. No, objected Robespierre, he should not. 'The question is not whether a man has performed any particular patriotic act, but what his whole career has been like ... In what way is Danton superior to Lafayette, to Dumouriez, to Brissot, to Hébert? What is said of him that may not be said of them? And yet have you spared them? ... Vulgar minds and guilty men are always afraid to see their fellows fall because, having no longer a barrier of culprits before them, they are left exposed to the light of truth. But if there exist vulgar spirits, there are also heroic spirits in this Assembly and they will know how to brave all false terrors. Besides, the number of guilty is not great. Crime has found but few culprits among us, and by striking off a few heads the country will be delivered ... Whoever trembles at this moment is also guilty.'

After this speech and another by Saint-Just who read the indictment in a dull, toneless voice – emphasizing his points, so a fellow-deputy recorded, with a threatening, chopping gesture of his outstretched hand, 'a motion like that of the knife of the guillotine' – objectors were silenced and the trial of Danton, Desmoulins and the other accused was approved.

It opened on 2 April. As Danton well knew, the verdict had already been decided upon, even though most of the charges seemed to be directed more at his character than at any provable crimes, and much of the rest of the indictment might as convincingly have been laid against his accusers. The Public Prosecutor was Antoine Fouquier-Tinville.

Fouquier-Tinville was the son of a rich farmer from the Vermandois who had died when he was thirteen, leaving a widow extremely well provided for but disinclined to provide much financial assistance for her son whose early years were spent as an impoverished clerk in a procurator's office in Paris. By the time he was twenty-seven, however, Fouquier-Tinville had been able to buy the practice of his employer and, as a clever, conscientious lawyer, was soon successfully established. Married to a cousin who brought him a respectable dowry, he became the tenant of a handsome apartment in the Rue Bourbon-Villeneuve as well as of a country house at Charonne, the master of a cook and a *valet de chambre*, and the father of five children. Having given birth to these five children within seven years, his wife died young and, after only a few months, Fouquier-Tinville married again. His second wife provided him with an even more handsome dowry than the first, as well as three more children. But although he soon afterwards sold his practice for a large sum, by the time the Revolution came, he was, for some unknown reason – his enemies blamed his passion for courtesans and dancing-girls – as needy as he had been in his youth. Claiming to be related to Camille Desmoulins, who had become General Secretary to the Ministry of Justice, he applied to him for an appointment and was thankful to be offered one on the Revolutionary Tribunal of Paris.

Pale and rather stout, with thick black hair, thin lips, a pockmarked nose, jutting chin and small, glittering eyes, he had thus suddenly become a powerful and dreaded figure. Invariably dressed in black, he was known to be as incorruptible as Robespierre himself; but, provided the processes over which he presided were conducted in an orderly fashion and with a proper regard for a show of legality, he was perfectly willing, indeed eager, to carry out the wishes of the authorities without too close an inquiry into the conduct of those whom they wished to destroy, even when he had cause to be grateful to them for past favours.

There were difficulties with Danton and Desmoulins, though. They both still enjoyed much popularity in the *sections*, and he had been given scarcely any time to prepare his case against them. Press censorship would ensure that the proceedings would be both briefly and tendentiously recorded, but the public would have to be admitted into the courtroom, as was customary, so that accounts of what passed there would spread rapidly throughout the city. Moreover, there could be no doubt, as Danton charged through the doors like an angry bull, that he was determined not to be a passive victim. He defended himself with such vehemence, indeed, that his bellowing voice could be heard through the open windows of the court on the far side of the Seine.

It is clear from the fragmentary records of the proceedings that at the outset he had little hope of being acquitted. When asked for his address by the Tribunal he gave it as 'soon in oblivion . . . in the future in history's pantheon'. And later he said, 'The court now knows Danton. Tomorrow he hopes to sleep in the bosom of glory. He has never asked for pardon and you will see him go to the scaffold with the calm of a clear conscience.' There were times during the course of the trial when both the President, Nicolas-François-Joseph Herman, and the Prosecutor were obviously rattled. The jury seemed impressed by Danton's loud defiance, and the spectators often cheered his stirring words. The President rang his bell in vain. 'Do you not hear my bell?' he asked. '*Bell!*' Danton shouted back at him. '*Bell!* A man who is fighting for his life pays no attention to bells . . . My voice, which has often been heard speaking in the people's name,' he continued more calmly but no less loudly, 'will have no difficulty in thrusting these vile charges aside. Will the cowards who have slandered me dare to meet me face to face? Let them show themselves and I will cover them with shame . . . I demand that the Convention establish a commission to hear my denunciation of the present dictatorship. Yes, I, Danton, will unmask the dictatorship which is now revealing itself in its true colours . . . You say I have sold myself. A man such as me has no price . . . Let the men who have proof step forward . . . Neither ambition nor greed has ever found a victim in me . . . I shall now speak to you about three *plats-coquins* [presumably Billaud-Varenne, Collot d'Herbois and Saint-Just] who have been the ruin of Robespierre . . . I have vital evidence to reveal. I demand an undisturbed hearing . . .'

The President interrupted him again, furiously ringing his bell. But Danton's voice boomed on while Fouquier-Tinville looked more and more alarmed, his countenance, in the words of his clerk 'depicting both rage and terror'. He was passed a note from the President which read, 'I am going to suspend Danton's defence in half an hour.' Yet even when he did so the prisoner refused to sit down until promised that he would be allowed to continue his speech the next day.

Terrified that the jurors might be persuaded to deliver the wrong verdict, Herman and Fouquier-Tinville now decided to write to the Committee of Public Safety:

A fearful storm has been raging since the session began. The accused are behaving like madmen and are frantically demanding the summoning of their witnesses. They are denouncing to the people what they say is the rejection of their demand. In spite of the firmness of the President and the entire court, their repeated requests are disrupting the session. They say that, short of a decree, they will not be quiet until their witnesses have been heard. We ask you what to do about their demands since our judicial powers give us no authority for rejecting it.

Rather than read out this compromising letter to the Convention, Saint-Just gave the deputies a false version of it, and informed them that the prisoners were in revolt against the Tribunal. He then produced a letter, allegedly written by a prisoner at the Luxembourg, which 'proved the existence' of a plot organized by Lucille Desmoulins and an aristocratic friend, to rescue the accused and murder the entire Revolutionary Tribunal. 'No further proofs are needed,' Saint-Just declared. 'The very resistance of these scoundrels proves their guilt.' He demanded and obtained a decree that 'every accused person who resisted or insulted the national justice should be forbidden to plead'.

Amar of the Committee of General Security hurried over to the courtroom with this decree which he handed over to Fouquier-Tinville with the words, 'This should make the job easier for you.' Fouquier took it from him with a smile of relief. 'Indeed we needed it,' he said.

'You are murderers,' shouted Danton when the decree was read out. 'Murderers! Look at them! They have hounded us to our deaths! ... But the people will tear my enemies to pieces within three months.'

The next day the trial was resumed an hour and a half earlier than usual, so few spectators were present to witness the final scenes. Fouquier-Tinville opened the proceedings by asking the jurors in an intimidating way if they had now heard enough against all the accused. They said they had and, on returning from their retirement, brought in the required verdicts.

That same day eighteen condemned men – Danton, Desmoulins, Delacroix and Fabre d'Églantine among them, as well as Hérault de Séchelles, who had been falsely accused of passing secrets to the enemy – were transported in three red-painted tumbrils to the guillotine. As with the Girondins, they were nearly all young men. Fabre d'Églantine was forty-three; Danton and Hérault de Séchelles both thirty-four; Desmoulins was also thirty-four, though he told the Revolutionary Tribunal that he was thirty-three, 'the same age as the *sans-culotte*, Jesus Christ, when He died'.

Desmoulins who had to be dragged from the courtroom to prison screaming, 'They are going to murder my wife', became so agitated in the cart that, though his hands were bound, he managed to tear the clothes from his body in a frenzy of protest as he shouted at the spectators. Danton, who had comforted him tenderly in prison, now lost patience with him and said, 'Be quiet! Leave the rabble alone.' But Desmoulins continued to rage and he arrived at the scaffold with his chest and shoulders scratched and bare. The sight of the guillotine seemed to calm him though. He looked at it for a moment then turned away 'with a contemplative expression on his face'. He waited for the end murmuring the name of Lucille.

The others had been calm throughout the journey. Hérault, the handsome philanderer, had nodded to various acquaintances and smiled as he saw a woman friend waving him goodbye from a window of the Garde-Meuble. Fabre d'Églantine appeared preoccupied with the thought that Billaud-Varenne would steal the manuscript of one of his unpublished plays and have it performed as his own. 'There are such beautiful verses in it,' he said. 'Beautiful *vers*, indeed,' Danton mocked him sarcastically, making outrageous play with the word that means worms as well as verses. 'You'll be making some beautiful *vers* next week!'

Danton's 'huge round head,' so Frénilly said, 'fixed its proud gaze on the crowds.' He saw David, once his friend who had agitated for his death, calmly sketching him and the other prisoners from a café table, and shouted an insult at him. He had cursed and ranted a good deal in prison. 'I'm leaving everything in a frightful mess,' he had called to one of the other accused in the next cell. 'There's not a single one of them who knows the first thing about government . . . If I left my balls to that eunuch Robespierre and my legs to Couthon the Committee of Public Safety might last a bit longer. But . . . as it is . . . Robespierre is bound to follow me, dragged down by me. Ah, better be a poor fisherman than muck about with politics.'

He was quite composed now, though. 'Oh, my wife, my dear wife,' he murmured. 'Shall I ever see you again?' But then he checked himself, stamping his foot as though in irritation at this outburst. 'Come, Danton. Courage. No weakness.' Hérault came up to kiss him goodbye. But the executioner separated them and pulled Hérault towards the steps. '*Coquin!*' Danton shouted. 'You'll not be able to prevent our heads touching each other in the basket.'

He was the last to be beheaded; and night was falling as he stepped up on to the platform, 'soaked with the blood of his friends, as though emerging from the tomb instead of about to enter it', so one observer recorded of a scene which time would never erase from his memory. 'I recall the full force of my feelings at Danton's last words which I did not hear myself but which were passed round with horror and admiration: "Above all, don't forget to show my head to the people. It's well worth having a look at."'

A week later more blood was shed. Chaumette was guillotined. So was Archbishop Gobel who, claimed by the Hébertists as one of their supporters, was condemned by Robespierre as an atheist. So was the widow of Hébert who was sentenced to death as an accomplice of her husband. And so was the pretty, twenty-three-year old widow of Camille Desmoulins, her one offence being a devoted attachment to her husband on whose behalf she had appealed in vain to Robespierre who was godfather to their baby son, Horace.

It is not enough for you to have murdered your best friend [her mother wrote to Robespierre when judgement upon Lucille had been pronounced]. You must have his wife's blood as well. Your monster, Fouquier-Tinville, has just ordered Lucille to be carried away to the scaffold. In less than two hours she will be dead . . . If Camille's blood has not driven you mad, if you can still remember the happy evenings you once spent before our fire holding our little Horace, spare an innocent victim. If not, then make haste and take us all, Horace, me and my other daughter, Adèle. Hurry up and tear us apart with your claws that still drip with Camille's blood . . . Hurry, hurry, so that we can all rest in the same grave.

The appeal went unanswered. Lucille Desmoulins prepared herself for death with a bravery which aroused the deepest admiration and sympathy even amongst her husband's bitterest enemies. 'I shall in a few hours again meet my husband,' she had exclaimed to her accusers when sentence of death was pronounced. 'In departing from this world, in which nothing now remains to engage my affections, I am far less the object of pity than you are.' Dressed with 'uncommon attention and taste', she climbed the steps to the scaffold with what was described as 'unaffected pleasure' and 'received the fatal blow without appearing to notice what the executioner was doing.'

'In heaven's name,' asked one who saw her die, 'when will all this bloodshed cease?'

It was not to cease yet. In June 1794 the Committee of Public Safety passed a decree, known as the law of 22 *Prairial*, which both greatly increased the numbers of those who could be regarded as 'public enemies' and expedited the processes by which they could be condemned to death – the only punishment now to be inflicted – by the Revolutionary Tribunal. Defence lawyers were dispensed with; so were witnesses unless 'the formality' of calling them was considered 'necessary to discover accomplices or for other important considerations of public interest'. The Tribunal was no longer required to interrogate the accused before their public trial, since this merely 'confused the conscience of the judges'; now, in the absence of positive proof, juries must be satisfied with 'moral proof'. 'For a citizen to become suspect,' said Georges Couthon who had been elected President of the Convention the previous December, 'it is sufficient that rumour accuses him.' After the law of 22 *Prairial* everything, indeed, went on much better, in the opinion of Fouquier-Tinville: heads fell 'like tiles'. 'Next week,' he said one day, 'I'll be able to take the tops off three or four hundred.'

In several provincial towns trials were conducted as expeditiously and summarily as they were in Paris. In Orange, for example, where one judge expressed his exasperation with another who had 'to have proofs just like in the courts of the *ancien régime*,' a commission established on 10 May had condemned 332 people to death by the end of July. It was in Paris, however, that most of the executions took place in that stiflingly hot summer. In an effort to centralize revolutionary justice, the Committee of Public Safety had suppressed various provincial courts and had brought those awaiting trial to the capital whose prisons were consequently crammed with 'enemies of the Republic' whom, so Couthon insisted, it was 'less a question of punishing than of annihilating'.

Many noblemen and noblewomen who had previously been spared were now brought to trial. One of them was the Princesse de Monaco who claimed to be with child since pregnant women were usually spared until their babies were born. While waiting for the prison doctor to examine her she cut off her hair which she succeeded in smuggling out of the prison for her children. She then wrote to Fouquier-Tinville: 'I inform you, citizen, that I am *not* pregnant. I did not tell this lie for fear of death ... but because I wanted to secure a day's grace so that I, rather than the executioner, could cut my hair. It is the only legacy that I can leave my children. It should at least be pure.'

Another noblewoman who was guillotined at this time was the aged widow of Maréchal the Duc de Noailles, Marie Antoinette's 'Madame L'Étiquette', whose senile eccentricity it had become to write long letters to the Virgin Mary on the subject of prudence and protocol in Heaven. They were answered by her confessor who signed himself Mary but who, on one occasion, committed on Her behalf some solecism which to led the Duchess to comment, 'But then one ought not to expect too much of Her. She was after all only a bourgeoise from Nazareth. It was through marriage that she became a connection of the House of David. Her husband, Joseph, would have known better.'

The old, demented Duchess was arrested in July with her daughter-in-law, the Duchesse d'Ayen, and her grand-daughter, the Vicomtesse de Noailles. They were taken to the guillotine watched by the Abbé Carichon who took advantage of a blinding rainstorm which slowed down the carts to give them absolution.

The carts halted before the scaffold [recorded the Abbé who described the chief executioner as a short young man with a markedly dandyish air]. There was a large circle of spectators, most of them laughing, 'There she is! Look at her! That's the Marshal's wife who used to have a grand carriage. Now she's in a cart just like the others' . . . I saw the chief executioner and his two assistants . . . [one of them had his hair drawn back in a pigtail and chewed on the stem of a red rose] . . . I must admit that . . . the sufferings of the [forty-five] victims were much mitigated by their business-like methods, the way they got all the condemned down from the carts before the executioner started, and placed them with their backs to the scaffold so they would not see anything. I felt the executioners deserved some gratitude for this and for the decorum they observed and their serious expressions which contained no traces of mockery or insult . . .

I now found myself facing the steps to the scaffold against which a tall, old white-haired man was leaning. He was to be beheaded first. He had a kindly air . . . Near him stood a pious-looking lady whom I did not know; Mme de Noailles was immediately opposite me. She was dressed in black and sitting on a block of stone with wide staring eyes . . . [Her daughter] stood in a simple, noble, resigned attitude with her eyes closed, looking as she did when receiving Holy Communion . . .

The executioner and his assistants climb on the scaffold and arrange everything. The chief executioner puts on a blue-red overall . . . When all is ready the old man goes up the steps. The chief executioner takes him by the left arm, the big assistant by the right and the other by the legs. They lay him quickly on his face and his head is cut off and thrown, together with his body, into a great tumbril, where all the bodies swim in blood. And so it goes on. What a dreadful shambles it is! The Duchess is the third to go up. They have to make an opening in the top of her dress to uncover her neck. Her daughter-in-law is the tenth . . . The chief executioner tears off her bonnet. It is fastened by a pin so her hair is pulled violently upwards and she grimaces with pain. When the daughter-in-law is gone the grand-daughter replaces her. She is dressed all in white. She looks much younger than she really is . . .

Day after day the executions continued until by the end of July over 1,500 people had been beheaded within the previous eight weeks. But only a small proportion of them were aristocrats. Less than nine in a hundred of those guillotined in the Terror were of noble birth; about six per cent were clergy. The rest, eighty-five per cent, came from that class of the people once known as the Third Estate. Among them were 'twenty peasant girls from Poitou', so one contemporary recorded:

All of them were to be executed together. Exhausted by their long journey, they lay in the courtyard of the Conciergerie, asleep on the paving-stones. Their expression betrayed no understanding of their fate . . . They were all guillotined a few days after their arrival . . . From one of them a baby she was feeding was taken from her breast.

Robespierre witnessed none of the victims perish. He had once expressed the opinion that public executions coarsened and brutalized the character of the people. But he made no move to stop them. He had to stay in power for, incorruptible, more virtuous than other men, he alone could save the Revolution. In justification of the Terror he declared in the Convention, 'At the point where we are now, if we stop too soon we will die. We have not been too severe . . . Without the revolutionary Government the Republic cannot be made stronger. If it is destroyed now, freedom will be extinguished tomorrow.' Besides, his own life was in danger. He had always said that the daggers of murderers were directed at him, that it was only by chance that Marat had been struck down before him. Since then two people, one a nobleman's former valet, the other an unbalanced girl of twenty who lamented the death of the King, had set out to kill him. He had cause to remember the words that Danton had shouted at the Revolutionary Tribunal and at the Duplays' shuttered house as the tumbrils rumbled past it on their way to the guillotine: 'You will follow us, Robespierre.'

THE DAYS OF *THERMIDOR*

22–28 July 1794

'Robespierre never forgave men
for the injustices which he had done them,
nor for the kindnesses which he had received from them,
nor for the talents which some of them possessed,
and he did not have'

BUZOT

On 18 *Floréal* Year III, that is to say on 7 May 1794, Robespierre delivered to the Convention a long speech which had taken him three weeks to prepare. In the course of it, having blamed his fallen enemies for putting the Republic in danger and vilified Danton, 'the most dangerous of the conspirators had he not been the most cowardly', he turned upon the atheists who had survived the recent purges and who were now trying to 'smother all the noble sentiments of nature' by elevating 'immorality into a cult'. Declaring that atheism was aristocratic, he propounded the necessity of a moral revolution to complete the work of the scientific revolution of the seventeenth and eighteenth centuries and proposed a decree which would announce unequivocally to the world the French people's recognition of the 'existence of the Supreme Being and the immortality of the soul'. To celebrate their acceptance of this new civic religion and their devotion to the principles and virtues of the Revolution, he then introduced a plan for a series of national festivals, the first of them to be held on Whit Sunday, 8 June, in honour of the Supreme Being.

On the morning of that day Robespierre dressed himself with even more than his accustomed care in a bright blue coat and buff cotton trousers. He left the house, without having had breakfast, carrying a bouquet of red, white and blue flowers and sheaves of corn. The sun shone brightly in a clear blue sky; the windows of the houses in the Rue Saint-Honoré were decorated with red roses; the pealing of church bells was punctuated by the boom of cannon and the tapping of drums. And to a young man, a 'very refined little dandy' named Vilate, a juryman on the Revolutionary Tribunal, who met him as he walked through the Tuileries gardens, Robespierre looked 'radiantly happy – for the first time'. Vilate invited him up to his apartment in the Pavillon de Flore.

He accepted my invitation without hesitation [Vilate recalled]. He was astounded to see the immense crowds of people that thronged the gardens below my windows. The women added to the gaiety of the scene by the elegance of their dresses ... Robespierre ate little. His glance was constantly directed towards the splendid spectacle below. He seemed to be intoxicated with enthusiasm. 'Behold the most interesting part of hu-

251

manity,' he exclaimed. 'Here is the universe assembled beneath us. Oh, Nature, how sublime, how delightful is thy power! How tyrants must turn pale at the idea of this Feast!' That was the extent of his conversation.

On the terrace of the Palace the members of the Convention were waiting impatiently for him to appear and, as President of the Convention, to open the proceedings. The minutes passed and Robespierre did not come. The deputies looked alternately at their watches and at an amphitheatre which had been built in front of the terrace. Surmounting the amphitheatre was a pyre on which was to be burned an ugly effigy representing atheism together with others symbolizing discord and selfishness in accordance with a scenario prepared by David, the painter. The deputies, many of whom had already derided the whole conception of the festival in private, did not trouble to disguise their resentment at being kept waiting so long. They grew even more restive when the President at last arrived upon the scene and delivered himself of a long speech in which he claimed that the world which the Supreme Being had created had never offered Him 'a spectacle so worthy of His sight' as the festival that Paris was celebrating this day.

Some deputies began to murmur to each other. One whispered, 'Just listen to the pontiff!' Another said sardonically that were it not for kind Monsieur de Robespierre they never would have known that there was a God or that the soul was meant to be immortal.

After Robespierre had finished speaking, he took a lighted torch that was offered to him and marched purposefully down towards the pyre. The evil effigies were satisfactorily consumed, but when the Goddess of Wisdom rose like a phoenix from their ashes to take their place her face was so blackened by soot that several spectators could not restrain their laughter.

Robespierre returned to his place where he delivered himself of a second speech after which the deputies at last moved off to the Champ de Mars, their irritation plain for all to see. Most of them pretended not to hear the orders of the ushers of the Convention who vainly endeavoured to get them to march in proper military fashion. Some walked arm in arm with their neighbours; others nodded significantly towards the neat figure of Robespierre who strode on, twenty paces ahead of the rest, a crown of feathers on his head.

In the middle of the Champ de Mars a tall tree spread its boughs over the summit of a mound covered with moss. The deputies sat down beneath the leaves of the tree surrounded by groups of little boys with garlands of violets on their heads, by young men with wreaths of myrtle, by older men wearing oak, ivy and olive leaves. Women, carrying baskets of flowers, held children by the hand. An orchestra began to play; the various groups began to sing; the young men drew swords and swore to their elders to defend the fatherland; the women lifted up their children in their arms; all raised their hands to heaven, paying homage to the Supreme Being. Robespierre made another speech. Then a barrage of artillery fire rent the air while the people cheered and hugged each other shouting, '*Vive la République!*'

For most of the spectators, if not for the deputies who had played their parts so resentfully, the festival had been an enjoyable one and had given them grounds for hope that the weeks of Terror and repression might be coming to an end – throughout the day the guillotine had been draped in velvet.

All citizens had been asked to decorate their houses with garlands and oak branches for the celebrations [the thirteen-year-old daughter of an architect told her father who had gone to design a theatre in the provinces]. We used all our artificial flowers. You may imagine that the previous night was an almost sleepless one for me because of the pleasures in store . . . I got up at six o'clock . . . and put on a lawn skirt, a tricolour sash round my waist and an embroidered fichu of red cotton . . . In our pockets we put some slices of bread and cooking chocolate . . . You cannot imagine what a sight the Champ de Mars presented. It looked as though someone had transported a huge cliff from the Pyrenees. On its peak was an obelisk surmounted by a statue representing the people of France holding aloft the statues of Liberty and Equality. It really seemed as though the French are fairies to have done such beautiful things in so short time . . . There were girls everywhere strewing flowers. My hair was simply full of them.

For Robespierre, however, the day which had begun so cheerfully in such auspicious sunshine, which should have been one of triumph, had ended in ultimate humiliation. He had overheard some of the remarks that the deputies had made, the references to the 'proud affectation' of 'the tyrant', to Brutus and Nemesis. He had been made well aware of the feelings amongst the *sans-culottes*, one of whom, standing near Vitale, had said, 'The bastard isn't satisfied with being the boss; he's got to be God as well'. And he could not have failed to hear the caustic comment that greeted his observation that it was the Supreme Being who had placed in the heart of the oppressor the sensations of remorse and terror: 'True, Robespierre, too true!' He went home with presentiments of danger and death. 'You will not see me much longer,' he said morosely to the Duplays before going to bed.

For some time past he had been becoming increasingly isolated from his equally overworked and, in some cases, equally didactic and authoritarian colleagues who were constantly getting on each others' nerves. After this festival, they felt more strongly than ever that he regarded himself as a dictator, while he in turn became more and more suspicious of them, particularly of Billaud-Varenne, the coarse Collot d'Herbois whom he suspected of conspiring against him, and of Carnot who always worked late in the Committee's offices, and was supposed by one of Robespierre's agents to do so in order to be the first 'to open all the letters that arrive'. There had been a period, after the destruction of both Hébertists and Dantonists when, closely associated with his principal supporters, Saint-Just and Couthon, he had been in unquestioned control of the Committee of Public Safety and hence of the Government. Through Fouquier-Tinville and Fouquier's associates he had controlled the Revolutionary Tribunal, and, through Hanriot, the National Guard. But always he had been as much feared and disliked as respected and revered. A revealing anecdote was related by Paul Barras, who said that a fellow-deputy awoke from a reverie with a cry of alarm when he realized that Robespierre's greenish eyes were upon him. 'He will now suppose,' the frightened deputy said, 'that I was thinking about something.'

'Fear was on every side, in the creak of a door, an exclamation, a breath,' wrote Louis Madelin of those early summer months when Robespierre had been in undisputed control of the government. 'Drawing-rooms were empty, wine-shops deserted: even the courtesans stopped going to the Palais Royal where (extraordinary sight!) virtue reigned supreme. The dreary city waited, under the burning summer sun.'

Plays were censored; Molière was banned. A performance at the Comédie Française was interrupted by a Jacobin who stood up to object to the line, '*les plus tolérants sont les pardonnables*'. When the audience told him to be quiet he went off to the Jacobin Club to denounce the actors who were all arrested. Few people dared talk freely, for the Committee of Public Safety's ubiquitous spies might well be listening. Even at the Fraternal Suppers, which were held in the streets outside houses whose owners were expected to cook and serve the food, conversation was guarded, while the quality of the meals provided was often governed by what interpretation might be placed upon it. Madame Rataud who kept a dress shop in the Rue des Petits-Champs commented upon the dilemma that faced her when a Fraternal Supper was held in her *section*: 'If I prepare a dish of haricots the *sans-culottes* will throw it in my face, yet if I provide roast pheasant the Jacobins will say it is too high-class.' In the event she cooked both and, after nervously waiting to see what her neighbours would provide before bringing out either, it seemed to her safe to produce them both. Other women wrote of the dangers to be encountered in the streets where spies watched out for 'enemies of the nation'. Madame Amé who ran a dressmaker's workshop in the Rue Traversière-Saint-Honoré kept a tricolour cockade for the use of her apprentices and insisted that whenever one of the girls went out on an errand she must pin it prominently to her hat.

Yet the fears that undoubtedly pervaded the lives of many citizens during these months were not universal. Gaily painted carriages no longer thronged the tree-lined boulevards of Paris, but families still strolled in the evening air down the Boulevard de la Comédie Italienne, and young ladies still went to drawing classes and had piano lessons.

This is how we spend our days [runs the entry for 16 January 1794 in the diary of a young governess in a bourgeois family in the Rue Saint-Marc]. Citizeness Ziguette [the youngest daughter in the family] leaves at ten o'clock after having eaten a light breakfast and practised her pianoforte fairly conscientiously. She trips away with a clatter of sabots, hoisting up her blue skirt to expose white under-petticoats much shorter than they should be and running like a Red Indian pulling along Thérèse [the cook] by the arm. Thérèse carries her bouillon and bread soup in a tin container. They arrive at Citizen Chaudet's. She draws, is complimented by her master. As soon as she comes home she gabbles what he has said to her . . . and as she reaches the top of the stairs I hear her shout, 'Food! I'm starving to death!' Quite alarmed by this ogrish hunger, we make haste to sit down to dinner where, over a good meal, we commend the merits of her sketches . . . Then there is pianoforte practice until lights are brought in, no longer wax but tallow candles, plain and simple. Then we read Ovid or Horace until about seven o'clock when we begin to read for instruction or entertainment such as learning by heart some lines from Racine or *Anarcharsis*.

If such bourgeois families as these had to make do with tallow rather than wax candles, they seem to have suffered few other deprivations. On the anniversary of the King's death Ziguette and her mother went to dinner with a Madame Houzeaux. They had soup, cold beef with gherkin and beetroot salad, skate with browned butter, stewed mutton and potatoes, fried sole, cheese and fruit. After dinner they sat by the fire to talk about the latest fashions, and on their way home they went into a shop in the Rue du Bac and bought 'a ravishing frock' for twenty-two livres. For families such as this the Terror was not of overriding concern, nor was Robespierre mentioned much in conversation.

Those more intimately concerned with politics, however, knew that Robespierre was now having difficulties with his colleagues. Differences of opinion had arisen in the Committee of Public Safety over a project, favoured by Robespierre, for the free distribution to impoverished patriots of estates confiscated from 'suspects', and over the speeding up of the procedures of the Revolutionary Tribunal, as well as over Robespierre's devotion to the religious ideas of Rousseau as exemplified by his inauguration of festivals such as those of the Supreme Being. At the same time there was growing rivalry between the Committee of Public Safety and the Committee of General Security. Robespierre, backed by Couthon and Saint-Just, had usurped many of the latter's powers, particularly those concerning the police. This added to the numbers of Robespierre's enemies among the members of the Committee of General Security without mollifying those who were jealous of his pre-eminence in the Committee of Public Safety. Even more dangerous for Robespierre was his gradual loss of control of the Convention. The radical members strongly disapproved of his recall to Paris of their representatives *en mission* in the provinces, while the more moderate members, still angry with the Jacobins for their destruction of the Girondins and appalled by the merciless manner in which the Revolutionary Tribunal had taken advantage of the law of 22 *Prairial*, had begun openly to condemn the continuance of the Terror at a time when the French armies' victories were making it inexcusable. On 26 June General Jean-Baptiste Jourdan, once a silk merchant's apprentice in Lyons, overwhelmed the Austrians at Fleurus and a fortnight later Brussels was occupied. Toulon had already been retaken and some sort of order had at last been restored in the Vendée. There being no longer any danger of invasion by foreign troops or any serious threat from either federalists or royalists, the continued dictatorship of Robespierre and his associates became increasingly insupportable.

For his part, Robespierre seems to have had little doubt that, with the help of the Commune and of the faithful members of the Jacobin Club, he could survive all attempts to defeat him. By carrying out further purges not only of the Convention but also of both Committees he could ensure himself of sufficient support in all of them. His confidence evidently restored after the doubts that had assailed him on the evening of the Festival of the Supreme Being, he quarrelled with Carnot, with Vadier and with Billaud-Varenne. After one particularly violent altercation with Billaud-Varenne, who described the dictatorship of Couthon, Saint-Just and himself as 'grotesque', he stormed out of the room, slamming the door behind

him and shouting, 'All right then, save the country without me.'
Thereafter he stopped attending Comittee meetings.

Some of his critics, more cautious than their colleagues and afraid
of losing their lives if they failed to overthrow him, attempted to
bring about a reconciliation. Paul Barras and Louis Stanislas
Fréron who had been jointly responsible for the excesses of the
Terror at Toulon and had been recalled to Paris at Robespierre's
instigation, called upon him at the Rue Saint-Honoré. Fréron had
been at school with him, and hoped that, at least 'for old times's
sake', Robespierre would receive them sympathetically.

Having passed through 'a long alley which led to an inner yard
full of planks, the owner's stock in trade', they found Robespierre
in his dressing-gown just returned from one of his regular visits to
his hairdresser.

He was not wearing his spectacles and his eyes turned on us with a
fixed look [Barras recorded]. He seemed quite amazed at our appearance
... and did not reply to our greeting. He turned first towards a mirror
that hung on the window, then to a smaller mirror, taking his toilet knife,
scraping the powder that covered his face and minutely inspecting the
arrangement of his hair. He then took off his dressing-gown, putting it
on to a chair near us so that we were dusted with the powder that flew off
it. He did not apologize, nor show any sign that he had even noticed our
presence. He washed himself in a bowl that he held in his hand, brushed
his teeth, spat several times on the floor by our feet as though we had not
been there ... Thinking that he detected a frown on Robespierre's face
and that his continued silence might be due to our use of the revolutionary
tu, Fréron substituted *vous* in the hope of appeasing this haughty and
touchy man. But Robespierre's expression did not alter. He remained
standing ... and still said nothing. I have seen no expression as impassive
on the icy marble faces of statues or on those of corpses.

Fouché, who had also been recalled to Paris on Robespierre's
orders and knew that he too stood in the shadow of the guillotine,
went to see Robespierre and was rebuffed in a different way. His
overtures were, it seems, furiously rejected; his activities at Lyons
were violently condemned; he was then abruptly told to leave the
house. For a time Fouché went into hiding, emerging occasionally

to spread rumours about Robespierre, persuading other members of the Convention that their lives were in as much danger as his own, uniting rivals by a common fear. Robespierre would have had him arrested, but the wily Fouché – like Talleyrand, a born trimmer and survivor – could not be found, and Robespierre had for the moment to be content with using his influence with the Jacobins to have him expelled from the Club.

Elsewhere Robespierre's influence was waning fast. The moderates in the Convention were growing daily more outspoken in their condemnation of the continuing Terror, no longer justified by the war; and towards the middle of July plans were laid for Robespierre's overthrow.

On 22 July (4 *Thermidor*) he was persuaded to attend a joint meeting of the Committees of Public Safety and General Security. He appeared there in a far from repentant or conciliatory mood, pacing about the room as he charged both Committees with all manner of misdemeanours and betrayals of the trust that the people reposed in them. After he had left, the Committees agreed to Saint-Just's issuing a statement indicating that some sort of understanding with Robespierre had been reached and that, as Couthon assured the Jacobin Club, while there might be differences of personality there was 'none of principle'. But, if Couthon and Saint-Just were prepared to compromise with their colleagues, Robespierre was not. He declined 'to adjust his principles for the sake of the Committees' and he refused to discuss them privately with the leaders of the Plain. He made up his mind to deliver a speech to the Convention in which he would clearly set forth his views and denounce all his enemies, all those 'perfidious rogues' who were responsible for the ills of the nation. He did not discuss his speech with either Couthon or Saint-Just. In long and solitary walks through the woods at Ville d'Avray and in contemplation, sometimes in tears, of the tomb of Rousseau, whose *Contrat social* was always by his bedside, he composed his stinging indictment. And on 26 July (8 *Thermidor*) he marched in to confront the deputies resplendent in nankeen silk breeches, white cotton stockings and the sky-blue coat which he had worn for the Festival of the Supreme Being six weeks before. He mounted the rostrum and remained there speaking for over two hours. Without actually naming any of them except Pierre Joseph Cambon, the Superintendent of Finance, he characterized and anathematized his opponents on the Committees, referring in particular and unmistakably to Billaud-Varenne and Carnot. He attacked Fouché, Collot d'Herbois and Vadier as well as Jean Lambert Tallien, who, while representative *en mission* at Bordeaux, had fallen in love with one of his prisoners, the divorced wife of the Comte de Fontenay, and who was consequently, despite his protestations of revolutionary zeal, suspected of having come under her moderating influence. Robespierre castigated Tallien with particular vehemence before turning upon all the deputies who had derided the Festival of the Supreme Being. He spoke darkly of purifying the Committee of Public Safety and dismissing the members of the Committee of General Security. He accused those responsible for military affairs of having dealings with the enemy, and Cambon of ruining the poor, depriving the people of national assets and disrupting the economy. He described himself, as he so often did when elaborating upon his own virtues, as 'a slave of freedom, a living martyr to the Republic, the victim as well as the enemy of crime'. 'Every scoundrel insults me,' he cried in growing indignation and sequential confusion. 'Let them prepare hemlock for me. I will wait for it on these sacred seats. I have promised to leave a formidable testament to the oppressors of the people. I bequeath to them truth . . . and death.'

His words, which had been listened to in silence, were at first greeted with that applause to which he had long been accustomed. But then Cambon, a brave as well as scrupulous man, infuriated by the unjust accusations made against him, strode to the rostrum to declare, 'Before I am dishonoured, I will speak to the French nation. It is time to tell the whole truth. One man alone is paralysing the will of the National Convention. *And that man is Robespierre.*'

Obviously taken aback by this furious counter-attack and the enthusiasm with which it was welcomed, Robespierre became apologetic rather than assertive. Encouraged by his faltering, other deputies, including Billaud-Varenne, rose to defend themselves vigorously and to assail Robespierre as heatedly as he had assailed them. 'The mask must be torn away,' Billaud-Varenne shouted. 'I would rather my corpse served as the throne of an ambitious man than that by my silence I should become the accomplice of his crimes.' Other deputies, fearing that their names were on the list of men whom Robespierre was condemning by implication, demanded that the names be announced. 'The list! The list!' numerous voices shouted. But Robespierre refused to divulge it. The time was not ripe, he said, thus alarming those who felt they might perhaps be on it as much as those who were sure they were and bringing them all in closer opposition to him. When the session was brought to a noisy conclusion it was clear that Robespierre's fall was imminent.

He himself still did not believe it so. That evening he went to the Jacobin Club of whose support he felt confident. Billaud-Varenne and Collot d'Herbois were already there, demanding to be allowed to speak first. But most members refused to listen to them and to cries of '*À la guillotine!*' they were both expelled from the hall. As they passed through the door the red-haired and red-faced René Dumas, now President of the Revolutionary Tribunal, shouted at their retreating backs that he would be waiting for them to appear before him next morning. To loud cheers Robespierre then rose to deliver the speech he had made in the Convention that afternoon, ending with the promise that, if they supported him, the 'new traitors' would share the fate of the old, but if they deserted him he would take hemlock and die with calm resignation. 'If you drink it I will drink it, too,' promised David, close to hysteria. 'Yes, yes,' others protested, they would all drink it; they swore to do so.

'What's new at the Jacobin Club, then?' asked Saint-Just tauntingly when Billaud-Varenne and Collot d'Herbois, his clothes torn and face scratched, returned to the offices of the Committee of Public Safety.

'How dare you ask that?' Collot yelled at him. 'You should know bloody well. You and Robespierre and Couthon are planning to have us guillotined. Why, you're drawing up an accusation against us now.'

'You may be right,' said Saint-Just who had, in fact, been doing so. He turned to Carnot who was also in the room and added, 'I shan't forget you, either. I've dealt with you in a masterly way.'

Collot then threw himself upon Saint-Just, grabbing him by the throat. Carnot pushed the two men apart, and Saint-Just, his normally icy composure evidently ruffled by Collot's fury, agreed not to deliver his report to the Convention until he had read it to the other members of the Committee. He was then left alone to complete it in the heat of the sultry night.

The atmosphere next day in the Convention was quite as emotional as it had been at the Jacobin Club and in the offices of the Committee of Public Safety the night before. Saint-Just, having broken his promise to return to the Committee first, rose to name the people that Robespierre had attacked by implication in his long speech the previous afternoon. But Tallien rushed up to the rostrum to interrupt him, to accuse both him and Robespierre of aggravating the ills of the nation. Tallien was followed by Billaud-Varenne, still enraged by Robespierre's remarks and by his expulsion from the Jacobin Club 'at the instigation of its most disreputable members' who planned 'to slaughter the Convention' and who 'spat out the vilest calumnies against men who had never once deviated from the true path of the Revolution'.

Robespierre attempted to reply, but his words were lost in the clangour of the President's bell. As he rushed to the rostrum, there were howls of protest and shouts of 'Down with the tyrant! *À la guillotine!*' Tallien, waving a dagger above his head, threatened to kill him if the Convention did not order his arrest. Refused permission to speak, Robespierre was compelled to listen while Vadier accused him of having hidden himself on the great *journée* of 10 August and of having deserted the Committee of Public Safety, by whose efforts the country was saved, at a time when the French armies were in danger of defeat.

As though driven frantic by these words, Robespierre rushed from side to side beneath the rostrum, and up and down the steps, shouting, 'Death! Death!' Pointing at Thuriot who was now in the President's chair repeatedly ringing his bell, he yelled 'For the last time will you give me permission to speak, President of murderers!' Then, in attempting to make further accusations, his voice failed him. 'Ah!' someone called out with satisfaction, 'Danton's blood chokes you.' 'President,' another voice shouted. 'Is this man to be master of the Convention a moment longer?' Robespierre was about to sit down in exhaustion when he was violently pushed away, 'Monster! How dare you! That was Vergniaud's seat.' He found another place and slumped down with a gesture of helpless defeat.

His arrest was proposed, immediately seconded and voted without a dissentient voice. His brother, Augustin, a handsome, pleasure-loving man whose tastes and temperament were so unlike his, courageously insisted on being arrested too. So did the Duplays' son-in-law, Philippe Lebas, when the Convention also decreed the arrest of his friend, Saint-Just, and that of Couthon. An usher, too frightened to hand the decree directly to Robespierre, placed it on the seat next to him. Robespierre ignored it. Eventually he and Saint-Just were escorted from the Convention by a party of gendarmes, one of whom carried the crippled Couthon on his shoulders.

As the prisoners were being marched away to the offices of the Committee of General Security a meeting of the Commune was urgently called at the Hôtel de Ville. It was agreed at this meeting that the Commune should declare itself in a state of revolt against both Committees and the Convention in protest against the arrest of the Robespierrists, and orders were issued calling upon the National Guard to muster on the Place de Grève. Less than half the Guard obeyed the summons. And when Hanriot, their commander, followed by a few of his men, drunkenly rode his horse through the streets of the Faubourg Saint-Antoine, brandishing a sword and calling out 'To arms! To arms!', his pleas were ignored. A man out walking with his wife heard Hanriot's loud, slurred shouts: 'Today must be another 31 May. Three hundred bastards sitting in the Convention must be exterminated!' 'You aren't a general anymore, Hanriot,' the man called back. 'You're a brigand. Don't listen to him. He's under arrest.'

At this moment [recorded Charles-André Merda, one of Hanriot's men] the General's aide-de-camp struck the citizen a blow with his sabre, ordering him to be taken to the guard-room of the Commune. And we pursued our course at the gallop [to the Committee of General Security] ... knocking down a lot of citizens with our horses ... and spreading terror around us ... Hanriot rode into the courtyard and, dismounting with his aides-de-camp, advanced towards the offices. The guards refused to let us in; and so he marched up to us in a fury, shouting 'Dismount! Come on! Help me release the patriots from these fucking bastards.' ... Six or seven of us followed the General. The guards crossed their bayonets in front of us; and a fight was on the point of breaking out when an usher from the Convention threw himself in front of us and said, 'Stop! He's no longer your General. He's under arrest. Here is the law. Obey it.' These words brought Hanriot to a halt.

To thwart any further attempts to rescue the prisoners they were now sent to separate prisons in different parts of Paris, Robespierre to the Luxembourg. But the gate-keeper there, in obedience to an order from the Commune, refused to admit him, and he sought refuge instead at the Mairie on the Quai des Orfèvres; but, at the insistence of his former henchman, Jean-Baptiste Lescot-Fleuriot, the Mayor, who did not want the responsibility of dealing with the situation himself, he was taken instead to the Hôtel de Ville. By now all was confusion. No one was sure who was in authority, who were considered traitors, who patriots. Robespierre's colleagues who had been taken to prison were released by order of the Commune and taken to Robespierre at the Hôtel de Ville. From there Robespierre himself, apparently confident that the Convention's vote against him would be reversed and that he would soon be called upon once more to guide the Revolution, sent a series of notes to the Commune urging them to close 'the city gates, to shut down all newspapers, to order the arrest of all journalists and traitorous deputies'. Couthon, carried to the Hôtel from the Port-Libre, advised an appeal to the army. Saint-Just spoke of a new dictatorship. Lescot-Fleuriot, exasperated by Robespierre's 'splitting hairs at such a time about small details of phraseology', boldly wrote out and signed a decree, outlawing Collot d'Herbois, Carnot, Fréron, Tallien, Fouché and other 'enemies of the people', which Robespierre could not bring himself to promulgate.

Meanwhile Hanriot and his men surrounded the Convention where Collot d'Herbois cried out dramatically, 'This is the time to die at our posts!' But Hanriot, unsure of his authority and too drunk to concentrate, refused to enter the building without specific orders and so the opportunity to occupy it was lost. Inside the hall arguments raged as to the best course to adopt. Fréron advised conferring the military command upon Barras who would be able to muster almost as many men from *sections* loyal to the Convention as Hanriot could from those supporting the Commune. Barras accepted the command and proposed to defend the Tuileries against possible assault. Billaud-Varenne argued that it was a time for attack not defence: the Convention's forces should advance upon the Hôtel de Ville and bring out Robespierre and his friends by force. 'The Hôtel de Ville must be surrounded at once,' he urged. 'We can't give Robespierre and the Commune an opportunity to murder us all.'

This suggestion was finally adopted in the early hours of the following morning. Two columns accordingly marched towards the Place de Grève, one of them led by Barras, the other by Léonard Bourdon, a leading Montagnard deputy and former Hébertist. Bourdon's column arrived first at the Place de Grève which they found deserted: Hanriot's men, having grown tired of waiting about in the now pouring rain and discouraged by reports that most *sections* had declared their support of the Convention, had gone home to bed.

Charles-André Merda, according to his own vainglorious account which has been largely discredited but not entirely disproved, was one of the first to enter the building:

The staircase was filled with supporters of the conspirators. We could hardly get by, marching three abreast. I was very excited ... The conspirators were in the secretariat to which all the approaches were closed. I got into the council chamber on the pretext that I was an orderly with secret despatches. I then took the passage to the left ... and reached the door of the secretariat ... Eventually the door was opened. I saw about fifty people inside in a state of great excitement ... I recognized Robespierre in the middle. He was sitting in an armchair with his left elbow on his knee and his head supported by his left hand. I leapt at him pointing my sword at his heart and crying, 'Surrender, you traitor!' He raised his head and replied, 'It is you who are the traitor. I shall have you shot.' At these words I reached for one of my pistols ... and fired. I meant to shoot him in the chest but the ball struck his chin and smashed his lower jaw. He fell out of his chair.

Robespierre had at last made up his mind to sign an appeal to arms. The pen had been in his hand. He had inscribed the first two letters of his name, Ro————, but there the writing stops. The bottom of the document is marked with blood.

Augustin Robespierre tried to escape by jumping out of a window, but he slipped and broke a leg. Couthon, helped to the top of a flight of stairs, fell to the bottom of them and cut open his forehead. Hanriot was hurled out of a window by Pierre Coffinhal, the immensely strong Vice-President of the Revolutionary Tribunal, who was enraged by the so-called General's incompetence; he fell on a dunghill from which he escaped to a builder's yard thence to a sewer where 'he was discovered by some soldiers who struck him with their bayonets and thrust out one of his eyes which then hung by the ligaments down his cheek'. Philippe Lebas shot himself. Saint-Just fingered a pistol as though toying with the idea of suicide himself but in the end he did not use it and quietly submitted to the gendarmes who escorted him with the other prisoners to the Convention. 'The coward Robespierre is outside,' Barras announced to the deputies. 'Do you wish him to enter?' 'To bring a man covered with crime into our hall would be to diminish the glory of this great day,' was the response. 'The body of a tyrant can only bring contagion with it. The proper place for Robespierre and his accomplices is the Place de la Révolution.'

Before being taken there Robespierre was carried on a plank to the offices of the Committee of Public Safety and dumped on a table in the green-painted anteroom, his head on a wooden ammunition box. For an hour he lay there without moving, his eyes closed, the blood still pouring from his shattered jaw. Then, at about four o'clock in the morning, he opened his eyes, and began quietly to wipe the clotted blood from his mouth with a pistol holster of soft white leather. One of the people who surrounded the table, looking down at him with more curiosity than pity, offered him a few pieces of paper which he used instead of the holster until they, too, were covered in blood. Some of the crowd in the room jeered at him: 'Well, you do seem to have gone quiet all of a sudden!' 'Oh, Sire! Is your Majesty in pain?'

At about six o'clock a surgeon came to stop him bleeding to

death. He put a key in his mouth, pulled out two or three teeth together with some fragments of broken bone, and then dressed the wound with a bandage that covered the whole of the lower part of his face. During these operations Robespierre remained silent, showing scarcely a trace of the agony he must have endured. When the surgeon had finished he pulled up the stockings which had fallen down to his ankles, pushed himself off the table and went to sit in a chair where he looked at the people who still surrounded him, his face as white as his stockings, the bandages round his jaw now red with blood.

At nine o'clock Couthon was brought into the room on a stretcher. Then Saint-Just and Dumas appeared. None of them spoke until Saint-Just, looking at the large placard proclaiming the Rights of Man that had been stuck on the wall, said, 'Well, whatever you say, that is *something* we did.' An hour later all the prisoners were taken to the Conciergerie where Robespierre indicated that he wanted pen and paper. 'What for?' the gaoler answered, refusing to bring them. 'Do you want to write to your Supreme Being?'

Arraigned before the Revolutionary Tribunal, Robespierre and his brother, together with Saint-Just, Couthon, Hanriot, Dumas, Fleuriot and sixteen other members of the *conseil general* of the Commune – a further seventy were to follow them – were condemned to death and taken by cart to the guillotine at five o'clock that afternoon. The crowds all along the route were immense and rowdy. They shouted insults and curses at the men in the carts, calling out 'To the guillotine! Long live the Republic! Down with the tyrant!' For a few moments the tumbrils stopped outside the Duplays' house while women danced about them and a boy, who had fetched a bucket from a butcher's shop, smeared the door with blood.

Robespierre's face was 'wrapped in a bandage of dirty, bloodstained linen', runs one report, 'and, from what could be seen of it, was fearfully disfigured . . . His eyes were lowered and almost closed . . . Just before arriving at the place of execution . . . a woman forced her way through the crowd . . . and, grasping the railing of the cart with one hand, raised the other threateningly in his face. "You monster spewed out of hell," she shouted at him. "Go down into your grave burdened with the curses of the wives and mothers of France . . . The thought of your execution makes me drunk with joy." '

Augustin Robespierre was also bandaged; so was Couthon; so also was Hanriot who, 'drunk as usual', presented a horrifying spectacle with his right eye still hanging from its socket. Saint-Just, who had once declared that the ship of the Revolution could arrive safely in port 'only by ploughing its way boldly through a Red Sea of blood', looked upon the crowd with stiff disdain, his pale brown breeches and white waistcoat still immaculate. They reached the Place de la Révolution at about half-past seven in the evening.

As Hanriot was 'about to ascend the scaffold, a bystander snatched out his loose eye'. Robespierre, who had to be lifted from the cart, lay flat on the ground, appearing to take no notice of what was happening. His eyes were closed and he did not open them until he felt himself being carried up on to the scaffold. The executioner threw off the coat which had been placed over his shoulders and then tore away the bandage and splint that the surgeon had applied to his wound. As his lower jaw fell from his upper, and the blood flew once more 'in torrents', he let forth 'a groan like that of a dying tiger, which was heard all over the square'.

'We are all throwing ourselves into each other's arms,' a newspaper reported the following day. 'The tyrant is no more.'

THE DAYS OF *GERMINAL*, *PRAIRIAL* AND *VENDÉMIAIRE*

1 April, 20 May and 4–6 October 1795

'*A burning fever is followed by complete prostration of strength*'

LA REVELLIÈRE-LÉPEAUX

The destruction of the Robespierrists and the wholesale purge of the Commune soon resulted in the Revolution's lurching to the Right. But the change of direction was not immediately apparent. In the general rejection of the Terror that followed the *journée* of 9 *Thermidor*, several former Hébertists and the *Enragés* who had escaped the guillotine were released from prison. Such extreme *sans-culotte* leaders as Jean Varlet came into prominence once more and, in a number of provincial towns, radicals reassumed that importance in the *comités revolutionnaires* of which Robespierre's recall of the *représentants en mission* had deprived them. But gradually the Plain began to assert itself as a more considerable body than it had ever done in the past. Some of its members, as well as some former Dantonists like Thuriot de la Rozère were elected to the Committee of Public Safety whose powers were severely reduced as were those of the Revolutionary Tribunal. Billaud-Varenne, Collot d'Herbois, Carnot and the time-serving Bertrand Barère de Vieuzac all left the Committee of Public Safety, and Fouquier-Tinville was removed from the Revolutionary Tribunal.

Moderates and Montagnards alike found it increasingly difficult to stem the rightward flow of the revolutionary tide. Robert Lindet proposed to the Convention that, while nobles and clergy should no longer be condemned merely because of their birth or calling, and while the Law of 22 *Prairial* against suspects which had been repealed should never be reintroduced, there should be no vendetta against those who had been responsible for the errors and violence of the past. But although the Convention voted unanimously in favour of this compromise, the revulsion against the Montagnards could not so easily be contained. Some of those who had once worked with Robespierre – and in the end had fallen foul of him, Fréron, Barras and Tallien amongst them – became positively reactionary as if to atone for the excesses of the Terror for which they had been responsible; and under their protection the *jeunesse dorée*, young men of mostly middle-class background, became as frightening a force as the *sans-culottes* had once been. These *jeunesse dorée*, who marched about the streets carrying short sticks weighted with lead, wore a kind of uniform of square-skirted coats and tight trousers, low boots and extremely high cravats. Their hair dangled in long locks over their ears and was plaited at the back of their heads. They constituted a dictatorship, so one of them boasted, 'a dictatorship which nobody opposed because it filled everyone's wish'. With their help the closure of the Jacobin Club was brought about, the red caps of liberty were banished from the streets and nearly all the Paris *sections* were taken over by the Right who, having stopped payments to workers for attending meetings, went further in keeping out unwanted *sans-culottes* by arranging to have the meetings held only in the middle of the day.

As the tide of reaction mounted, as pamphlets and newspapers attacked 'Robespierre's Tail', as theatre audiences applauded anti-Jacobin plays and the actors of the Comédie Française were released from prison, the surviving Girondins were recalled to the Convention from which David's paintings of the deaths of Marat and Lepeletier were removed. At the same time demands for the punishment of the men who had been responsible for the Terror grew louder. Jean Baptiste Carrier, the lawyer, who had supervised the cruelties of the Terror at Nantes was guillotined on 16 November. Collot d'Herbois, Billaud-Varenne, Barère and Vadier, were all brought to trial. So were Le Bon and Herman. Fouquier-Tinville and fifteen men who had served with him on the Revolutionary Tribunal were executed to the undisguised delight of those artisans and shopkeepers, domestic servants, journeymen and tradesmen whose families had provided the guillotine with most of its victims.

In many French provinces, also, reaction led to demands for the punishment of those who had carried out the bloody policies of the fallen régime and in some areas, particularly in the south, to outbreaks of what became known as the White Terror. Officials responsible for the former Terror were beaten, maimed, lynched and murdered by friends and relations of those who had suffered, by fanatical extremists of the Right as merciless as their victims, or by groups of assassins like that known as the *Compagnie du Soleil*. In several towns in Provence and Languedoc, in Ain and Gascony, in Marseilles and Lyons, Aix and Nîmes, in Tarascon and Lons-le-Saunier hundreds of prisoners were massacred in their cells or in the courtyard of the gaols in which they had been confined for offences committed in the time of Robespierre.

Elsewhere in France the change of government provoked less violence. In certain departments, indeed, there were no reprisals at all, in others no cause for them. At Rheims, for instance, the few 'Terrorists' brought to trial were all acquitted, while in Seine-et-Marne the Terror had not been accountable for a single death.

In other areas it proved impossible for the central Government to exercise any firm control over the local authorities. Lyons, though nominally supervised by moderate republicans, became once more a kind of royalist stronghold; while in the Vendée the rebels who had risen up against the Republic were able – by a series of armistices highly favourable to themselves– to exercise an authority which left them in virtual control not only of their own territory but also of large parts of the north-west.

Both in these areas and in most departments of France this was an even more unpleasant time than usual for the poor. The rate of inflation and the numbers of unemployed soared. Bread was rationed, fuel scarce. Brigandage was common in the countryside. And the winter of 1794–5 was an exceptionally severe one: first temperatures fell so low that many rivers, including the Seine, froze from bank to bank and starving wolves abandoning the snow-bound forests, invaded villages and towns, then a sudden thaw led to widespread floods. Spring came at last, but no end to the suffering. By April 1795 food prices in certain towns had doubled since the beginning of the year while bread, for instance, had risen to over forty-five *sous* the pound. *Assignats* were worth no more than eight per cent of their original value.

To the *sans-culottes* it seemed that the gap between rich and poor was becoming almost as wide as it had been before the Revolution. Sudden fortunes were being made by profiteers and speculators who spent money as rapidly as they made it. They and their women sped through the streets in ornately painted carriages to expensive restaurants where meals were devoured at prices that would have provided two month's food for a worker's family, to gambling dens, to theatres whose private rooms, in the words of a police report, were 'absolute sewers of debauchery and vice', and to dance halls which now sprang up all over Paris. Dandies known as *incroyables*, affecting lisps and dressed in the most outlandish fashions, with hair cut short in front and raised up by a comb at the back, appeared in the Tuileries gardens and were seen enjoying boating parties on the Seine accompanied by *merveilleuses* whose scanty, revealing clothes were equally exotic and whose wigs were marvels of the *perru-quier's* art. At *bals des victimes*, entertainments at once riotous and ghoulish, guests whose friends or relations had perished in the Terror wore hair arranged as though prepared for the blade of the guillotine and thin bands of red silk round their necks.

The *sans-culottes* grew more and more resentful, but they had no effective leaders now. They were not supported by the *sections* any more, nor, as they had been in the past, by a powerful Commune. An attempt was made to mount one of those revolutionary *journées* which had once been so successful: on 1 April (12 *Germinal*) demonstrators, women and men 'with bare arms and chests', marched upon the Convention demanding cheaper bread, the proscription of the *jeunesse dorée* and the resurrection of the Constitution which the Montagnards had framed in 1793. But the Convention, unlike that of June 1793, was not to be intimidated – the National Guard was on its side – and after a party of *muscadins* armed with whips and cudgels had been called in by Legendre, the demonstrators were thrown out with ease. Far from winning either sympathy or concessions the *journée* of 12 *Germinal* provoked repression. Some of the *sans-culotte* leaders were arrested, and many of their adherents, both in Paris and the provinces, were dismissed by their employers and refused passports which might have enabled them to go in search of other work. At the same time, the opportunity was taken to get rid of several Montagnards: eight of the most notable were arrested, and Billaud-Varenne, Collot d'Herbois and Barère were all sentenced to transportation, Billaud-Varenne and Collot to Guiana, Barère to the Isle of Oléron.

Undeterred by these punishments and angered by yet another cut in the bread ration, the Parisian *sans-culottes* made a further attempt a few weeks later to force the Convention to attend to their complaints. But, as in other towns where there were demonstrations and riots, and even cries of 'Bread and a King', the workers had no effective leadership.

Even so, the demonstration planned for 20 May (1 *Prairial*) threatened to be massive and intimidating. The night before, crowds of people, many of them women, could be seen rushing about the streets of the Faubourgs Saint-Antoine and Saint-Marceau, the Rues Saint-Denis and Saint-Martin and throughout the Cité, urging people to join them next day in a march upon the Convention, to stick slogans in their hats reading '*Bread and the Constitution of '93*' and to let the women march in the front as the Government's troops would never dare to open fire on them. They declared that the Convention had executed Robespierre and his friends only to take their place as tyrants, that the people were being deliberately starved, that avaricious shop-keepers were being encouraged to keep their prices at a level that no poor family could afford. The next morning, as church bells rang, as the tocsin was pealed, cannon fired and drums beaten, a vast crowd of people, accompanied by three battalions of National Guard, though not by their officers, marched towards the Tuileries, carrying placards, pikes and swords, some unarmed shouting, 'This is the struggle of the black hands against the white.' They arrived at the hall of the Assembly at about ten o'clock, closing all the roads that led towards it. Then, bursting through the doors, they shouted for food that they could afford. The President, Vernier, putting on his hat, called for silence and order; and, when his pleas were ignored, was replaced in the chair by the more authoritative André Dumont whose commands were no more successful. 'No talk!' the mob cried. '*Bread!*' At length an army officer appeared with a party of fusiliers and a number of *jeunesse dorée*, equipped as before with cudgels and postboys' whips. They slashed at the backs of the demonstrators, men and women alike, 'who fled with tremendous screams, amidst the loud applause on the part of the spectators in the tribunes'.

Within a few minutes, however, there was a renewed assault upon the locked doors, one of which was forced off its hinges with a splintering of wood and a shower of plaster. Once more the mob rushed in as the deputies on the lower seats scrambled towards the upper benches, out of harm's way. At this moment, men armed with muskets and bayonets from one of the *sections* loyal to the Convention, appeared on the scene and managed to drive the assailants back. But the crowd outside the hall was constantly growing until, shortly before three o'clock, though the men who had come to the Convention's defence stood by the doors with crossed bayonets, the mob forced their way in yet again, those in front being pushed forward by the pressure of bodies behind. The deputies rose from their seats shouting 'The Republic for ever!' as shots were fired and musket balls ricochetted about the walls. One brave deputy, a young man from the valley of the Douro named Jean Féraud, came forward to face the invaders, throwing himself down in front of them, and crying out, 'Kill me! You will have to pass over my body before you take another step.' The invaders ignored him, trampling over him and, while some sat down in the seats vacated by the deputies who had moved to those higher up the hall, others advanced towards the President's chair, now occupied by Boissy d'Anglas instead of the exhausted Dumont.

Seeing his new President thus threatened, the intrepid Féraud jumped to his feet, ran to protect him and was shot and killed in the ensuing scuffle. His body, kicked by wooden sabots, was dragged outside, decapitated by a tavern-keeper who 'sliced off his head like a turnip' and threw it back to the crowd. It was then taken back into the hall, impaled upon a pike, to intimidate the President. Boissy d'Anglas remained calm and collected, at first holding up his arm to screen his eyes from the horrible sight of Féraud's dripping head, then bowing sadly and respectfully towards it. And while the crowd shouted, beat drums and rattled the staffs of their pikes on the floor, various deputies endeavoured to make themselves heard above the uproar, the Montagnards amongst them apparently ready to give way to some of the demonstrators' demands. But exactly what these demands were it was difficult to determine. Some, amidst cries for bread and the 1793 Constitution, called for the release of all patriots, others for the re-establishment of the Commune. One man repeatedly shouted for the arrest of all *émigrés*, another for house to house searches for hidden food, and a third kept up for half an hour an insistent chant of 'The arrest of all rogues and tyrants! The arrest of all rogues and tyrants!' For two hours the wild confusion continued unabated until one of the leaders of the demonstrators, whose name was never discovered, proposed that the deputies should be brought down from the seats to which they had climbed for refuge, collected on the floor of the hall and forced to discuss the people's plight. This was done, and there followed an inconclusive debate in which nothing of importance was decided and votes were registered in such a chaotic manner that it was impossible to determine who had voted for what. In any case the Government Committees had already decided that no measures which might be adopted under duress were to be considered binding.

The Committees had by now assembled sufficient forces to disperse the rioters, and at about half-past eleven the leading columns arrived at the Tuileries. Their commander, Danton's friend, the butcher Legendre, who had become one of the principal proponents of reaction, mounted the rostrum and shouted above the din, 'I exhort the Convention to stand firm. And, in the name of the law, I command the citizens who are here to withdraw.'

He was shouted down by the rioters, but, after a brief struggle in which a few men were wounded, the insurgents were at long last cleared out of the building. As they fled through the doors and jumped from the windows, a deputy stood up to speak. 'So this assembly,' he said, 'the cradle of the Republic, has once more almost become its tomb. Fortunately the crimes of the conspirators have been averted. But, fellow-representatives, you would not be worthy of the nation if you were not to avenge them in a signal manner.' Cheers and clapping greeted these words from all sides, and fourteen Montagnards who had spoken in defence of the demonstrators, or were believed to be in sympathy with them, were immediately arrested. The names of other Montagnards who had earned unfortunate reputations for themselves in the provinces were then called out and the arrest of these men, too, was demanded to enthusiastic shouts of 'The Convention for ever!'

'Let us have no more half measures,' cried Tallien, whose behaviour at Bordeaux had for a time been far more merciless than that of any of the commissioners now denounced. 'The aim of today's violent demonstration was to re-establish the Commune and to restore the Jacobins to power. We must destroy all that remains of them . . . We must have vengeance . . . We must profit by the inefficiency of these men who fancy themselves the equals of those who overthrew the throne, who try to bring about revolutions and succeed only in provoking riots . . . We must lose no time in punishing them and putting an end to the Revolution.'

Tallien's words also were loudly applauded. But when the session was closed and the deputies departed at three o'clock in the morning, the men whose condign punishment he had advocated were already planning another attempt to overawe the Convention. It was to take place that very day. Setting out from the Faubourg Saint-Antoine a large body of demonstrators, better armed and disciplined than those who had marched the day before, were to advance upon the Tuileries and to threaten the Convention with cannon. The march began as planned, and the deputies who had reassembled in their hall after only a few hours' sleep were soon to learn that their own gunners had defected to the insurgents, taking their cannon with them. Legendre stood up in an attempt to reassure them. 'Representatives,' he said, 'keep calm and remain at your posts . . . Good citizens are ready to defend you.'

The hall had, indeed, been surrounded by troops and by several units of the National Guard; yet the desertion of the artillery made it seem likely that, were fighting to break out, the forces at the Convention's disposal might be unable to hold the assailants back. For several minutes conflict appeared imminent as the opposing forces faced each other, their muskets loaded. But then men from both sides began to protest at having to fight their fellow-citizens. Gradually they broke ranks and walked across to talk to each other, and eventually it was agreed that twelve members of the Convention should be invited to leave their hall and to come down to discuss the grievances of the hostile *sections*. Twelve deputies were accordingly selected and went to fraternize with the *sans-culottes* who, after prolonged negotiations, persuaded them to allow a deputation of demonstrators to present a petition to the Convention. Upon their appearance in the hall, where they reiterated their demands, there were loud shouts of 'Down with the Jacobins!' from the public galleries. The President called for silence, and, having imposed it, addressed a few mollifying remarks to the deputation whose colleagues in the streets outside were already beginning to abandon their posts and go home.

So the *journée* of 1 *Prairial* was no more successful than the far more violent one of 12 *Germinal* – yet the repression that followed it was even more severe. The immediate trial of all prisoners taken from among the rioters was ordered. The beating of the *générale* without proper authority was made a capital offence, and a military commission was set up to pass sentence upon everyone, left-wing deputies and *sans-culotte* leaders alike, who were held responsible for the disturbances. The first of the accused brought before this military commission was the assassin of Féraud who had only just been apprehended and who was sentenced to be guillotined that same day.

This man was actually on the scaffold when a mob stormed up the steps, knocked aside the gendarmes and executioners and bore him away into a warren of narrow streets in the middle of the Faubourg Saint-Antoine. The Convention responded to this new provocation with a prompt display of determined force. Almost 25,000 men, including nearly 4,000 regular soldiers, were called up to surround the faubourg into which about 1,200 excited *jeunesse dorée* dashed with bravado ahead of them. These young men were soon themselves surrounded by the angry inhabitants of the neighbourhood and might not have escaped with the beating to which several of them were subjected had not the Convention's formidable army and its numerous cannon persuaded the *sans-culotte* leaders to agree to surrender their arms and to deliver up Féraud's murderer when they had found him.

Having put down this latest popular revolt, the Convention's agents turned with renewed vigour upon its promoters and upon the Montagnard deputies who were supposed to have looked upon it with indulgence. Well over 3,000 suspects were rounded up, and although most of these were later released, they were closely watched thereafter by the police and frequently re-arrested when further disturbances were threatened. Reports of an uprising at Toulon, which was, however, soon put down, increased the Convention's determination to be ruthless. Former members of the Committees of Public Safety and General Security, whose services to the country had previously protected them from punishment, were no longer immune. Carnot was spared as the 'organizer of military victory', but David's reputation as a distinguished artist

279

could no longer save him and he was imprisoned. Robert Lindet, whose responsibility for food-supplies on the Committee of Public Safety had been discharged with tireless efficiency, was also arrested. Among the thirty-six men condemned to death were six Montagnard deputies. The wife of a young army officer, Laure Junot, described their end:

One day my brother returned home dreadfully agitated. He had witnessed an awful scene. Romme, Soubrany, Duroi, Duquesnoi, Goujon and Bourbette [the six deputies] exhibited the most admirable fortitude during their trial . . . When sentence was pronounced on them they looked at each other calmly; and, on descending the staircase, which was lined with spectators, Romme looked about as if seeking somebody . . . who did not appear. 'No matter,' he said. 'With a firm hand this will do, *Vive la Liberté!*' Then drawing from his pocket a large penknife he plunged it into his heart, and, drawing it out again [fearing he had not struck hard enough, inflicted several more wounds on his chest, throat and face. He then] gave it Goujon who, in like manner, passed it to Duquesnoi. All three fell dead instantly without uttering a groan. The weapon, passed on to Soubrany by the trembling hand of Duquesnoi, found its way to the noble hearts of the rest; but they were not so fortunate as their three friends. Grievously wounded, yet alive, they fell at the foot of the scaffold which the executioner made them ascend, bleeding and mutilated as they were.

After their deaths and the final destruction of the Montagnards as a political force, the reaction continued apace. The *sans-culottes*, already virtually powerless, were further weakened by the reconstitution of the National Guard which became once more a largely bourgeois organization. The word 'revolutionary' was decreed as no longer applicable to institutions which had previously been thus described, a commemorative festival was instituted in honour of the Girondins, and an amnesty was offered to all those who had fled from France after the uprising of May 1793.

So fast was the tide of reaction flowing, indeed, that royalists began to hope for a restoration. The late King's son, whom they recognized as Louis XVII, had contracted tuberculosis of the bones during his incarceration in the Temple and died there aged ten on

8 June 1795. But the Comte de Provence, who had been surrounded by the most intransigent counter-revolutionaries during his exile and was then living at Verona, proclaimed himself King Louis XVIII. He announced that on his return to the throne he would restore the traditional three orders in France, have those who had voted for the death of his brother brought to trial, and give back to the Church the power and prestige it had formerly enjoyed.

Already plans had been laid for a royalist restoration by force. It was intended that the Prince de Condé, father of the Duc de Bourbon, who had fought against the Revolution in conjunction with the Austrians, should advance with a royalist army from the east; that an insurrection should be simultaneously provoked in the south; that the extravagant and pleasure-loving General, Charles Pichegru, commander of the Rhine Army, should be suborned by huge bribes, by the promise of his promotion to marshal and the offer of the château and park of Chambord; and that an expeditionary force of *émigrés*, for which the English government were to provide money, naval support and uniforms, should be landed in the north-west to link up with the *Chouans*. But, as with so many other royalist plots, the execution bore little relation to the planning. General Pichegru proved an unreliable accomplice; the plans for the insurrection in the south were discovered and thwarted; the Breton *Chouans* of 1795 lacked the fervent courage of the earlier *Vendéens*; and in General Lazare Hoche, a former private in the *Gardes-françaises*, the republicans had a commander as skilful as he was decisive. When the *émigré* forces landed on the southern coast of Brittany on 27 June 1795, Hoche soon forced them to surrender, having pushed the *Chouans* who tried to come to their support back into the Quiberon peninsula. Over 700 prisoners, most of them nobles and many of them former naval officers, were shot in their English uniforms for high treason.

The immediate results of this dismal failure were a fresh outbreak of the cruel civil war in the north-west, where savage reprisals were taken against republican prisoners by the rebels, and a vigorous campaign by the Government against both royalists and the few surviving Montagnards. Several royalist journalists were arrested; so were some Montagnards, including that cunning intriguer, Fouché, while determined efforts were made to track down those of the *jeunesse dorée* to whose evasion of military service the authorities had hitherto turned a blind eye. At the same time the Convention debated the draft of a new constitution which was presented by Boissy d'Anglas.

In introducing this Constitution of the Year Three, Boissy d'Anglas, in a speech which might almost have been written by Vergniaud, declared:

> Absolute equality is a chimera. If it existed one would have to assume complete equality in intelligence, virtue, physical strength, education and fortune in all men ... We must be ruled by the best citizens. And the best are the most learned and the most concerned in the maintenance of law and order. Now, with very few exceptions, you will find such men only among those who own some property, and are thus attached to the land in which it lies, to the laws which protect it and to the public order which maintains it ... You must, therefore, guarantee the political rights of the well-to-do ... and [deny] unreserved political rights to men without property, for if such men ever find themselves seated among the legislators, then they will provoke agitations ... without fearing their consequences ... and in the end precipitate us into those violent convulsions from which we have scarcely yet emerged.

After two months' debate the Constitution, which in effect returned the country's political and economic leadership to men who were reasonably well off, was approved by the Convention. Legislative power was to be entrusted to two Councils, a Council of Five Hundred composed of men over thirty years of age who were to have the right to initiate laws, and a Council of Ancients of two hundred and fifty members, married men or widowers at least forty years old, who were to approve or veto the laws proposed. A third of the members of each Council were to be required to retire each year. Executive power was to be entrusted to a Directory of five members who were to be appointed by the Council of Five Hundred and who were to be given a magnificent uniform 'as a protest', so Boissy d'Anglas said, 'against *sans-culottism*'.

Conscious that they commanded limited support in the country as a whole, the Thermidorians – as Boissy d'Anglas and his col-

leagues were called in allusion to the season in which the Robespierrists had been overthrown – decreed that two thirds of the new
deputies should be chosen from amongst the members of the Convention. Both this Law of the Two-Thirds as it was known and the
Constitution itself were submitted to a plebiscite; and, despite
enormous numbers of abstentions, both were approved, the Constitution by a majority of over a million votes to less than 50,000,
the Two-Thirds Law by about two to one.

The comparatively widespread opposition to this law, particularly in Paris, the South and the West, gave the royalists an opportunity to organize the last *journée* of the Revolution. Protesting that
there had been fraud in the counting of votes, that the troops which
had been brought into the capital had been called in for some sinister
purpose, and that the Convention's attempt to perpetuate itself was
an affront to freedom, the royalist plotters were able to play on the
people's distress to win their support. For there was, indeed, much
distress in France that summer and autumn of 1795. The bread
ration fell as the price of meat rose, and wages could not keep up
with the rising cost of everything else. Sugar soared from eleven to
sixty-two *livres* a pound, firewood from 160 *livres* a wagon-load in
May to 500 in September. The cost of living had by then risen
almost thirty times higher than it had been in 1790. The police were
accordingly not surprised when the annual celebrations commemor-
ating the fall of the monarchy passed off in what they termed 'a state
of apathy'.

To the royalists and their fellow-conspirators the time, then,
seemed ideal for an attack upon the Convention. They induced a
number of *Chouan* leaders and *émigrés* to come to Paris, and went
about the *sections* fostering the people's inclination to blame their
sufferings and misfortunes upon the Government, persuading them
that they were threatened with a renewal of the Terror, inciting
young men to march about the streets shouting 'Down with the
Two-Thirds'. In several *sections* there were serious riots in which
musket shots were exchanged with the soldiers of the Convention.

The Convention responded to the danger from the royalists by
turning to the staunchly republican *sans-culottes*, issuing arms to all
citizens 'faithful to the Revolution' who applied for them, and by

forming three battalions of 'Patriots of '89'. At least seven of the disaffected *sections* thereupon declared themselves in rebellion, beat the *générale* in defiance of the law and seized arms for the fight that now appeared inevitable. By the beginning of October, after news had reached Paris of the eruption and repression of royalist uprisings at Châteauneuf-en-Thimerais and Dreux, as many as 25,000 *sectionnaires* were under arms. The *section* of Lepeletier became the centre of the insurrectionary movement, and it was here that the Government's first attempt to suppress it took place. General J. F. de Menou, commander of the Army of the Interior, was ordered to march into it with a strong force of infantry, cavalry and artillery to overawe the rebel *sectionnaires* and to insist that they deliver up their arms. Menou, a kind officer of a somewhat hesitant nature and moderate political opinions, accepted his orders with reluctance and carried them out both late and indecisively. He advanced towards the convent of the Filles St Thomas, where the leaders of the Lepeletier *section* were in session, with his troops in so close a formation that, had they been called upon to do so, they would have had little chance of conducting a successful engagement against the massed ranks of their armed opponents who filled the streets and looked down upon them from the roof tops. General Menou entered the convent, his cannon drawn up behind him and levelled at the door. He found the *section*'s committee armed and defiant. To his almost apologetic request that they hand over their weapons, they replied that they would do nothing of the sort, defying him to use force. So, having obtained an undertaking that the *section* would disperse its forces if he withdrew his, he led his columns out of the area while the men he had been sent to subdue fulfilled their promise, only to reassemble again immediately in more challenging mood than ever.

Well aware now that Menou was far from the kind of general they needed in such a crisis, and suspecting that he might well be in complicity with the rebels, the Convention dismissed him and appointed in his place Paul Barras, who had proved so energetic a leader during the *journée* of *Thermidor*. But Barras had never been a particularly successful commander of regular troops – his years in the army, spent mostly in India, had not been in the least distinguished – and it was considered essential that he should be given some more experienced assistants. One of these, introduced to him by Fréron, was the Corsican Brigadier Napoleon Bonaparte.

Bonaparte, then aged twenty-six, had come to the notice of the Convention through his exceptional skill as an artillery officer during the siege of Toulon and had risen from the rank of captain to that of brigadier-general within the space of four months. Unlike several of his friends, including his closest, Alexandre des Mazis, who had chosen to emigrate, he had demonstrated his support of the Revolution from the beginning. While stationed at Valence as a subaltern he had been appointed secretary of the Society of Friends of the Constitution. He had publicly condemned the King's flight to Varennes, and had made it known that he approved both of the sale of land confiscated from the Church and the nobility, and of the decree by which the clergy were to be elected by their congregations. Since the capture of Toulon, however, Bonaparte's career had not prospered. He had become friendly with the sociable, gregarious Augustin Robespierre and, after the fall of the Robespierrists, had thus become suspect to the Thermidorians. For a time he was placed under house arrest. Then, after his release, he was transferred from the artillery to the infantry for having tried to rescind an order posting him to the Army of the West which was engaged in the unpleasant duty of fighting the *Chouans*. He applied for sick leave which he spent in Paris in a dreary hotel on the Left Bank, complaining of the shabby way he had been treated and even on occasion threatening suicide. He walked disconsolately about the city in his now frayed uniform, or in what Mme Junot described as 'a grey greatcoat, very plainly made, buttoned up to his chin . . . and a black cravat very clumsily tied', his long ill-combed hair falling over his collar. When his leave was over, he asked for a command in the field, but was given instead a staff appointment which he found so irksome that he decided to go to Constantinople to help reorganize the Turkish artillery. He had obtained his passport and was ready to leave when Fréron, whom he had met in the South while they were on duty together there, took him to Barras.

'Will you serve me?' Barras asked him abruptly. 'You have three minutes to decide.'

Bonaparte needed no time to consider the offer. He assented

immediately, asking only where were the guns which would be needed if they were to repel the threatened attack by the rebels who outnumbered the Convention's forces by about six to one. Joachim Murat, a handsome, swaggering cavalry officer, an innkeeper's son who was one day to become King of Naples, was sent to fetch them from a camp, six miles to the south. A rebel force was already on its way to the camp, but, galloping at the head of 200 horsemen, Murat arrived there first and brought back forty guns with him to Paris. Eight of these were allocated to Bonaparte who was given the task of defending the Tuileries from any attack that might be made upon it from the north.

The total number of men at the Convention's disposal was about 8,000, of whom some 5,000 were regular troops of the line. Most of these were disposed so as to guard all approaches to the Tuileries in the Rue du Cul de Sac Dauphin, the Rue l'Échelle, the Rue Rohan and the Rue St Nicaise, on the Pont Neuf, the Pont Royal and the Pont Louis XVI, and around the Place de la Révolution and the Place Vendôme. The cavalry were held in reserve on the Carrousel and in the Tuileries gardens. An ammunition depot, a hospital and stores of provisions were established in the Tuileries itself. The heights of Meudon were occupied so that the Convention could retire there if compelled to retreat from their hall, and arms were sent to the radical Faubourg Saint-Antoine whose 'attachment to the cause of liberty' Barras – prepared to accept any allies so long as the emergency lasted – described as being well known and whose inhabitants Fréron was exhorting to come to the defence of the Revolution.

While these preparations were being made, the insurrectionary committee, which had been set up in the *section* of Lepeletier, was also making its dispositions. It appointed as commander-in-chief of its forces General Danican, an officer from a poor noble family who had served against the *Vendéens* but had been dismissed on suspicion of being secretly a royalist. He had come to Paris, thoroughly dis-illusioned by the present Government, and prepared to assist in any plans for its subversion. The misconceived plan which the insur-rectionaries adopted was to make a concerted attack upon the Tuil-eries. Instead of building barricades around it, encircling it with sharpshooters in the surrounding houses, and bringing about its downfall by a siege of attrition, they decided to storm the Tuileries with columns of troops marching upon it from the Odéon, from the streets that led down to it from the Rue Saint-Honoré, and from the Pont Neuf.

The Convention's forces waited all morning for the expected attack in a drizzling rain. The deputies sat in silence in their hall. Eight hundred muskets and cartouche boxes were stored in an ante-room, ready for their use should they have to defend themselves. Noon came and still there was no attack. Barras, on horseback, and Bonaparte on foot, waited in the courtyard of the Tuileries. Two eight-pounders, loaded with case-shot had been placed at the end of the Rue Neuve Saint-Roch, their barrels levelled at the church of Saint-Roch at the end of the street. After hours of silence, there came the sound of drums and musket fire. Bonaparte approached the guns and waited there for Barras's orders.

It was soon after three o'clock when the leading columns of the rebels appeared in the Rue Saint-Honoré. The Convention's troops opened fire on them with their muskets, but they came on, returning the fire, into the Rue Neuve Saint-Roch. Barras gave Bonaparte the order to open up with his eight pounders. Immediately the gunners responded. The shots tore into the advancing ranks, mowing many of them down and blasting chunks of masonry from the walls of the church. The rebels faltered, then came on again, wavered as the shot tore into them and finally fell back as the guns were wheeled to the right and left and fired down the Rue Saint-Honoré from top to bottom. The *sectionnaires*, scattered now, fled backwards towards the Lepeletier.

Here, in the convent of the Filles Saint Thomas, Danican and the insurrectionary committee decided upon another assault from the Faubourg Saint-Germain towards the Pont Neuf which was still occupied by men under the command of a young *émigré* named Lafond. Here they would be joined by a column under a *Vendéen* leader, the Comte de Maulevrier. The combined force would then advance along the Quai Voltaire to the Pont Royal. But once again the rebels could not withstand the barrage of artillery. A storm of grape-shot from the Pont Royal tore into their ranks from the front, while other guns opened up on them from the *quai* of the Tuileries. Lafond made a gallant effort to storm the bridge, but his men were driven back by the relentless fire of the Convention's gunners. By six o'clock, when two to three hundred men had been killed or wounded on both sides, the fighting was over.

After the *journées* of *Vendémiaire* there was to be no further threat from the royalists. With the influence of the Montagnards and the *sans-culottes* also destroyed, the largely well-to-do and conservative Thermidorians were now in control of the Revolution. But it was to prove an extremely unsteady and insecure control, maintained only by devious compromises, by successive purges, by hitting out alternately at reactionaries and radicals alike, and by an increasing reliance upon the army.

THE ADVENT OF BONAPARTE

*'It appears that France must soon be governed by a single despot . . .
a dictator produced by the Revolution'*

GOUVERNEUR MORRIS

On 3 November 1795, the day after their election, the Directors met in a small room in the gloomy deserted Luxembourg. Taking off their melodramatically plumed hats, they sat round a rickety table on straw-bottomed chairs which the porter had brought into the otherwise unfurnished room together with some logs for the fire. Only one of them was well known and he not much respected. This was Paul Barras who, so a foreign Minister said, would have 'thrown the Republic out of the window tomorrow if it did not pay for his dogs, his mistress, his food and his gambling'. The others, all of whom had voted for the King's death, were Louis-Marie La Revellière-Lépeaux, Jean-François Reubell and Étienne-François Letourneur. La Revellière, an anti-clerical former Girondin, was a hunchback with a huge head and thin legs who, it was said, had escaped the guillotine only because a Montagnard had scornfully complained of time being wasted on such a 'paltry fellow as that'. Reubell, like La Revellière, had been a deputy in the Constituent Assembly but had sat as a Montagnard. An arrogant, red-faced lawyer he had also been on the Committee of Public Safety and had once been heard to declare that 'any deputy who opposed the Revolution ought to be put in a sack and thrown into the river'. Letourneur, an officer in the Engineers, had been an unassertive member of the Plain. The fifth Director, Sieyès, was not there. He had refused to serve, and his place was subsequently taken by Carnot.

Two days after this first meeting the Directors issued a statement proclaiming their intention of replacing 'the chaos which always accompanies revolutions by a new social order'. They intended to 'wage vigorous war on royalists, revive patriotism, sternly suppress all factions, extinguish party spirit, destroy all desire for vengeance ... revive industry and commerce, stamp out speculation, revitalize the arts and sciences, re-establish public credit and restore plenty'.

These were formidable tasks. For not only were the royalists 'reviving their intrigues', as the Directors themselves put it, not only were the Left also endeavouring to bring the Directory down, but the financial and economic plight of the country was disastrous. The value of the *assignat* had fallen so low that one hundred *livres'* worth could now be exchanged for no more than fifteen *sous*; and when 2,400,000 *livres* of a new paper currency, *mandats territoriaux*, were issued, these depreciated in value so rapidly that by the beginning of 1797, when they were withdrawn, they were worth only one per cent of their face value. Beggars pushed them away when offered them. Peasants, too, only accepted metal currency for their produce, protesting that they would only take 'the other stuff' if their horses would eat it. And their produce was far from plentiful. The 1795 harvest was so poor, in fact, that the already meagre bread ration had to be severely curtailed and in certain places supplemented by rice which the poor could not cook because of the exorbitant prices demanded for fuel.

The discontent of the poor was aggravated by the ever increasing flamboyance of the rich. 'The thirst for pleasure,' reported one newspaper, 'the stream of fashion, a succession of dinners, the luxury of their splendid furniture and their mistresses, are the objects that chiefly employ the thoughts of the young men of Paris.' New restaurants and dance-halls opened every week, the thirty-two theatres were crowded every night, and so were the gambling rooms in one of which the wife of a deputy 'lost two millions on a single card'. There were firework displays at the Tivoli and the Pavillon de Hanovre, a new circus in the garden of the Capucines, lively entertainments in the gardens of Marboeuf, and daring *tableaux vivants* in the Jardins d'Idalie. Carriages once more bowled along to Longchamp, and at Frascati's heads turned and men stood on tiptoe to catch a glimpse of the delicious young Madame Récamier, or of Madame Tallien in a gauze dress split down the side, with jewels in her black hair, bracelets round her ankles and rings on her painted toes.

Fashions became more and more *outré*. There was a passion for pseudo-classical styles, for long diaphanous high-breasted robes, for 'Athenian' coiffeurs with triple rows of curls, for Grecian, bejewelled sandals and plumed and spangled fans, for dressing *à la sauvage*, 'the arms and breasts bare, a gauze skirt with flesh coloured tights beneath it . . . and circlets set with diamonds round the legs and thighs'. 'No one,' wrote Mallet du Pan, 'thinks of anything now but eating and drinking and pleasures.'

There were millions, though, for whom there could be no pleasure, who were saved from starvation only by the free distribution of food requisitioned from the peasants, whose plight was cited by the Jacobins as further evidence of the Directory's appalling incompetence. Initially the Directors had been tolerant towards the Left in their anxiety to bind all parties together in a stabilized regime. They had appointed Jacobins to various administrative posts, they had been indulgent towards the appearance of various radical clubs, including the Panthéon Club, and they had allowed freedom to the left-wing press. But they had soon felt obliged to reconsider their policy of toleration when there seemed a danger that the Jacobins might combine to overthrow them. They dismissed the most troublesome or suspect of them from the posts to which they had been appointed, they prosecuted left-wing journalists, they closed the Panthéon Club, and they issued a warrant for the arrest of François-Noël Babeuf, the tactless and obtuse journalist, who declared in his *Tribun du peuple* that the Revolution was being betrayed, that, 'despite all obstacles and oppositions', it had advanced up to 9 *Thermidor* but had been retreating ever since.

Babeuf, who chose to call himself Gracchus, was born at Saint Quentin in November 1760, the son of a petty official and of an illiterate maidservant. He had worked as a young man for a land surveyor at Roye where his distaste for his ill-paid work and his sympathy for the unfortunate peasants living in the rural poverty of Picardy drew him to the career of political journalist. A compulsive, tedious writer, he was also resilient, indefatigable and persistent. The more often he was derided the more sure he was that his theories constituted the answer to the problems of mankind. In his earlier days as a political philosopher he had supported the idea of the *loi agraire*, but he had now come to the view that 'perfect equality' and 'common happiness' could only be achieved by the suppression of individual property and the private ownership of land. Men, working at their chosen occupations, should place the fruits of their labour into a common store, and there should be established 'a simple administration for food supplies' which would 'take note of all individuals and all provisions and have the latter divided up according to the most scrupulous equality'. Babeuf had also come to the view that this form of communism could only be realized by violence. He and his fellow-conspirators therefore set up an insurrectionary committee and dispatched agents all over Paris to spread the word of their 'Plebeians' Manifesto'. But from the beginning Babeuf's organization had been infiltrated by spies, and the Government were well informed as to his intentions, knowing the names of most of his confederates. Even so, the Directors were unsure how best to proceed against the so-called 'Conspiracy of Equals'. Reubell feared that to take strong action might play into the hands of the royalists; La Revellière was more concerned with the activities of refractory priests; Barras, characteristically, waited until he was quite sure which way the wind was blowing. Carnot, however, insisted on firm repression. So, on 10 May 1796 Babeuf, a most incompetent conspirator, was arrested, and in August he and his fellow-conspirators were taken to trial in iron cages to Vendôme. On 26 May 1797 after an immensely long trial, he and one fellow-conspirator were condemned to death, the others being acquitted. He was guillotined the following day.

Although joined by numerous former terrorists and financed by Jacobins bent upon the Directory's destruction, Babeuf's conspiracy had never presented a danger to the Government as had the royalists. Supported by hundreds of *émigrés* and non-juring priests now returning to France and supplied with money by the English Government through an agent in Switzerland, the royalist campaign was gathering strength week by week. In April 1797 the majority of the new members returned in the elections were constitutional monarchists; and had they been a united, well-led party, able to come to terms with the *émigrés*, they might well have overthrown the Directory, restored the throne and made peace with France's foreign enemies. But they were disunited, had no outstandingly capable leaders and were repeatedly rebuffed by the diehard *émigrés*. Moreover, there was strong feeling in France against a return of the monarchy. Those who owed their wealth and appointments to the Revolution were as anxious not to lose them as were the peasants who had acquired confiscated lands and been freed from seigneurial dues.

Yet the Directors, discredited and financially inept, knew that they must take action against the royalists if they were to survive. The two convinced republicans, Reubell and La Revellière, even proposed annulling the elections. This, Carnot strongly resisted. But, after his usual hesitations, Barras threw in his lot with the republicans, and a *coup d'état* was decided upon. There could be no question, though, of a popular uprising. As on the *journées* of *Vendémiaire*, the army would have to be called in.

The mood of the army was not as it had been at the time of Valmy. The tradition of antagonism towards King, priests and nobles was still strong, but spirits in the ranks were no longer kept up by enthusiastic support for the republican cause. Soldiers felt cut off from the Government at home; they took pride in their regiments and in French might rather than in the Revolution. It was their generals they looked to for leadership now, not the civilians at home, certainly not to the 'army commissioners' whom the Directors had appointed to succeed the Convention's *représentants en mission*. Above all, they looked to Bonaparte who had promised them 'rich provinces, great cities . . . honour, glory and wealth'.

After Bonaparte's services on the *journée* of 13 *Vendémiaire* – for which Barras and Fréron both gave him more credit than was his proper due – he was appointed first a divisional general, then commander of the Interior, and, on 2 March 1796, Commander-in-Chief of the Army in Italy. This last appointment was unanimously approved by the Directors, all of whom recognized in him a man who would not scruple to replenish the country's empty coffers with treasure looted from his defeated enemies. It was also warmly welcomed in the country as a whole. The economist, Dupont de Nemours, was almost alone in condemning it. 'I can hardly believe you have made such a mistake,' Dupont wrote to Reubell as soon as he heard of Bonaparte's promotion. 'Don't you know he is one of those Corsicans? They are all on the make.'

A week after his appointment to the command in Italy, Bonaparte married Josephine de Beauharnais, a former mistress of Barras and widow of the Vicomte de Beauharnais who had been guillotined in June 1794. And within three days of his marriage to this fetching, extravagant young woman from Martinique, Bonaparte was on his way to his headquarters near Genoa.

Certain members of the Government were not at all sorry to see Bonaparte leave Paris, but they had not foreseen the consequences of what was to prove a triumphant campaign in Italy. It had been the Directory's original intention to make an attack upon Vienna the main threat to the Austrian armies. Of secondary importance were to be advances by the Army of the Alps under Kellerman into Piedmont, by the Army of Italy into Lombardy, and a landing on the Irish coast by the Army of Ireland under Hoche. But the attack upon Vienna did not go well, while the Irish expedition was thwarted when the ships carrying Hoche's men were dispersed in a storm. It was only from Italy that news of great victories was received. From there came reports that the King of Sardinia's forces had been overwhelmed and that he had been obliged to cede Savoy and the area around Nice to France; that the Austrians, defeated at the bridge of Lodi on the Adda, at Arcola and at Rivoli, had been compelled to sign peace preliminaries at Leoben leading up to the Treaty of Campo-Formio at Passariano; that the Austrian Emperor had been forced to recognize the annexation by France not only of what had formerly constituted the Austrian Netherlands but also the left bank of the Rhine, and had been obliged as well to acknowledge the creation of a Cisalpine Republic out of the territories which the French had conquered in northern Italy. As a recompense the Venetian Republic, which Bonaparte had occupied, had been handed over to the Austrians after the French had stripped Venice of great quantities of her treasures including the famous bronze horses outside Saint Mark's basilica which, made in classical times, had been looted by the Venetians from Constantinople.

These famous horses formed part of an enormous amount of treasure which Bonaparte shipped back to France. Works of art, pictures, statuary, rare books and huge amounts of bullion reached French ports or were trundled across the frontier in loaded wagons. Delighted as they were to receive their share of these millions of *livres*' worth of loot, the Directors could not but be concerned by Bonaparte's independence. They had intended to satisfy themselves with what Danton had referred to as France's 'natural frontiers', with a few modifications here and there in France's favour, and to seize territories beyond these frontiers so that they could negotiate with their defeated enemies from a strong position. But Bonaparte had ignored their instructions. The peace negotiations, like the campaign, were largely conducted and concluded in accordance with his own ideas. Bonaparte had thus become an irresistible force in the conduct of France's foreign affairs. He was now also to become profoundly influential in affairs at home.

Anxious to have his Italian policies ratified by the Directors, Bonaparte had listened sympathetically to their overtures when the elections of April 1797 had resulted in hostile majorities in the Councils. He had agreed to send home the huge and vulgar, foul-mouthed Pierre Augereau, one of his roughest generals. Augereau had been born into a poor family in Paris and, having enlisted in the carabiniers at the age of seventeen, had had to flee abroad after drawing his sword on an officer. He had subsequently served in the Russian, Prussian and Neapolitan armies before the Revolution had brought him back to France again. Bonaparte considered him 'an ignoramus' but just the man for the job in hand. Augereau thought so himself. 'I have come here,' he announced confidently on his arrival in Paris, 'to kill the royalists.' Reubell judged him 'a splendid brigand'.

Under his command the Directory's forces occupied the city for the *coup d'état* of 18 *Fructidor*. General Pichegru, the royalist general who, having been elected for the Jura, was now President of the Five Hundred, was arrested. So was François Barthélemy, Letourneur's successor, the one Director, other than Carnot, who was in sympathy with the Councils. Carnot himself escaped and fled abroad. The Councils were then purged, the elections in forty-nine departments being annulled and 177 deputies displaced. Journals antagonistic to the Directory were suppressed, various opponents of the three Directors who had organized the *coup* were transported to Guiana where a large number of them perished, and others were arraigned before military tribunals, condemned to death and shot. *Émigrés* were given a fortnight to leave France on pain of death. Deported priests who had returned to France were also ordered to leave the country or risk sentence to the 'dry guillotine' of Guiana. All other priests were required to swear an oath of hatred of both the monarchy and the Constitution of 1793.

The victory of the Directory was for the moment complete. But only for the moment, for it had been achieved by a fatal reliance upon the army; while the Councils, provoked by the methods of the Government which became more and more authoritarian and anti-clerical as time went by, awaited an opportunity for revenge.

The Jacobins also were mustering their forces for an onslaught against the Directory, which was given little credit for the un-doubtedly beneficial administrative reforms carried out by the Ministries of Finance and of the Interior. Unfortunately, it was unable to profit from England's remaining the only country still at war with France after the signing of the Treaty of Campo-Formio. The appear-ance of a large French army at Brest had provoked such forceful reac-tion from the British Government that Bonaparte advised against the projected invasion of England and pressed instead for an Egyptian expedition, the beginning of the realization of his 'Eastern dream'.

The Directory approved Bonaparte's plan, thankful to be at least temporarily rid of a man whose ambitions were as alarming as his intentions mystifying, and seeing in his schemes a possible means of damaging English commerce and of establishing a base for the cre-ation of a French Empire in the East. So, on 19 May 1798, the four hundred ships of the Egyptian expedition set sail from Toulon, carrying 38,000 troops and nearly 200 scholars, writers and artists. It was a romantic adventure and, initially, successful. Malta was cap-tured on the way, Alexandria taken by assault, the Mameluke cavalry were overwhelmed in the shadow of the pyramids, and on 23 July Bonaparte marched into Cairo. A week later, however, he was trapped; the French fleet, riding at anchor near Aboukir, was surprised by Nelson who put out of action all but two of its ships. Nor was this all. The Egyptian expedition had alarmed Turkey as well as Russia which, with its Eastern interests evidently threatened, resolved henceforth to play a more determined part in the war. France's enemies rapidly multiplied again. Naples turned against her, so did Austria; so, eventually, did Sweden. The Directory responded by a new *levée en masse*. Even so, it could not call upon as many men as could the combined forces of her enemies, nor could it produce the necessary equipment. Both in Italy and in Germany the French armies suffered a series of setbacks and defeats, and, had it not been for the mutual jealousies and mistrust of the ill-assorted allies opposing them, they might well have been overwhelmed.

At home the discontent which conscription had aroused grew more bitter as taxes were increased and the economy stagnated. And the Councils now seized their opportunity to revenge themselves for the treatment they had received at the hands of the Directory in the purges that had followed the *coup d'état* of 18 *Fructidor*. 'You have destroyed public feeling,' declared a deputy in one of many attacks upon the Directors. 'You have muzzled liberty, persecuted republicans, destroyed a free press, suffocated truth ... The French people in Year VI [1797] appointed to public office men worthy of their confidence and you had the effrontery to say that the elections were the result of a conspiracy and, making that your excuse, you meddled disgracefully with the representatives of the nation.'

Harried by such vituperation two of the most disliked Directors were prevailed upon to resign. The place of one of them was taken by Roger Ducos, a compliant protégé of Barras, who had voted for the death of the King in the Convention. Other figures familiar in the earlier days of the Revolution were once more seen at the Ministries: Fouché became Minister of Police, and Robert Lindet, Minister of Finance. General Bernadotte, who had distinguished himself in Italy, was appointed Minister of War.

Under the influence of these men the Government once again lurched to the Left. Old clubs were allowed to reopen their doors and new ones proliferated, Jacobin newspapers reappeared in cafés and on the streets, and a forced loan was imposed upon the well-to-do. Sieyès, who had at first encouraged the Councils in their assault upon the Directory, did not much care for the way events were now turning. In May 1799 he replaced Reubell, the Director most closely associated with the war policy of the Government, and, with the authority of a Director himself, he warned against a return to those 'disastrous times' when those who were 'not officially in charge of anything were obstinately determined to take everything in hand'. In denouncing 'those who by their frantic provocations' proved themselves to be 'not republicans at all', he called upon his audience to remember with horror the 'Terror so justly abominated by Frenchmen'.

Such sentiments were widely shared. Proposals put forward in one of the most celebrated of the clubs, the Club du Manège, that the time had come to 'resurrect the pikes' and reconstitute the Committee of Public Safety met with furious shouts of 'Down with the Jacobins!' and with hails of stones hurled through the windows of the hall. And when the club was closed by the police, the acclamations were far louder than the protests. The continuing military disasters kept Jacobinism alive for a time. But General Jourdan's call for a reissue of the 1793 decree of '*la patrie en danger*' was hotly resisted. Bonaparte's brother, Lucien, who had entered the Council of Five Hundred the year before, insisted that it was better 'to extend the constitutional powers of the Directory than to be exposed to the danger of being carried off by a revolutionary wave', while another deputy warned of 'a return to the 1793 régime'. Jourdan's motion was easily defeated in the Council of Five Hundred, and by the middle of October 1799 there was no longer any need for such a motion as the foreign threat had passed: the English had been defeated at Bergen and Castricum, Switzerland had been conquered again, and the Tsar had withdrawn his troops to Russia. The Jacobin cause was lost.

Only in Egypt did French prospects still appear gloomy. Bonaparte had triumphed over the Turkish army at Aboukir but was still confined in the country by the English blockade. Well aware that for the moment there was no further glory to be won in the East, he gave up his command to a subordinate and, slipping past the English ships, sailed home to France. 'I am going home,' he said, 'to drive out the lawyers.'

He landed at Fréjus on 9 October and entered Paris less than a week later. He was greeted as a hero, the victorious conqueror, the peacemaker of Campo-Formio and, although France had already been saved, the saviour of France. 'Everyone is intoxicated,' the *Moniteur* reported. 'Victory which is Bonaparte's constant companion, has anticipated him for once. He arrives in time, however, to strike the final blows against the dying Coalition.' Yet there were no more blows to be struck that year, and Bonaparte had already determined that his services were to be of a different kind.

He knew that a *coup* was imminent and that the country, tired of war and tired of revolution, was ready to accept it. The brief resurgence of Jacobinism had alarmed those classes which were now predominant in France, and they were looking for a man who would stamp it out for good. The landowning peasants dreaded a change in the political climate which might lead to the *loi agraire* as much as they feared the consequences of a royalist restoration. The commercial and business interests of the bourgeoisie demanded political stability, an end to forced loans, a régime that would establish property owners as the rightful beneficiaries of the Revolution.

Sieyès was ready to help them. Convinced now that the authority of the executive must be expanded at the expense of the Councils and that this could only be achieved by a *coup d'état* organized by a popular general, he had first approached General Joubert. But within a few days Joubert had been killed in action. He had then sounded out General Moreau, but Moreau had expressed doubts and raised objections. Then Bonaparte had appeared on the scene and Bonaparte was almost ideal: he had a Jacobin past, so the suspicions of the Jacobins would be allayed; he was unscrupulous; he had placed himself in a potentially dangerous position by deserting his post and coming home without authority. He was also ambitious – more ambitious than perhaps Sieyès suspected: he was unlikely to stand aside when the *coup* had been effected, particularly for Sieyès, a man whom he despised, 'the mole of the Revolution'. He was moreover in the turmoil of an emotional crisis. While in Egypt he had learned that Josephine was having an *affaire* with a handsome young hussar and that they were both involved in financial dealings with corrupt army contractors. He had come home determined to divorce her; yet, once he was with her again, her contrite tears, her beguiling charm, and the entreaties of her children overcame his resolve. They were reconciled. He undertook to give up the lively young woman with whom he had been consoling himself in Egypt while Josephine, in turn, promised to be faithful to him thereafter. His marriage mended, Bonaparte began to plan the *coup d'état* with his fellow-conspirators.

Much work had been done already. General Bernadotte, who had proposed that Bonaparte should be arrested for desertion and evasion of the quarantine regulations, was dismissed from the Ministry of War. Fouché, as Minister of Police, indicated that he would not interfere. Barras, as usual, was equivocal, ready to jump to the winning side, agreeing for the moment to raise no objections. The election of Lucien Bonaparte as President of the Five Hundred was contrived. The President of the Ancients gave satisfactory assurances. Talleyrand undertook to negotiate between Sieyès and Bonaparte who finally met on 1 November. The meeting disturbed Sieyès, for Bonaparte immediately made it clear to him that he was not going to be the mere 'sword' of the operation. He was after political power, and Sieyès had no alternative but to give way to him.

The next step was to persuade the Ancients to vote for the transfer of both Councils to Saint-Cloud in accordance with a provision of the Constitution of Year III which provided for such a move when the deputies were deemed to require the protection of troops against popular disturbances. A rumour was, therefore, spread abroad that a Jacobin plot was afoot to 'convert the two Councils into a national convention', in the words of the *Moniteur*, 'to remove from the Convention all deputies not in sympathy with its aims and to entrust the government to a committee of public safety'. Referring to this plot, a deputy warned the Ancients on 9 November (18 *Brumaire*) that the conspirators were waiting only for a signal to 'raise their daggers against the representatives of the nation'. The required vote was, therefore, given; and General Bonaparte was invested with the command of the Paris garrison 'to ensure the safety of the national representation' when the Councils moved to Saint-Cloud. Barras now decided that the conspirators were playing too dangerous a game. Followed shortly by two of the other five Directors, he resigned 'in protest', leaving Sieyès and Ducos, the only survivors of the Second Directory.

As their meeting places, the Orangery and the Galerie d'Apollon, were not ready for them, the Councils were unable to meet at Saint-Cloud until about one o'clock on 19 *Brumaire*. And when they did at last assemble, the sessions of both were stormy, some deputies protesting that the Jacobin plot was an invention to secure their removal to the château which was now surrounded by troops, and others insisting that every representative should take an oath swearing to maintain the Constitution. As President of the Five Hundred, Lucien Bonaparte felt compelled to give way to this request though the swearing would take at least an hour. By half-past three, however, his brother had lost all patience and, accompanied by his aides-de-camp and secretary, Fauvelet de Bourrienne, he entered the hall of the Ancients to make a speech himself. Though confident with his troops, Napoleon Bonaparte was never at ease in civilian assemblies. His speech turned into a long and badly delivered harangue in which he maintained, fumbling for words, that there was no longer a Directory and that there were men sitting in the hall of the Five Hundred 'who would be willing to restore the revolutionary committees and the scaffold'. 'If there is talk of declaring me *hors la loi*,' he declared, turning towards his aides, 'I shall appeal to you, my brave companions in arms. Remember that I march accompanied by the god of victory and the god of fortune.' Outside, he added, there were more of his men whose bayonets he could see. 'General,' whispered Bourrienne, tugging at his arm, appalled by the impression he was creating, 'General, you don't know what you are saying.'

He allowed himself to be led away; but in the courtyard he was given a message from Fouché and Talleyrand in Paris who wrote to say that there was not a moment to lose, that the time for decisive action had come. Surrounded by soldiers, he thereupon marched into the Orangery where the deputies of the Five Hundred rose to their feet in horror at this illegal intrusion. Some of them left their seats, shaking their fists in his face, punching him in the chest, seizing hold of his collar. 'Outlaw him!' they shouted. 'Down with the military dictator!' Looking shocked and pale and as though about to faint – he afterwards admitted that he lost his nerve that day – he was dragged from the hall by four of his grenadiers.

When the rest of the men heard what had happened to their General, they furiously demanded orders to clear the *péquins* out of the Orangery. And when shouts of 'Outlaw him! Outlaw him!' reached Bonaparte's ears through the windows of the hall, he realized that he must act if only to save himself. Resolving to make an appeal to the Council's bodyguard who seemed as yet reluctant to support him, he sent a message to his brother to come out to help him.

Lucien had been presiding over the increasingly rowdy session, firmly resisting the demands for a vote to be taken on a motion declaring the General an outlaw. He came out of the hall immediately in response to his brother's request and went over with him to the Council's guards.

'The President of the Council of Five Hundred declares to you that the great majority of the Council is, at this very moment, terrorized by certain deputies,' Lucien announced to them. 'They are armed with daggers . . . and probably in the pay of England.' He added that an attempt had been made to assassinate the General whose pale face, bleeding where he himself had scratched it in his excitement, lent force to the suggestion. The Guards were at first hesitant, but when Lucien, pointing a sword at his brother's chest, cried out, 'I swear to kill my own brother if he ever interferes with the freedom of Frenchmen,' they allowed themselves to be persuaded by his lies, and stood by while a column of soldiers, led by Joachim Murat, marched upon the Orangery with drums beating and bayonets fixed. At the sight of their approach the deputies fled from the building, several of them jumping out of the windows, the braver among them shouting, 'Long live the Republic!' as they ran off through the park.

Both Councils were thus demolished and later replaced by two commissions of twenty-five members each. These commissions were required to prepare a new Constitution; and in this they were to take the advice of the 'Consuls of the French Republic' – Sieyès, Ducos and Bonaparte.

Bonaparte's name came last of the three. But no one doubted that his was the one that mattered. The other two, priest and lawyer, soon faded into the background, and before long Bonaparte was First Consul. Five years later he was Emperor. It was he, the soldier, who was the Revolution's heir, and ultimately its victim.

APPENDIX I

The fate of characters whose end is not recorded in the text

ALIGRE. Emigrated to England, then moved to Brunswick where he died in 1798.

AMAR. Lived in obscurity during the Consulate and Empire and was still in Paris in 1815. Having accepted no employment under Napoleon and taken no oath, he escaped the law which forced other regicides into exile. He died in Paris in 1816.

ARTOIS. Became King Charles X on the death of his brother Louis XVIII in 1824. A characteristic Bourbon, he could neither learn nor forget. His reactionary rule ended with the July Revolution of 1830 when the former Duc de Chartres, now Duc d'Orléans, became King Louis Philippe.

AUGEARD. After the arrest of the royal family at Varennes he went to Brussels where he publicized the royalist manifesto against the Constitution of 1791. He soon returned to Paris and took part in various intrigues. Emigrated in 1792. Returning to France after 18 *Brumaire*, he died in Paris in 1805.

AUGEREAU. Became a marshal in 1804 and distinguished himself at Jena and Eylau where he was badly wounded and thereafter never recovered his former powers. He agreed to serve Louis XVIII at the first Restoration, then, during the Hundred Days, offered his services to Napoleon who refused them, calling him a traitor. He was deprived of his rank and pension at the second Restoration of Louis XVIII in 1815 and died the following year.

BARBAROUX. After the fall of the Girondins he escaped to Caen, then moved to Saint-Émilion where he wrote his *Mémoires*. His hiding place discovered in June 1794, he tried to shoot himself but missed his aim, shattered his jaw and mutilated his tongue. Thus painfully wounded he was taken to Bordeaux and there guillotined.

BARENTIN. Emigrated in 1790, first to Piedmont, then to Germany and finally to England. Returned to France after the First Restoration but on account of his age was not reappointed Keeper of the Seals. He died in Paris in May 1819.

BARÈRE. Removed from the Isle of Oléron to Saintes, he escaped to Bordeaux and remained there in hiding for some years. On his emergence, Bonaparte employed him as a secret agent. At the restoration of the Bourbon dynasty he was banished from France as a regicide – 'the tree of liberty could not grow if it were not watered with the blood of Kings', he had declared during Louis XVI's trial. He went to live in Belgium, returning to France after the revolution of July 1830. He was granted a pension by King Louis Philippe and died in 1841 at the age of eighty-five, the last survivor of the Committee of Public Safety.

BARRAS. His political life came to an end with the fall of the Directory. Having amassed a great fortune he lived in luxurious comfort until his death in 1829.

BARTHÉLEMY. Escaped from French Guiana to the United States, thence to England. Returned to France after 18 *Brumaire* and entered the Senate. Deserted Napoleon in 1814, went into hiding during the Hundred Days, and was created a marquis after the second Restoration. He died in 1819.

BERNADOTTE. Appointed a marshal of France under the Empire, he was elected successor to the Swedish throne in 1810. He became King Charles XIV of Sweden in 1818 and died at Stockholm in 1844.

BESENVAL. Arrested after the fall of the Bastille, he was brought to trial by the tribunal of the Châtelet and acquitted. He died in obscurity in Paris in 1794.

BILLAUD-VARENNE. Deported to French Guiana after the insurrection of 12 *Germinal* 1795, he survived the 'dry guillotine' in a hut made of palm leaves and refused a pardon offered him by Napoleon after 18 *Brumaire*. He left Guiana in 1816 for Haiti where he died of dysentery three years later.

BOISSY D'ANGLAS. Suspected of royalism by the Directory whom he vigorously attacked, he was proscribed on 18 *Fructidor* 1797 and went to live in England. Returning to France after 18 *Brumaire*, he was elected a member of the Tribunate, a senator in 1805 and a peer of France in 1814. He served Napoleon during the Hundred Days and was consequently for a time excluded from the chamber of peers. He died in 1828.

BONAPARTE, LUCIEN. Became Minister of the Interior during the Consulate but differences of opinion with his brother led to his dismissal. He was appointed Ambassador in Madrid in 1800 but disagreed with his brother there, too. The final break with Napoleon came when he married his mistress instead of the widow of the King of Etruria as was required of him. He went to live in Italy, and subsequently lived in England having been captured by a British ship on his way to the United States. He returned to Rome in 1814, but went back to France to support Napoleon, with whom he was by then reconciled, during the Hundred Days. Returning once more to Italy at the Second Restoration, he died in Rome in 1840.

BOURDON, LÉONARD. Arrested after 12 *Germinal* and imprisoned in the Château de Ham from which he was released by the Directory to establish a *comité de propagande* in Hamburg. Soon recalled, he was appointed a member of the administrative council of the military hospital at Toulon under the Consulate. He died shortly before the Restoration.

BOURDON DE L'OISE. Arrested after 18 *Fructidor*, he was deported to French Guiana where he died soon after his arrival.

BOURIENNE. Sent to Hamburg as French envoy in 1802, he was recalled in disgrace in 1810, having accumulated an enormous fortune. He went over to the Bourbons in 1814, and thereafter lived in obscurity, dying at Caen in 1834.

BRETEUIL. After the fall of the Bastille, he fled to Switzerland, one of the first of the *émigrés*. For some time he acted for Louis XVI in negotiations with the European courts and with the Comtes de Provence and Artois; but, following the execution of Marie Antoinette, he retired into private life in Germany. He returned to France in 1802 and died in Paris in 1806.

BRIENNE. Returned to France from Italy at the outbreak of the Revolution and took the oath of the Civil Constitution of the Clergy. Tried to explain his conduct to the Pope who would not excuse it and accepted his resignation as a cardinal. Distrusted also by the revolutionary Government, he was arrested at Sens in November 1793 and died in prison soon afterwards either of poisoning or of a stroke.

BROGLIE. An early *émigré*, he commanded the 'army of the princes' for a short time in 1792. He died at Münster in 1804.

BUZOT. After the fall of the Girondins, he fled to Normandy thence, when the uprising there failed, to the Gironde. Hunted by police spies with trained dogs he was forced to leave his hiding place and on 18 June 1794 his body, partly devoured by animals, was found on the outskirts of a wood near Châtillon.

CALONNE. After being dismissed by Louis XVI and exiled to Lorraine, he went to live in England where he corresponded with Necker. Forbidden to return to France to offer himself for election to the Estates General in 1789, he joined the *émigrés* at Coblenz. He went back to France with Napoleon's permission in 1802, but died a few weeks after his arrival.

CAMBON. During the Thermidorian reaction he was proscribed as a former Montagnard and felt compelled to leave France. He returned in 1795 and went to live in retirement near Montpelier. Condemned as a regicide in 1816 he had to go abroad again. He died in Brussels in 1820.

CARNOT. Fled abroad after the *coup d'état* of 18 *Fructidor*, returning after 18 *Brumaire* and becoming Minister of War in 1800. He resigned the following year and in 1810 published his celebrated work on fortifications, *De la défense des places fortes*. When France was threatened in 1814 he offered his services to Napoleon and was appointed Governor of Antwerp. Minister of the Interior during the Hundred Days, he had to go abroad again on the second Restoration. He died at Magdeburg in 1823.

CAZALÈS. Emigrated after the fall of the monarchy in 1792. He fought with the *émigré* army. Returning to France in 1802, he died two years later.

CHABOT. Compromised in financial speculations in 1794, he was executed with the Dantonists who protested against being associated with this former Franciscan friar, the *'fripon'*, who had claimed Christ as the 'first of the *sans-culottes*'.

CHARTRES. Driven from France by the hostility of Louis XVIII, he went to live in England. He became Louis Philippe after the deposition of Charles X in 1830. Following the revolution of 1848 he fled to England and died at Claremont, Surrey, in 1850.

CHOISEUL. Arrested after the flight to Varennes and imprisoned at Verdun. Transferred to Orléans, he was released when the King accepted the Constitution and returned to Paris where he was appointed *chevalier d'honneur* to the Queen. After the Queen's imprisonment in the Temple, he fled to England in the guise of a Spaniard. On his return he was accused of taking part in a conspiracy against Bonaparte and exiled. At the Restoration he was created a peer of France and later became aide-de-camp to Louis Philippe and Governor of the Louvre. Died in Paris in 1838.

CLERMONT-TONNERRE. Having advocated Louis XVI's right to an absolute veto, he was murdered by the mob during the insurrection of 16 August 1792.

CLÉRY. Remained in the Temple until March 1793 when he was released and went to live at Juvisy. He was rearrested in May and imprisoned in La Force. Saved by *Thermidor*, he went to Strasbourg where he wrote his memoirs which were published in London in 1798. He returned to Paris in 1802 where he tried to get a new edition of the memoirs published. The authorities refused to allow this unless an apology for the new régime was included. He declined the compromise and later angered Napoleon by turning down the offer of becoming First Chamberlain to the Empress Josephine. He left France and died at Vienna in 1809.

COFFINHALL. Escaped from the Hôtel de Ville on 9 *Thermidor* and hid in a boat on the Seine near the Île des Cygnes for three days. Anxious for news, he went to his mistress's house in the Rue Montorgueil where he was arrested. His identity being established he was executed the same day.

COLLOT D'HERBOIS. A victim of the 'dry guillotine', he died at Cayenne in 1796, less than a year after his transportation there.

CONDORCET. His outspoken support of the Girondins and condemnation of the Montagnards led to his being declared *hors la loi*. Concealed for a time by Madame Vernet, the widow of a sculptor, he left her house for the country where he died in April 1794, evidently of exposure and exhaustion.

CORDAY. Perfectly composed during her trial, she moved her position so that a man who was sketching her portrait could get a better view of her. In the tumbril Sanson said to her conversationally, 'It's a long journey, isn't it?' 'We're bound to get there,' she replied, 'in the end.' Sanson, profoundly impressed by her beauty and courage, considerately stood up when they came in sight of the guillotine so that she should not see it, but she asked him to sit down: a person in her position was 'naturally curious'. After her execution Sanson's assistant picked up the head to show to the crowd and slapped it across the cheek. Some said they saw her face blush; others maintained it was the effect of the red stormy sunset. '*Elle nous perd,*' Vergniaud said, '*mais elle nous apprend à mourir.*'

CORNY. Dismayed by the course the Revolution was taking, he fell ill and died in November 1790.

DAVID. As enthusiastic a supporter of Napoleon as of the Jacobins, David's portrait of Napoleon pointing the way to Italy is a characteristic apotheosis. At the Restoration he was exiled as a regicide and went to live in Brussels. He died in December 1825.

DROUET. Declining a reward of 30,000 francs for his part in the capture of the King at Varennes, he was elected to the Convention where he became notorious for the violence of his proposals which included one for the execution of all English residents in France. While on a mission to the army he was captured by the Austrians, later being released with a group of other prisoners in exchange for Madame Royale. Elected to the Council of Five Hundred, he was arrested for his part in Babeuf's conspiracy. He escaped, fled to Switzerland and then to Teneriffe. Returning to France, he was forced into exile again by the second Restoration. He went back secretly, however, and settled down under an assumed name at Mâcon where he died in 1824.

DUCOS. Voted for Napoleon's deposition in 1814, but gained no favour with the Bourbons. Exiled as a regicide in 1816, he died in a carriage accident at Ulm the same year.

DUMONT. Died of natural causes in January 1830.

DUMOURIEZ. Intrigued against Louis XVIII and endeavoured to establish an Orléanist monarchy. He went to live in England and was granted a pension by the Government to whom he gave military advice during the Napoleonic wars. He died at Turville Park, Henley-on-Thames in 1823 and was buried in Henley parish church.

DUPONT DE NEMOURS. Emigrated to the United States in 1799. He returned to France in 1802 but refused office under Napoleon. Appointed a Councillor of State on the first Restoration, he returned to America in 1815 when Napoleon escaped from Elba and died near Wilmington, Delaware in 1817.

DUPORT. As one of the King's apologists he was arrested on 10 August 1792, but managed to escape abroad. He returned to France after 9 *Thermidor*, but left again after 18 *Fructidor* and died in Switzerland in 1798.

EDGEWORTH. Escaped to England in 1795 with a farewell message from Madame Elisabeth to her brother, the Comte d'Artois. He then took some papers to her other brother, the Comte de Provence, whom he accompanied to Mittau where he died of fever in 1807.

ELISABETH. The King's sister was accused of supplying *émigrés* with money and of encouraging the resistance of the royalist forces on 10 August 1792. She was condemned to death by the Revolutionary Tribunal and executed on 10 May 1794.

EPRÉMESNIL. Imprisoned in the Abbaye as a staunch monarchist, he was released before the September Massacres. Arrested at Le Havre, he was taken to Paris, accused of being an agent of the English Government, arraigned before the Revolutionary Tribunal and guillotined on 21 April 1794.

ESTAING. On the strength of compromising letters which had passed between him and Marie Antoinette, on whose behalf he spoke at her trial, he was condemned to death and executed on 28 April 1794.

FAUCHET. Having warmly supported the earlier phases of the Revolution, preached a funeral oration for those citizens killed at the storming of the Bastille and blessed the tricolour flag for the National Guard, he opposed the execution of the King and the marriage of priests. Accused of encouraging the federalist movement at Cannes, he was brought before the Revolutionary Tribunal and executed with the Girondins on 30 October 1793.

FERRIÈRES. Died of natural causes at the Château de Marsay in July 1804.

FERSEN. Returning to Paris in February 1792, Fersen was convinced that a second attempt to get the royal family out of France was not practicable. He was promoted *Riksmarskalk* in the Swedish army in 1801. On the death of the popular Prince Christian Augustus of Augustenburg in 1810, Fersen was slanderously accused of having been implicated in a plot to poison him. As *Riksmarskalk* he received the body on the outskirts of Stockholm and conducted the funeral cortège into the city. The mob threw stones and hurled abuse at him, then battered him to death on the steps of the senate house.

FOUCHÉ. Having intrigued against Robespierre, he then intrigued against Napoleon and Louis XVIII. But, although widely distrusted, he took part in every government from 1792 to 1815. He was for several years Minister of Police. Proscribed as a regicide he had to go abroad in 1816. He died at Trieste as Duc d'Otrante, in 1820.

FOUQUIER-TINVILLE. After the uprising of *Thermidor*, his defence that he had merely obeyed the orders of the Committee of Public Safety was not accepted. He was executed on 7 May 1795.

FRÉRON. Elected to the Five Hundred, he was prevented from taking his seat. He was also disappointed in his hopes of marrying Bonaparte's sister, Pauline. He died in 1802 at Santo Domingo where he had been sent as commissioner in 1799.

GRÉGOIRE. An early supporter of the Revolution, he later denounced Gobel's apostasy and declared in the Convention that he would not abjure his faith nor resign as Bishop of Blois. He wore episcopal dress in Paris during the Terror and read Mass in his house, but resigned his bishopric in 1801 in protest against the concordat with Rome. He died in 1831.

GUADET. A warrant was issued for his arrest on the fall of the Girondins. He fled to Caen, then to his father's house at Saint-Emilion, but he was discovered and guillotined at Bordeaux on 17 June 1794.

GUILLOTIN. Survived the punishment which his machine is often alleged to have inflicted on him and died in 1814.

HERMAN. Condemned to death on 7 May 1795 he displayed great contempt for his judges, throwing his hat at the man who occupied the seat from which he himself had pronounced sentence of death during the Terror.

HOCHE. Became Minister of War in 1797 but died at Wetzlar of consumption in September that same year at the age of twenty-nine.

ISNARD. One of the surviving Girondins who were recalled to the Convention after 9 *Thermidor*. He was elected to the Council of Five Hundred, but played little part in its deliberations and retired to Draguinan in 1797. Professing himself a convinced royalist he avoided proscription as a regicide and survived until 1825.

JOSEPHINE. Napoleon arranged for the nullification of their marriage in 1810 when he hoped to make a politically more advantageous match with Marie-Louise, daughter of the Emperor Francis I of Austria, and by her to have the son with whom Josephine could not provide him. She retired to her private house at Malmaison outside Paris where she lived and entertained as extravagantly as ever, and where she died in May 1814.

JOURDAN. Became a marshal of France in 1804 and, after submitting to the Bourbons, a peer of France in 1819. He lived until 1833.

LAFAYETTE. Denounced as a traitor by the Assembly in 1792, he spent five years in Austrian and German prisons. He returned to France in 1802 and, after a period of rustic retirement on his Lagrange estate during the First Empire, he was elected deputy for the Sarthe which he represented until 1824. He was placed in command of the National Guard in the 1830 revolution and died in 1834.

LALLY-TOLLENDAL. Emigrated to England in 1789. He offered to defend the King but was refused permission to return to Paris. Louis XVIII created him a peer of France. He died in 1830.

LAMETH, ALEXANDRE. Accused of treason in August 1792, he escaped abroad and was imprisoned by the Austrians. He returned at the time of the Consulate and became deputy for Seine-et-Oise after the Restoration. He died in 1829.

LAMETH, THÉODORE. Died at the age of ninety-eight in 1854.

LAMOIGNON. Committed suicide on 15 May 1789.

LANJUINAIS. Escaped to Rennes on the fall of the Girondins and remained in hiding until recalled to the Convention after 9 *Thermidor*. He died in Paris in 1827.

LA ROCHEFOUCAULD LIANCOURT. Emigrated to England in 1792 and went to the United States of America in 1794. He returned to France after 18 *Brumaire* and died in 1827.

LA TOUR DU PIN. She survived the Revolution, having moved to Bordeaux and then having escaped to the United States. She died at Pisa in 1853 at the age of eighty-three.

LAZOWSKI. A warrant was issued for his arrest in March 1793 but he escaped to Vaurigard where he died almost immediately of a fever following a drunken debauch. He was buried at the foot of the tree of liberty on the Place du Carrousel.

LEGENDRE. Elected a member of the Council of Ancients, he died in December 1797.

LETOURNEUR. Appointed Prefect of the Loire-Inférieure in 1800. Banished as a regicide in 1816, he died near Brussels the following year.

LINDET, ROBERT. Declined office under both the Consulate and the Empire. Left France in 1816 as a proscribed regicide, but returned shortly before his death in 1825.

LINDET, THOMAS. Elected to the Council of Ancients, he lived in obscurity under the Consulate and Empire. Banished as a regicide in 1816, he went to live in Italy, then Switzerland. Receiving permission to return to France, he died at Bernay in August 1825.

LINGUET. Moved into the country to escape the Terror, having written a defence of Louis XVI, but was discovered and brought back to Paris to be guillotined on 27 June 1794.

LOUSTALOT. Died of natural causes in October 1790.

LOUVET. Elected to the Council of Five Hundred, he retired in May 1797. In the royalist reaction of that summer the *jeunesse dorée*, who regarded him as a Jacobin, insulted him in the street and smashed his bookshop which he was compelled to move from the Palais Royal to the Faubourg Saint-Germain. He died in obscurity in August 1797 looking 'like an old man at thirty-seven'.

MAILLARD. An agent of the Committee of General Security, he disappeared after 9 *Thermidor*. Still alive under an assumed name in the early years of the Empire, the date of his death is unknown.

MALLET DU PAN. Exiled to Berne for an attack on Bonaparte and the Directory, he went to London in 1798 and died at Richmond, Surrey, in 1800.

MALOUET. Emigrated to England in 1792. Appointed Minister of Marine by Louis XVIII. He died in 1814.

MANUEL. Refused to vote for the death of Louis XVI and retired to Montargis. He was arrested there and brought back to Paris to be guillotined in 1793.

MARAT, Albertine. The English historian, J. W. Croker, saw her in Paris, where she was still living in the late 1830s. Told that she was 'as like her brother as one drop of water is like another', he found her 'very small, very ugly, very sharp and a great politician'. She died in 1841.

MARIE THÉRÈSE (MADAME ROYALE). Remained in prison throughout the Terror. She was released in December 1795 in exchange for some French prisoners held by the Austrians including Drouet. She married the eldest son of the Comte d'Artois, the Duc d'Angoulême, who renounced his rights to the throne in 1830 when his father abdicated.

MAURY. Emigrated in 1792. He returned in 1804 and became Archbishop of Paris in 1810, holding the office until 1814 despite the Pope's prohibition. He died in 1817.

MERCY. Appointed Austrian Ambassador to the Court of St James's in 1794 but died a few days after his arrival in London.

MERDA. For his services on 9 *Thermidor* the Convention recommended him to the notice of his superiors. He was promoted captain, colonel in 1807 and later brigadier-general. He died at Moscow in 1812. His account of Robespierre's death has been discredited. Others claimed that Robespierre shot himself.

MOMORO. Arrested, brought before the Revolutionary Tribunal on 22 March 1794 and condemned to death.

MONTESQUIOU. Accused of royalist sympathies, he escaped to Switzerland. He returned to Paris in 1795 and died there three years later.

MOREAU DE SAINT MÉRY. Arrested after 10 August 1792 but escaped to the United States and started a bookshop in Philadelphia. Returned to France in 1799 and became historiographer to the navy. A relative of the Empress Josephine, he was appointed administrator of the Duchies of Parma, Piacenza and Guastalla in 1802 but was dismissed in 1806. He died in 1819.

MOUNIER. Disapproving of the course of the Revolution after his proposal of the Tennis-Court Oath, he emigrated to Switzerland in 1790, returning in 1801 when Bonaparte appointed him prefect of the department of Ille-et-Vilâine. He died in 1806.

MURAT. Married Napoleon's sister, Caroline, after 18 *Brumaire*. Promoted marshal in 1804, he later succeeded Napoleon's brother, Joseph, as King of Naples in 1808. Defeated by the Austrians at Tolentino, he escaped to Corsica. Taken prisoner in an attempt to recover his kingdom, he was shot on 13 October 1815.

NARBONNE. Emigrated in 1792. Returned in 1801 and was later appointed aide-de-camp to Napoleon. In 1813 he became French ambassador in Vienna. He died in 1813.

NECKER. Returned to Switzerland in 1792 and settled down on his estate near Geneva where he devoted himself to writing until his death in 1804. His wife, who had sorely missed her salon in Paris, had died ten years before.

PÉTION. After the fall of the Gironde, escaped to Caen thence to Saint-Émilion. Tracked down by police spies, he left the wigmaker's house where he had been sheltered and on 18 June his body, with that of Buzot, was found on the outskirts of a wood partly eaten by animals.

PICHEGRU. Implicated in a plot to restore Louis XVIII, he offered his resignation to the Directory who accepted it. Arrested on 18 *Fructidor*, he was deported to Cayenne. He escaped to London and returned to Paris in 1803 to organize a royalist insurrection against Napoleon. He was betrayed, arrested, and on 15 April the following year he was found strangled in prison.

POLIGNAC, Gabrielle de. Emigrated in 1789 and died abroad shortly after the death of the Queen.

PROVENCE. Remained in England until 1814 when he returned to France as Louis XVIII. Obliged to leave Paris again on Napoleon's escape from Elba, he returned to France after Waterloo and reigned until his death in 1824.

REUBELL. Retired from public life after 18 *Brumaire* and died at his birthplace, Colmar, in 1807.

REVELLIÈRE-LÉPEAUX. Forced to resign on 30 *Prairial*, he went to live in retirement in the country. He returned to Paris in 1809 but took no part in public affairs, dying in 1824.

RIVAROL. Emigrated in 1792 and lived at first in London, then in Hamburg and Berlin where he died in 1801.

ROCHAMBEAU. Arrested during the Terror but managed to escape execution. Pensioned by Bonaparte, he died at Thoré in 1807.

ROEDERER. Went into hiding after 10 August 1792. He appeared again after *Thermidor* and was appointed to a chair in political economy. Created a senator by Napoleon, he became Joseph Bonaparte's Minister of Finance at Naples and a peer of France during the Hundred Days. He was deprived of his offices on the Restoration, but his title of peer of France was restored in 1832. He died three years later.

ROLAND. Went into hiding at Rouen but, on learning of his wife's execution, he walked out into the countryside, pinned a paper to his coat declaring that since her murder he could 'no longer remain in a world stained with enemies', and stabbed himself to death with a swordstick.

ROSSIGNOL. Achieved high rank in the war against the Vendéens. Involved in the Babeuf conspiracy, he was tried and acquitted but exiled in 1800 to the Seychelles where he died two years later.

ROUGET DE LISLE. Although he wrote a few songs other than the *Marseillaise*, for which he composed the words and perhaps the music – though this has been disputed – none was to achieve much success. A less than ardent republican he was cashiered and imprisoned for a time. He died at Choisy-le-Roi in 1836, and his ashes were transported to the Panthéon.

ROUX. Condemned to death by the Revolutionary Tribunal on 15 January 1794, he stabbed himself with a knife and was carried away to Bicêtre where he died.

SANSON, Charles. Remained the public executioner of Paris until 1795 when he handed over to his son, Henri, who died in 1840.

SANTERRE. Relieved of his command of the Paris National Guard in 1793, he was sent to command a force in the Vendée. Blamed for the failure of this expedition and accused of having written a prejudiced report upon it, he was sent to prison where he remained until *Thermidor*. He then resigned his command and returned to his business. The brewery, however, was not the prosperous concern it had been and he died in poverty in 1809.

SÈZE. Retired to a house he owned in the hamlet of Brevannes in the spring of 1793. Created a count by Louis XVIII, he lived on until 1828.

SIEYÈS. Lived in retirement during the Empire but prudently left France at the time of the Restoration. He returned after the 1830 revolution and died in Paris six years later.

TALLEYRAND. 'Treason,' said Talleyrand 'is merely a matter of dates.' Foreign Minister under the Directory and Napoleon, he also served Louis XVIII in that office. After representing France at the Congress of Vienna he became King Louis Philippe's ambassador to the Court of St James's. He died in Paris in 1838.

TALLIEN. He was elected to the Council of Five Hundred, but, distrusted by the moderates as a former terrorist and by the Left as a reactionary, he made little mark. He sailed to Egypt with Bonaparte in 1798 and edited the official journal, the *Décade Egyptienne*. He then became consul at Alicante. Having contracted yellow fever and lost the sight of an eye he returned to Paris where, having failed to obtain a pension, he died in poverty in 1820. He had married the fascinating Comtesse de Fontenay in 1794 but obtained a divorce from her in 1802. She married the Comte de Caraman, later Prince de Chimay, in 1805.

TARGET. Having disappeared from view during the Terror, he emerged to become a member of the Institute and of the Court of Cassation. He died in 1807.

THURIOT. After 18 *Brumaire* became *juge au tribunal criminel* of the *département* of the Seine. Replaced at the first Restoration, he took up his functions again during the Hundred Days. Banished as a regicide in 1816, he obtained permission to practice law in Liège where he died in 1829.

TOURZEL. When the royal family were imprisoned at the Conciergérie she asked to be taken there with them. This request and a subsequent one to share Madame Royale's imprisonment were both refused. She was imprisoned for five months but survived the Terror and died at her château at Abondant in 1832 at the age of eighty-two.

TRONCHET. A deputy of the Council of the Ancients during the Directory and president of the Court of Cassation during the Consulate. He died in March 1806.

VADIER. Condemned to deportation under the Directory, he escaped and remained in hiding in Paris until May 1796. Tried with the Babeuf conspirators, he was acquitted but kept in prison for four years at Cherbourg. Released after 18 *Brumaire*, he went to live in Toulouse where he was kept under police surveillance. Exiled as a regicide in 1816, he died at Brussels in 1828.

VILATE. Executed 7 May 1795.

APPENDIX 2

Glossary

aides: excises on various goods such as wines, playing cards and soap.

ami du peuple, L': founded by Marat in September 1789 and, like *Le Père Duchesne*, circulated widely among the people. Often suppressed, it changed its name to *Publiciste de la République française* in March 1793. The last issue appeared the day after Marat's murder.

armée révolutionnaire: armed force of Jacobins and *sans-culottes* raised in several places in the late summer of 1793. Its principal purpose was to force farmers to release their stocks for Paris and other towns. It was disbanded after the execution of the Hébertists.

Assignats: interest-bearing bonds which – with a face value of 1,000 *livres* each – were intended to be used in payment for *biens nationaux*. Further issues were made from time to time to ensure a regular flow of money, and in this way France was given a new paper currency. *Assignats* stopped bearing interest in May 1791; and, by the time of the Directory, 100 *livres* in *assignats* were worth no more than fifteen *sous*.

banalités: the exclusive rights of a *seigneur* to maintain a mill, an oven or a winepress, often exacted by a *fermier*. They were renounced on the famous night of 4 August 1789 and declared subject to redemption.

barrières: customs posts surrounding Paris.

biens nationaux: 'national lands', the former properties of the Church.

bourgeoisie: generally used to define the fairly well-to-do urban middle class, the families of both professional and businessmen.

319

Brissotins: the name by which the Girondins were at first more usually known.

Brumaire: the second month of the Revolutionary Calendar which corresponded with the days from 22 October to 20 November, from *brume*, mist.

cahiers de doléances: lists of grievances drawn up by each of the three orders before the meeting of the Estates General in 1789. The clergy and nobility drew up their lists in assemblies in the towns which were the centres of their electoral districts. The more numerous Third Estate usually met in parish churches where preliminary *cahiers* were prepared and written down by some respected lawyer, schoolmaster or *coq du village*. Delegates were then selected; and the preliminary *cahiers* were absorbed into general *cahiers* at electoral assemblies. Model *cahiers* were circulated to suggest lists of grievances and how to frame them.

ça ira!: Revolutionary song sung to the tune of a country dance by Bécourt, *Le carillon national*. First heard in Paris during the preparations for the *Fête de la Fédération* of 14 July 1790. The refrain, which was said to have been written by a street-singer named Ladre, originally ran:

> *Ah! Ça ira, ça ira, ça ira!*
> *Le peuple, en ce jour, sans cesse répète:*
> *Ah! Ça ira, ça ira, ça ira!*
> *Malgré les mutins, tout réussira*

The words were altered during the Terror to:

> *Ah! Ça ira, ça ira, ça ira!*
> *Les aristocrates à la lanterne!*

Bonaparte prohibited the song when he became First Consul.

capitation: a kind of poll-tax levied in rough correspondence to income. Established in 1701, it was originally intended to be levied on all Frenchmen who were divided into twenty-two classes, the Dauphin, at at the top of the first class, being assessed at 2,000 *livres*, soldiers and day-labourers, at the bottom of the last class, at only one *livre*. The clergy bought themselves out in 1710 for 24,000,000 *livres*. The nobility had also become exempt by the time of the Revolution when the *capitation*, levied only on commoners, had become a supplement of the *taille*.

carmagnole: originally, perhaps, a short jacket with metal buttons introduced into France by workers from Carmagnola in Piedmont. It became popular in Marseilles and was brought to Paris by the Marseillais *fédérés*. Worn with black woollen trousers, red or tricolour waistcoats and red caps it was taken up by the Jacobins. It was also the name of a dance and of a popular Revolutionary song – the words of which were constantly being altered – that accompanied it. Like the *Ça ira*, it was banned by Bonaparte when he became First Consul.

certificats de civisme: documents issued during the Terror as proof of political orthodoxy by the vigilance committees of the sections. Passports could not be obtained without them.

Chouans: royalist insurgents who took their name from four brothers named Cottereau, known more often as Chouan, a corruption of *chat-huant*, screech-owl, because they imitated that bird's cry in order to recognize each other in the woods at night. Three of the four brothers were killed in battle. *Chouans* were active in La Vendée, Brittany and Normandy.

comités de surveillance: watch-committees formed in each commune in March 1793 to assist the police, keep an eye on officialdom and supervise public security and order. They were usually controlled by extreme Jacobins and often took the place of local government. They later became known as *comités revolutionnaires* and after Thermidor as *comités d'arrondisements*.

Commune: the revolutionary local government authority of Paris. It was formed in July 1789 and disbanded after *Thermidor*. The official Commune was displaced by an Insurrectionary Commune on 9 August 1792, the day before the attack on the Tuileries.

Cordeliers: the Parisian district that today includes the Odéon and the Hôtel de la Monnaie. It was inhabited by many actors and playwrights (Fabre d'Églantine and Collot d'Herbois both lived here) and by many booksellers, publishers, printers and journalists, Marat and Camille Desmoulins among them. Danton also lived here and became a powerful figure in the area. So did Fréron, Billaud-Varenne, Chaumette, Momoro and Loustalot.

Cordeliers' Club (Society of the Friends of the Rights of Man and of the Citizen): Formed when the Commune redivided Paris and the Cordeliers' District was absorbed into the *section* Théâtre Français. It took as its model the Jacobin Club and styled itself the 'elixir of Jacobinism'. Its emblem was an open eye, representative of its aim to keep a close watch on the government. Its members met first in the church of the monastery of the Cordeliers (Franciscan Observantists), then in a hall in the Rue Dauphine. After 10 August 1792 the more moderate members such as Danton and Desmoulins stopped attending, and the *Enragés* began to dominate it.

corvées royales: direct taxes paid in service rather than money. They consisted of *corvées royales*, by which peasants were called upon to lend carts for the transportation of troops and military supplies, and *corvées des routes*, by which peasants who lived within ten miles of main roads were required to supply not only carts but labour and animals to keep these roads in repair.

décade: the ten-day week of the Revolutionary Calendar introduced in October 1793.

décadi: the tenth day of a *decade*.

département: territorial and administrative sub-division of France. By a decree of 15 January 1790, the Assembly created eighty-three of them. They were named after their geographical features.

droits de colombier: feudal rights which enabled the seigneur's pigeons to be fed at the peasants' expense.

Encyclopédie: one of the great masterpieces of the eighteenth century, a dictionary of the arts, sciences and trades. It was conceived when two publishers approached Denis Diderot for a translation of Ephraim Chamber's *Cyclopaedia* of 1728. Diderot persuaded them to bring out a more ambitious work. Seventeen volumes of text and eleven of plates appeared between 1751 and 1772. Seven additional volumes were published 1776–80.

Enragés: extremist revolutionaries, led by Jacques Roux and Jean Varlet, who became a powerful force in Paris in 1793. They were particularly antagonistic to those whom they suspected of hoarding or speculating.

faubourgs: these former suburbs originally lay outside the walls of the old city but by the time of the Revolution they had all been enclosed within the city's boundaries.

Fédéralisme: a movement, supported by the Girondins, which sought to grant provincial areas the running of their own affairs.

fédérés: the citizen soldiers who came to Paris from the provinces for the Festival of the Federation on 14 July 1792. Prominent among them were units from Brest and the men from Marseilles who popularized the *Marseillaise*.

fermier: an agent contracted to collect dues. *Fermiers généraux* paid large sums for the right to collect various indirect taxes and made fortunes by exploiting them.

Feuillants: constitutional monarchists who resigned from the Jacobin

Club in July 1791 in protest against moves by certain Jacobins to have the King deposed.

Floréal: the eighth month of the Revolutionary Calendar which corresponded with the days from 20 April to 19 May, from the Latin *florens*, flowery.

Frimaire: the third month of the Revolutionary Calendar which corresponded with the days from 21 November to 20 December, from *frimas*, hoar-frost.

Fructidor: the twelfth month of the Revolutionary Calendar which corresponded with the days from 18 August to 16 September, from the Latin *fructus*, fruit, plus *doron*, Greek gift.

gabelle: the government salt monopoly by which people were made to buy specific amounts of salt at prices far higher than they would have fetched on an open market. Several rich noblemen bought shares in the Tax Concession which managed the monopoly and collected customs duties.

Garde Nationale: the citizens' militia which was formed by the Paris districts in 1789. Originally a predominantly bourgeois institution, it gradually changed its character – as did so many other institutions and terminologies – as the Revolution progressed.

Gardes-françaises: royal troops stationed in the capital when the Revolution began. Most of them proved sympathetic towards the *Vainqueurs de la Bastille*. 'While the rabble hacked, tore up, threw down and burnt the barriers of the Chausée d'Antin and the railings, offices and registers of the customs officers,' wrote an eye-witness of an attack on a *barrière* in July 1789, 'the *Gardes-françaises* came up to stand between the fire-raisers and the spectators, leaving the former free to act.'

générale: drum-beat; *battre la générale*, to beat to arms.

Germinal: the seventh month of the Revolutionary Calendar which corresponded with the days from 21 March to 19 April, from the Latin *germen*, bud.

Indulgents: those, mostly Dantonists, who advocated a policy of clemency during the height of the First Terror.

insoumis: men who evaded conscription.

intendants: local agents of the King during the *ancien régime*.

Jacobin Club: founded at Versailles in 1789 and then known as the Breton Club as most of its members came from Brittany. On the removal of the Assembly to Paris it became known as the Jacobin Club because it met in the convent of the Jacobin friars, Dominican friars who were called Jacobins since their first house in Paris was in the Rue

Saint-Jacques. In 1791 the Club was named *Société des amis de la constitution, séante aux Jacobins* and, after the fall of the monarchy *Société des Jacobins, amis de la liberté et de l'égalité*. Fairly moderate at first, the Club became increasingly revolutionary. It was closed in November 1795.

jeunesse dorée: gangs of young anti-Jacobins, armed with whips and weighted sticks, who were encouraged by Fréron to attack left-wing agitators and recalcitrant workers. They were mostly drawn from that class of youth to whom the *sans-culottes* referred as *muscadins*.

journée: an important day, particularly one upon which some violent action of revolutionary significance occurred.

lanterne: a lamp-post which served as a gibbet in the early part of the Revolution, such as that upon which Foullon was hanged in the Place de Grève. '*À la lanterne!*' was consequently an earlier version of the threatening cry '*À la guillotine!*'

lettre de cachet: a royal decree, in the form of a sealed letter, by which the King could have a person imprisoned without explanation or trial.

levée en masse: the mobilization of the country's total human and material resources. It was approved reluctantly by the Convention on 23 August 1793.

lit de justice: a special session of the Paris *parlement* in which the King could force its members to register his decree.

livre: unit of weight and monetary value. 4 *liards* = 1 *denier*, 12 *deniers* = 1 *sou*, 20 *sous* = 1 *livre*, 3 *livres* = 1 *ecu*, 8 *ecus* = 1 *louis*. The journalist, Linguet (1736–1794) said that a man needed 300 *livres* a year to live in reasonable comfort.

loi agraire: a policy favoured by some *Enragés* by which wealth would be more equally distributed by the enforced division of property.

Marais: the group in the Convention, also known as the Plain, that occupied the middle ground between Girondins and Jacobins.

Marseillaise, La: first called the *Chant de guerre pour l'armée du Rhin* when published at Strasbourg, became known by its present title when popularized by the Marseilles *fédérés* in Paris. It was banned for a time by Napoleon and after the Restoration.

maximum: declaration of maximum prices. The *maximum des denrées* fixed the maximum for foodstuffs, the *maximum des salaires* for wages. The *maximum* of May 1793 imposed a limit on the price of grain only, that of September 1793 on most essential articles. The *maximum* was abolished in December 1794. Many shopkeepers had flagrantly disregarded it. 'So much for fixed prices,' butchers were heard to say as they flung bits of heads and hooves into the meat on the scales, 'and if you don't like it you can bloody well lump it.'

menus plaisirs: now pocket-money or pin-money, but in the context of Versailles those 'small pleasures' of the Court unconnected with hunting.

Messidor: the tenth month of the Revolutionary Calendar which corresponded with the days from 20 June to 18 July, from the Latin *messis*, harvest, and Greek *doron*, gift.

Montagnards: Jacobin deputies, collectively known as the Mountain, who occupied the higher seats in the Convention. Originally led by Danton and Robespierre, they helped to form the government after the overthrow of the Girondins.

muscadins: name given to *bourgeois* youth, particularly the *jeunesse dorée*, by the Jacobins.

Nivôse: the fourth month of the Revolutionary Calendar which corresponded with the days from 21 December to 19 January, from the Latin *nivosus*, snowy.

noblesse de robe: magistrates of the *ancien régime* who had acquired the status of nobility either by buying or inheriting their office.

ouvriers: urban citizens who worked with their hands, small manufacturers as well as workers.

péquin (pékin): epithet used by soldiers for a civilian.

Père Duchesne, Le: Hébert's notorious journal which appeared three times a week between 1790 and 1794 took its name from a stock character of the Théâtre de la Foire. He was depicted as a stove merchant in a vignette at the head of the front page with a pipe in his mouth and tobacco in his hand. Beneath the vignette were the words, '*Je suis le véritable Père Duchesne, foutre.*'

philosophes: the writers and philosophers of the middle of the eighteenth century who substituted for traditional beliefs an ideal of social well being based on a trust in the progress of humanity and science. Their ideas influenced many of the revolutionary leaders, as Robespierre was, for instance, influenced by Rousseau and his *Contrat social.*

physiocrates: writers on economics who believed that the source of national wealth was agriculture and advocated free trade.

Plain: See *Marais.*

Pluviôse: the fifth month of the Revolutionary Calendar which corresponded with the days from 20 January to 18 February, from the Latin, *pluvia*, rain.

Poissarde: fishwife, but also applied to other market-women.

Prairial: The ninth month of the Revolutionary Calendar which corresponded with the days from 20 May to 19 June, from *pré*, meadow.

rentier: person whose income comes from investments, man or woman of property.

répresentants en mission: delegates sent out by the Convention to the army and the provinces to explain and enforce its policies.

sans-culottes: literally meaning without breeches, a form of dress associated with aristocrats and the well-to-do; workers wore trousers. The term had political as well as economic significance. Santerre, the brewer, who was rich, liked to consider himself a *sans-culotte*; so did numerous shopkeepers and master craftsmen who read revolutionary newspapers and pamphlets and influenced their illiterate workmen. But *sans-culottes* were generally poor, if not so poor that they were more concerned with getting enough to eat than with politics. Pétion defined them, cierks as well as artisans, petty traders and craftsmen as well as labourers, as the 'have-nots as distinct from the haves'. 'A great many *sans-culottes* did *not* work with their hands,' Professor Richard Cobb has written, 'could *not* tile a roof, did *not* know how to make a pair of shoes, were *not* useful. The trouble was that there was a vast range of disagreement about what constituted a *sans-culotte*, and as in the Year II it was a good thing to be, if one could not get in under one count – social origin, economic status, category of employment – one could go round to the back and get in under quite another – moral worth, revolutionary enthusiasm, simplicity of dress or of manner, services rendered to the Revolution . . . past sufferings at the hands of various oppressors . . . The *sans-culotte* is not an individual with an independent life of his own. It could not be said of him "once a *sans-culotte*, always a *sans-culotte*"; for, apart from the difficulties of an exact definition of the status . . . he exists at all only as a unit within a collectivity, which itself exists only in virtue of certain specific, unusual, and temporary institutions: once the sectionary institutions have been destroyed, or tamed, the *sans-culotte* too disappears; in his place, there is what there had been before – a shoemaker, a hatter, a tailor, a tanner, a wine merchant, a clerk, a carpenter, a cabinet-maker, an engraver, a miniaturist, a fan-maker, a fencing-master, a teacher. There is nothing left save perhaps the memory of militancy and a hankering after Brave Times, that appear all the braver when remembered under very hard ones. The *sans-culotte* then is not a social or economic being, he is a political accident.'

sans-culottides: the five days of the Revolutionary Calendar left over after the year had been divided into twelve months of thirty days each. The Convention agreed that they would be feast days celebrating respectively Virtue, Intelligence, Labour, Opinion, Rewards. The sixth extra day in leap year was to be the *sans-culottide* on which Frenchmen were to come 'from all parts of the Republic to celebrate liberty and equality, to cement by their embraces national fraternity, and to swear, in the name of all on the altar of the country, to live and die as brave *sans-culottes*'.

séance-royale: a royal session of the Estates General.

sections: Before the Revolution, Paris was divided into sixty districts. The Commune redivided it into forty-eight *sections.* Each *section* had its own particular flavour, its own revolutionary committee and armed force upon which it could rely in times of trouble.

septembriseurs: those responsible for the prison massacres of September 1792, later, like *bouveur de sang,* a term of opprobrium.

taille: basic tax of the French monarchy during the *ancien régime* which varied from province to province, being paid in the north on total income and in the south on income from landed property only (*taille réelle*). The privileged and influential managed to escape paying it so that in practice it was paid almost entirely by the poor, principally the peasants.

taxation populaire: the enforced sale by bakers, grocers and other food merchants of goods at lower prices by mobs that invaded their premises.

Terreur, la: method of revolutionary government by intimidation during which the powers of the state – economic, judicial and military – were used to direct the life of the nation and draconian punishments were inflicted on those who opposed it. Also applied to those periods from October to December 1793 and March to July 1794 when the Jacobins imposed such a government upon France.

Thermidor: the eleventh month of the Revolutionary Calendar which corresponded with the days from 19 July to 17 August, from the Greek *therme,* heat, plus *doron,* gift.

tricoteuse: a woman who sat and knitted during the sessions of the Revolutionary Tribunal and around the guillotine.

Vainqueurs de la Bastille: title bestowed upon those who were able to satisfy the authorities that they had taken an active part in the storming of the Bastille. As they enjoyed a pension and uniform as well as an honoured title, applications to join their number were numerous; and it seems that many *Vainqueurs* may well have been present in spirit rather than in person.

Vendémiaire: first month of the Revolutionary Calendar which corresponded with the days from 22 September to 21 October, from the Latin *vindemia*, vintage.

Ventôse: the sixth month of the Revolutionary Calendar which corresponded with the days from 19 February to 20 March, from the Latin *ventosus*, windy.

vingtième: originally intended as a five per cent tax on income, it had either been compounded for a lump sum by the privileged orders and by various corporate organizations of the bourgeoisie or had been largely evaded by them by the concealment of their real income. By the time of the Revolution it was mostly paid by the peasants.

APPENDIX 3

Table of principal events

1789

July–August	The Great Fear
4 August	Renunciation of feudal rights in National Assembly
26 August	Declaration of Rights of Man and of the Citizen
5 October	March of women to Versailles
6 October	Royal Family brought to Paris followed by National Assembly
10 October	Louis XVI decreed King of the French
29 October	'Active' and 'Passive' citizens distinguished by decree
2 November	Church property nationalized
7 November	Decree excluding deputies from Ministry
14–22 December	Local government reorganized
19 December	*Assignats* issued

1790

4 February	King speaks to Assembly
13 February	Religious orders, except those engaged in teaching or charitable work, suppressed
19 June	Titles of hereditary nobility abolished
12 July	Civil Constitution of the Clergy
14 July	First *Fête de la fédération*
4 September	Resignation of Necker
27 November	Decree imposing civic oath on clergy
26 December	King sanctions clerical oath

1791

9 February	Election of first bishops of constitutional church
20 February	King's aunts move to Rome
10 March	Pope condemns Civil Constitution of the Clergy
2 April	Mirabeau dies
20 June	Flight to Varennes
25 June	King suspended from his functions on being brought back to Paris
17 July	The 'Massacre of the Champ de Mars'
17 August	Frenchmen abroad summoned to return within one month
27 August	Declaration of Pillnitz
14 September	King accepts Constitution and is restored to functions
1 October	Legislative Assembly meets

Appendix 3

1791

9 November	Decree ordering return to France of *émigrés* suspected of conspiracy against nation
12 November	King vetos decree against the *émigrés*
19 November	King vetos decree against non-juring priests
29 November	Assembly passes decree against non-juring priests

1792

9 February	Property of *émigrés* decreed forfeit to nation
10 March	Assembly brings about resignation of Ministry; administration sympathetic to Girondins takes its place
20 April	War declared
29 April	General Dillon murdered by his troops
12 June	Ministry dismissed by King
19 June	King vetos proposed military camp near Paris
20 June	Mob invades Tuileries
28 June	Lafayette returns to Paris
11 July	Decree of '*La patrie en danger*'
25 July	Brunswick Manifesto
25–30 July	Arrival of *fédérés* from Brest and Marseilles
3 August	All but one of the Paris *sections* petition for deposition of King
9 August	Insurrectionary commune formed in Paris
17 August	Storming of the Tuileries. King suspended from functions. Ministers dismissed in June reappointed
19 August	Lafayette defects to Austrians. Brunswick crosses frontier
23 August	Longwy falls to Prussians
25 August	Redemption charges for seigneurial dues abolished
2 September	Verdun surrenders to Prussians
2–6 September	Prison massacres
8 September	Brunswick enters Argonne Forest
20 September	Battle of Valmy. Convention constituted
21 September	Convention abolishes monarchy
22 September	Convention decrees that all acts from now on are to be dated from Year One of the Republic
29 September	French army occupies Nice
6 November	Battle of Jemappes. French army advances into Belgium

1792

19 November	Decree of *Fraternité et secours*
27 November	Savoy becomes 84th French *département*
15 December	Decree of *Guerre aux châteaux*

1793

14–17 January	Convention debates the fate of the King
21 January	The King is executed
1 February	War declared against England and Holland
14 February	Monaco annexed
7 March	War declared against Spain
9 March	Convention authorizes representatives *en mission*. Levy of 300,000 men authorized
10 March	Revolutionary Tribunal established
11 March	Revolt in La Vendée begins
18 March	Battle of Neerwinden
21 March	*Comités de surveillance* established in every commune
26 March	Committee of Public Safety established
4 April	General Dumouriez deserts to Austrians
6 April	Committee of Public Safety reduced to nine members.
13 April	Marat arraigned before Revolutionary Tribunal
4 May	First *maximum*
May–October	Federalist revolts in provinces against the Convention
28 May	Insurrectionary Committee formed
29 May–2 June	Overthrow of the Girondins
3 June	*Émigrés'* land sold in small lots
5 June	Couthon, Saint-Just and Hérault de Séchelles join the Committee of Public Safety
24 June	Constitution of 1793
13 July	Murder of Marat
17 July	Final abolition of all feudal rights without compensation
27 July	Robespierre joins Committee of Public Safety
28 July	Fall of Valenciennes
14 August	Carnot joins the Committee of Public Safety
23 August	Decree of *levée en masse*
27 August	Toulon surrenders to Admiral Hood
5 September	Attempted coup by Hébertists
6 September	Billaud-Varenne and Collot d'Herbois join the Committee of Public Safety

Appendix 3

1793

17 September	Law of Suspects
29 September	Law of General *maximum*
7 October	Adoption of Revolutionary Calendar: Year II deemed to have begun on 22 September
9 October	Lyons retaken
10 October	Government declared to be 'revolutionary until the peace'
16 October	Marie Antoinette executed
31 October	Girondin leaders executed
6 November	Duc d'Orléans executed
8 November	Madame Roland executed
11 November	Bailly executed
29 November	Barnave executed
19 December	English evacuate Toulon
23 December	*Vendéens* defeated at Savenay

1794

24 March	Execution of Hébertists
2 April	Danton's trial begins
5 April	Execution of Dantonists
8 June	Festival of the Supreme Being
10 June	Law of *22 Prairial*
26 June	Battle of Fleurus
23 July	*Maximum des salaires*
26 July	Robespierre calls for purge in his last speech in the Convention
27 July	The *journée* of 9 *Thermidor*. Arrest of Robespierrists. Abolition of Paris Commune by Convention. Liège and Antwerp captured by Jourdan and Pichegru
28 July	Execution of Robespierre and his followers. Repeal of Law of *22 Prairial*.
29 July	Execution of Robespierrists on Paris Commune
30–31 July	Reorganization of Committee of Public Safety
31 July	*Maximum des salaires* withdrawn
10 August	Reorganization of Revolutionary Tribunal
12 November	Jacobin Club closed

1794

8 December	Return of some surviving Girondins to the Convention
24 December	*Maximum* abolished

1795

23 January	Amsterdam occupied
17 February	Hoche brings temporary peace to La Vendée
21 February	Decree separating Church and State
5 March	Carnot leaves Committee of Public Safety
1 April	*Journée* of 12 *Germinal*
5 April	Peace with Prussia signed at Basle
16 April	Peace with Holland signed at the Hague
20–23 May	*Journées* of *Prairial*
23 May	Parisian *sections* disarmed
May–June	The White Terror
8 June	Death of Dauphin
24 June	Comte de Provence, self-styled Louis XVIII, issues proclamation from Verona
27 June	*Émigrés* land at Quiberon Bay
20 July	*Émigrés* defeated by Hoche.
22 July	Peace with Spain signed
22 August	Convention approves Constitution of the Year III
4–6 October	*Journées* of *Vendémiaire*
26 October	Convention is dissolved. Directory is inaugurated

1796

2 March	Bonaparte becomes General of the Army of Italy
28 April	Armistice of Cherasco with Piedmont
10 May	Bonaparte defeats Austrians at Lodi
16 November	Bonaparte's victory at Arcola

1797

12 May	Democratic republic set up at Venice
27 May	Babeuf executed
15 June	Ligurian republic set up at Genoa
9 July	Cisalpine republic set up at Milan
4 September	*Coup d'état* of 18 *Fructidor*

Appendix 3

1797
18 October   Peace with Austria secured by Treaty of Campo-Formio

10 December   Bonaparte returns to Paris

1798
15 February   Proclamation of Roman republic

12 April   Proclamation of Helvetian republic

18 May   Bonaparte sails for Egypt

1 August   Battle of the Nile

1799
26 January   Proclamation of Parthenopean Republic at Naples

12 March   War declared on Austria

20 May   Sieyès joins the Directory

15 August   Suvarov defeats Joubert at Novi

26 September   Massena defeats Russians at Zurich

9 October   Bonaparte lands at Fréjus

9 November   *Coup d'état* of *Brumaire*

PRINCIPAL SOURCES

A complete biography (if it were possible to compile one) would occupy far more pages than there are in this book. There is a good selective bibliography in Lefebvre's history, and shorter ones in the histories by Soboul, Roberts, Goodwin and Hampson. This list is a highly personal selection.

ASCHERSON, NEAL (ed.), *The French Revolution: Extracts from* The Times, *1789–1794*, Times Books, 1975

AULARD, ALPHONSE, *The French Revolution: A Political History, 1789–1804*, trans. Bernard Miall, 1910

BEIK, P. H. (ed.), *The French Revolution*, Macmillan, 1971

BERNARD, J. F., *Talleyrand: A Biography*, Collins, 1973

BIENVENU, RICHARD (ed.), *The Ninth of Thermidor: Fall of Robespierre*, Oxford University Press, 1968

BIRÉ, EDMOND, *The Diary of a Citizen of Paris during the Terror*, trans. John de Villiers, 1896, 2 vols.

BLANC, LOUIS, *Histoire de la Révolution française*, Paris 1847–1862, 12 vols.

BOULOISEAU, M., *La République jacobine – 10 août 1792 – 9 Thermidor an II*, Paris, 1972

BRADBY, E. D., *The Life of Barnave*, Oxford, 1915, 2 vols.

BRAESCH, F., *La Commune du 10 août 1792*, Paris, 1911

BRINTON, CRANE, *A Decade of Revolution 1789–99*, 1934

BRUCKNER, GENE A., *Jean-Sylvain Bailly: Revolutionary Mayor of Paris*, University of Illinois Press, 1950

BUCKMAN, PETER, *Lafayette: A Biography*, Paddington Press, 1977

Cambridge Modern History, vol. VIII., The French Revolution, Cambridge University Press, 1934

CAMPAN, MADAME, *Mémoires*, 1833

CARON, PIERRE, *Massacres de septembre*, Paris, 1935; *Paris pendant la Terreur*, Paris, 1910–58, 5 vols.; *La Première Terreur*, Paris, 1950

CLAPHAM, J. H., *Abbé Sieyès*, 1912

COBB, RICHARD, *Les Armées Revolutionnaires*, Paris, 1961–3, 2 vols.; *Death in Paris, 1795–1801*, Oxford University Press, 1978; *Paris and its Provinces, 1792–1802*, Oxford University Press, 1975; *The Police and the People. French Popular Protest, 1789–1820*, Oxford University Press, 1970; *Reactions to the French Revolution*, Oxford University Press, 1972; *Terreur et subsistances 1793–1795*, Paris, 1965

COBBAN, ALFRED, *Aspects of the French Revolution*, Cape, 1968; *A History of Modern France*, Volume 1: 1755–1799, third edition, Pelican Books, 1963; *The Social Interpretation of the French Revolution*, Cambridge University Press, 1964

COLE, HUBERT, *Fouché: The Unprincipled Patriot*, Eyre & Spottiswoode, 1972

COOPER, DUFF, *Talleyrand*, Cape, 1938

CRONIN, VINCENT, *Louis and Antoinette*, Collins, 1974; *Napoleon*, Collins, 1971

CURTIS, E. N., *Saint-Just, Colleague of Robespierre*, London, 1935

DAWSON, CHRISTOPHER, *The Gods of Revolution*, Sidgwick & Jackson, 1972

DAWSON, PHILIP (ed.), *The French Revolution*, Prentice Hall, Inc., 1967

DESMOULINS, CAMILLE, *Le Vieux Cordelier*, Paris, 1936

ELLIOTT, SIR JOHN, *The Way of the Tumbrils*, Rheinhart, 1958

FERRIÈRES, MARQUIS DE, *Mémoires*, Paris, 1822, 3 vols.

FERSEN, HANS AXEL VON, *Rescue the Queen: A Diary of the French Revolution, 1789–1793*, Bell, 1971

FISHER, JOHN, *The Elysian Fields: France in Ferment, 1789–1804*, Cassell, 1966

FUNCK-BRENTANO, F., *Scènes et tableaux de la Révolution*, Paris, 1934

GARNIER, JEAN-PAUL, *Barras*, Paris, 1970

GAUTHIER, FLORENCE, *La voi paysanne dans la Révolution française: L'exemple picard*, Maspero, Paris, 1977

GAXOTTE, PIERRE, *The French Revolution*, trans. Walter Alison Phillips, Scribner's, New York, 1932

GERSHOY, LEO, *Bertrand Barère: A Reluctant Terrorist*, Princeton

University Press, 1962; *The Era of the French Revolution 1789–99*, 1957

GODECHOT, JACQUES, *La Prise de la Bastille*, Paris, 1965, trans. Jean Stewart, Faber, 1970

GOODWIN, A., *The French Revolution*, fifth edition, Hutchinson, 1976

GOODSPEED, D. J., *Bayonets at St Cloud: The Story of 18th Brumaire*, Hart-Davis, 1965

GOTTSCHALK, LOUIS, *Jean Paul Marat: A Study in Radicalism*, Greenberg, New York, 1927

GREENLAW, R. W. (ed.), *The Economic Origins of the French Revolution: Poverty or Prosperity*, 1958

GREER, DONALD, *The Incidence of the Terror during the French Revolution*, Harvard University Press, 1935

HAMPSON, NORMAN, *Danton*, Duckworth, 1978; *The Life and Opinions of Maximilien Robespierre*, Duckworth, 1974; *A Social History of the French Revolution*, Routledge & Kegan Paul, 1963

HEARSEY, J. E. N., *Marie Antoinette*, Constable, 1972

HERISSAY, JACQUES, *Les Journées de septembre 1792*, Paris, 1945

HUFTON, OLWEN, *The Poor of Eighteenth-Century France 1750–1789*, Clarendon Press, 1974

JACOB, L., *Les Suspects pendant la Terreur*, Paris, 1952

JAURÈS, JEAN, *Histoire socialiste de la Révolution française*, ed. Soboul, new edition Paris, 1968–72

JOHNSON, DOUGLAS (ed.), *French Society and the Revolution*, Cambridge University Press, 1976

JONES, R. BEN, *The French Revolution*, University of London Press, 1974

A Journal of the Terror: Being an Account of the occurrences in the Temple during the confinement of Louis XVI by M. Cléry the King's valet de chambre together with a description of the last hours of the King, by the Abbé de Firmont, Folio Society, 1955

KERR, WILFRED B., *Reign of Terror 1793–4*, University of Toronto Press, 1927

LAMARTINE, ALPHONSE DE, *History of the Girondins*, 1839, 3 vols.

LA TOUR DU PIN, MADAME DE, *Memoirs*, ed. and trans. Felice Harcourt, introduction by Peter Gay, McCall, New York, 1971

LAFAYETTE, MARQUIS DE, *Mémoires, Correspondance et Manuscrits*, Paris, 1838, 6 vols.

LEFEBVRE, GEORGES, *The Coming of the French Revolution*, trans. R. R. Palmer, Princeton University Press, 1967; *Études sur la Révolution française*, second edition Paris, 1963; *The French Revolution: From its*

Origins to 1793, trans. Elizabeth Moss Evanson, Routledge & Kegan Paul, 1962; *The French Revolution: From 1793 to 1799*, Routledge & Kegan Paul, 1964; *Paysans du Nord pendant la Révolution française*, Lille, 1924

LENOTRE, G., *The Flight of Marie Antoinette*, trans. Mrs Rodolph Stawell, 1906; *The Last Days of Marie Antoinette*, trans. Mrs Rodolph Stawell, 1907; *Paris révolutionnarie: Vieilles maisons, vieux papiers*, Paris, 1930; *Les Quartiers de Paris pendant la Révolution*, Paris, 1896; *The September Massacres*, 1929; *The Tribunal of the Terror: A Study of Paris in 1793–1795*, trans. Frederic Lees, 1909

LEWIS, GWYNNE, *Life in Revolutionary France*, Batsford, 1972

LOOMIS, STANLEY, *The Fatal Friendship: Marie Antoinette, Count Fersen and the Flight to Varennes*, Davis Poynter, 1972; *Paris in the Terror, June 1793–July 1794*, Cape, 1965

LUCAS, COLIN, *The Structure of the Terror: The Example of Javogues and the Loire*, Oxford University Press, 1973

LYONS, MARTIN, *France under the Directory*, Cambridge University Press, 1975

MADELIN, LOUIS, *Fouché 1759–1820*, Paris, 1930, 2 vols.; *The French Revolution*, 1916; *Talleyrand*, 1948

MALLET, BERNARD, *Mallet du Pan and the French Revolution*, 1902

MARKHAM, FELIX, *Napoleon*, Weidenfeld & Nicolson, 1963

MATHIEZ, ALBERT, *Les Grands Journées de la Constituante 1789–1791*, Paris, 1913; *Le Directoire*, Paris, 1934; *The French Revolution*, trans. Catherine Alison Phillips, 1928

MATRAT, JEAN, *Robespierre, or the Tyranny of the Majority*, trans. Alan Kendall with Felix Brenner, Angus & Robertson, 1975

MAUROIS, ANDRÉ, *A History of France*, trans. Henry L. Buisse and Gerard Hopkins, third edition, Cape, 1960

MCMANNERS, J., *The French Revolution and the Church*, S.P.C.K., 1969

MICHELET, JULES, *History of the French Revolution*, trans. Charles Cocks, ed. with and introduction by Gordon Wright, University of Chicago Press, 1967

MICHON, Georges, *Correspondance de Maximilien et Angustin Robespierre*, Paris, 1926

MIGNET, F. A. M., *History of the French Revolution from 1789 to 1814*, 1919

MORRIS, GOUVERNEUR, *A Diary of the French Revolution*, ed. Beatrix Cary Davenport, Harrap, 1939, 2 vols.

MORSE-STEPHENS, H., *Speeches of the Statesmen and Orators of the Revolution, 1789–1795*, Oxford University Press, 1892, 2 vols.

MORTON, J. B., *The Bastille Falls and other Studies of the French Revolution*, 1936; *Brumaire: The Rise of Bonaparte. From the Death of Robespierre to the Establishment of the Consulate*, 1948; *Saint-Just*, 1935

ORIEUX, JEAN, *Talleyrand: The Art of Survival*, Secker & Warburg, 1974

PALMER, R. R., *Twelve Who Ruled: The Year of the Terror in the French Revolution*, Princeton University Press, 1941; *The World of the French Revolution*, Allen & Unwin, 1971

PATRICK, ALISON, *The Men of the First French Republic*, John Hopkins University Press, 1972

PERNOUD, GEORGES, *The French Revolution*, with Sabine Flaissier, trans. Richard Graves, Secker & Warburg, 1960

REINHARD, MARCEL, *La Chute de la royauté 10 août, 1792*, Paris, 1969; *France du Directoire*, Paris, 1956, 2 vols.; *Le Grand Carnot*, Paris, 1950

ROBERTS, J. M., *The French Revolution*, Oxford University Press, 1978; *French Revolution Documents*, ed. with John Hardman and R. C. Cobb, Basil Blackwell, 1966, 1973, 2 vols.

ROBIQUET, JEAN, *Daily Life in the French Revolution*, Weidenfeld & Nicolson, 1964

ROEDERER, P. L., *Chronique de Cinquante Jours*, 1832

ROGERS, CORNWELL B., *The Spirit of Revolution in 1789*, Princeton University Press, 1949

ROSE, R. B., *Gracchus Babeuf: The First Revolutionary Communist*, Arnold, 1979

ROSS, MICHAEL, *Banners of the King: The War of the Vendée, 1793–4*, Seeley Service, 1975

Royal Memoirs of the French Revolution, London, 1823

RUDÉ, GEORGE, *The Crowd in History, 1730–1848, A Study of Popular Disturbances in France and England*, Wiley, 1964; *The Crowd in the French Revolution*, Oxford University Press, new edition, 1967; *Paris and London in the Eighteenth Century: Studies in Popular Protest*, 1970; *Revolutionary Europe 1783–1815*, Fontana, 1964; *Robespierre: Portrait of a Revolutionary Democrat*, Collins, 1975

SALVEMINI, GAETANO, *The French Revolution, 1788–1792*, trans. I. M. Rawson, Cape, 1954

SCOTT, WILLIAM, *Terror and Repression in Revolutionary Marseilles*, Macmillan, 1973

SOBOUL, ALBERT, *The French Revolution, 1787–1799*, trans. Alan

Principal Sources

Forrest and Colin Jones, N. L. B., 1974, 2 vols.; *The Parisian Sans-Culottes and the French Revolution, 1793–4*, trans., G. Lewis, Oxford University Press, 1964; *Le Procès de Louis XVI*, Paris, 1966

STAËL, MADAME LA BARONNE DE, *Considerations sur les evénéments de la Révolution française*, 1818, 3 vols.

STEWART, J. H. (ed.), *Documentary Survey of the French Revolution*, Collins/Macmillan, 1951

SYDENHAM, M. J., *The First French Republic, 1792–1804*, Batsford, 1974; *The French Revolution*, new edition, Methuen, 1969; *The Girondins*, Athlone Press, 1961

TAYLOR, I. A., *Life of Madame Roland*, 1911

THIERS, LOUIS ADOLPHE, *History of the French Revolution, 1789–1800*, 1895, 5 vols.

THOMPSON, J. M., *Eye-witnesses of the French Revolution*, Blackwell, 1938; *The French Revolution*, Second edition, Blackwell, 1944; ed., *French Revolutionary Documents, 1789–1794*, Blackwell, 1933; *Leaders of the French Revolution*, Blackwell, 1932; *Robespierre and the French Revolution*, English University Press, 1952

THOMSON, DAVID, *The Babeuf Plot*, Routledge, 1947

TILLY, CHARLES, *The Vendée*, Arnold, 1964

TOCQUEVILLE, ALEXIS DE, *The Ancien Régime and the French Revolution*, trans. Stuart Gilbert with an introduction by Hugh Brogan, Collins/Fontana, 1966

TØNNESON, K. D., *La Défaite des Sans-Culottes*, Paris, 1959

VOVELLE, M., *La Chute de la monarchie, 1789–1792*, Paris, 1972

WATSON, S. J., *Carnot*, Bodley Head, 1954

WELCH, O. J. G., *Mirabeau*, Cape, 1951

WILLIAMS, G. A., *Artisans and Sans-Culottes: Popular Movements in France and Britain during the French Revolution*, Arnold, 1968

WOLOCH, ISSER, *Jacobin Legacy*, Princeton University Press, 1970

WRIGHT, D. G., *Revolution and Terror in France, 1789–1795*, Longman, 1974

YOUNG, ARTHUR, *Travels in France*, 1792, 2 vols.

INDEX

'active' citizens, 147, 153
Adélaïde, Daughter of France, 119
Aiguillon, Armand, Duc d', 42, 94
Alembert, Jean le Rond d', 29, 205
Aligre, Étienne d', 38, 305
Amar, J. A. B., 229, 242, 305
Ancients, Council of, 282, 297, 298, 299, 302
army, its state in 1792, 145; conscription, 216; purges demanded, 168, 215; mood of, 295
Artois, Charles, Comte d', later King Charles X (1757–1836), 162; personality, 25, 305; and Third Estate, 60; at séance royale, 61, 62; flees abroad, 89; his colour, 90; counter-revolutionary, 117; advocates war, 143; later life, 305
Assembly of Notables, 38, 39, 44
Auch, Martin d', 60
Augeard, 95, 305
Augereau, Pierre-François, 297, 305
Austria, Declaration of Pillnitz, 143; France at war with, 145, 202; battle of Jemappes, 193; battle of Fleurus, 257; defeated, and Treaty of Campo-Formio, 296
Ayen, Duchesse d', 247
Azéma, Michel, 159

Babeuf, François-Noel, called Gracchus Babeuf (1760–97), 293–4
Bailly, Jean-Sylvain (1736–93), and Estates General debates, 53, 58; and National Assembly, 60; seeks admission to séance royale, 60; supports Mirabeau, 62; on enthusiasm in Paris, 87, 89; Mayor of Paris, 88; on popularity of Louis XVI, 91; on state of anarchy, 92; confronts mob at Tuileries, 118; and flight of royal family, 124; monarchien, 133; and Champ de Mars massacre, 135; ultimate fate, 135, 142; execution, 224–5
bals des victimes, 274
Barbaroux, Charles, 141–2, 200, 306
Barentin, Charles de, 40, 51, 52, 61, 306
Barère, Bertrand (1755–1841), 90, 271, 272, 274, 306
Barnave, Antoine (1761–93), demands recall of Necker, 88; apologist for murder, 93; and return of royal family to Paris, 128, 129; and Queen, 133; execution, 142, 225
Barras, Paul-François, Vicomte de (1755–1829), Terror at Toulon, 227; on fear of Robespierre, 254; and Robespierre, 258, 266; takes military command, 265; becomes reactionary, 271; and insurrection of Lepeletier sectionnaires, 284; and Bonaparte, 285; and journées of Vendémiaire, 286, 287; unrespected Director, 291; and 'Conspiracy of Equals', 294; and coup d'état of 18 Fructidor, 295; and Josephine de Beauharnais, 295; and Ducos, 299; and coup d'état of Brumaire, 302; resigns from Directory, 302; later life, 306
Barthélemy, François, 297, 306
Bas, Laurent, 213, 214
Bastille, conditions in, 71; prisoners, 72; governor of, 72–3; preparations against attack, 73; guns withdrawn, 74; storming of, 75–80; vainqueurs, 82–3; sightseers and souvenirs, 83; Brissot in, 137
Bayon, Captain, 125, 126–7
Belgium, 193, 257
Bernadotte, Jean-Baptiste, 299, 302, 306
Besenval, Baron de, 69, 70, 306

342

Index

Louis XVI, King—*contd.*
larity, 90–91; withholds consent to National Assembly decrees, 95; banquet for arrival of Flanders Regiment, 95, 96; and market-women's bread riot, 98, 99, 100; advised to flee from Versailles, 98, 100; Lafayette reassures, 101; and the Dauphin, 102, 129; appears on balcony, 103, 104; journey to Tuileries, 104–5; 'the baker', 105; change in title, 109; and Mirabeau, 110, 111; at *Fête de la Fédération*, 114; and Civil Constitution, 115, 117, 118; hopes to recover lost authority, 116–17; decides to escape, 118–19; and Fersen, 120; flight to Varennes, 121–7; destroys papers, 128; the return to Paris, 128–30; and Lafayette, 130; vetoes Assembly's decrees, 138; journalists attack, 140; and Revolutionary Wars, 144–5; replaces Ministers with Feuillants, 146; in despondency, 149; and invasion of Tuileries, 149; and state of emergency, 151; and 14 July celebrations, 151–3; his abdication demanded, 154; and storming of Tuileries, 155, 156; seeks refuge in National Assembly, 158; to be imprisoned, 161–2; Convention sends for, 182; daily routine in prison, 182–3; condemned to death, 185; and his family, 185–6; execution, 186–9; and young Robespierre, 205

Louis-Charles, Duke of Normandy, Dauphin *from 1789, later* King Louis XVII (1785–95), birth of, 23; and Louis XVI, 102, 182, 186; and Marie Antoinette, 103–4, 118; on Tuileries, 105; at *Fête de la Fédération*, 114; flight to Varennes, 120, 121, 122; return journey to Paris, 129; kicks up leaves, 157; soldier carries, 158; imprisoned, 182, 183; taken from his mother, 221; death of, 280

Louis Joseph Xavier, Dauphin (1781–9), 23, 54

Louis Philippe, *see* Chartres, Duc de

Louvet de Couvrai, Jean Baptiste (1760–97), 197, 228, 314

Lyons, depression, 34; outbreaks of fighting, 194; civil war, 202–3, 215; execution by cannon fire, 227; prisoners massacred, 272; royalist stronghold, 273

Maillard, Marie Julien Stanislas, 81, 97, 100, 172, 314

Malesherbes, Chrétien Lamoignon de (1721–94), 184

Mallet du Pan, Jacques, 41, 292, 314

Manège, Assembly established at, 104, 109; mob marches on, 148; royal family in, 158, 161; Convention transferred from, 197

Manuel, Louis-Pierre (1751–93), 150, 151, 157, 314

Marat, Albertine, 213, 314

Marat, Jean-Paul (1743–93), targets for his literary attacks, 140; appearance and personality, 140–41, 142; history, 141–2; urges violence, 146; urges attack on prisoners, 169; and *septembriseurs*, 176, 178; Girondins arraign, 196; Dr Moore on, 196–7; acquitted, 197; extreme popularity, 197–8; rings tocsin, 199; and overthrow of Girondins, 201; Charlotte Corday murders, 212–13; David's 'Marat Assassinated', 214, 216; and Custine, 215; busts of, 231, 232

Maria-Theresa, Empress of Austria (1717–80), 20

Marie Antoinette, Queen (1755–93), appearance, 20, 21, 51, 103, 221; personality, 20, 25, 26–7, 150; wedding, 20–21; and her husband, 21–2, 25, 98, 100, 118, 128, 149, 184, 185, 186; scurrilous rumours about, 22; birth of her children, 23; domestic routine, 24, 25; attitude to Court protocol, 25–6; Turgot annoys, 35; and Calonne, 38–9; and Necker, 44; at convention of Estates General, 50, 51, 52; and Third Estate, 59; applauded, 87; urges withdrawal of Court to Metz, 89; and market-women's bread riot, 99, 100; escapes to King's apartments, 101–2; shows herself to mob, 103, 104; leaves Versailles, 104–5; and Mirabeau, 111; at *Fête de la Fédération*, 114; becomes less unpopular, 117; mob at Tuileries, 118; aid from foreign powers, 119; and Fersen, 120; flight to Varennes, 120, 121, 122; and Assembly's decree, 127; return journey to Paris, 128, 129; journalists attack, 140; and Revolutionary wars, 145; and invasion of Tuileries, 149; and Lafayette, 151; and 14 July celebrations, 152; Roederer advises, 157; fears for Dauphin's safety, 158; life in prison, 182, 183; trial authorized, 215; Dauphin taken from, 221; trial and execution, 221–2

Marie Thérèse, *see* Royale, Madame

Marseillaise, 153–4

Marseilles, 91, 153, 194, 202, 272

Martin, Jeanne, 97, 103

Maurepas, Jean Frédéric, Comte de (1701–81), 27, 28, 29, 37

Maury, Jean Siffrein, Abbé, 49, 53, 314

Menou, Jacques-François, 284

Mercier, Sébastien, 185, 233

Index